Memo from Alamut

Memo from Alamut

by

Vernon Frazer

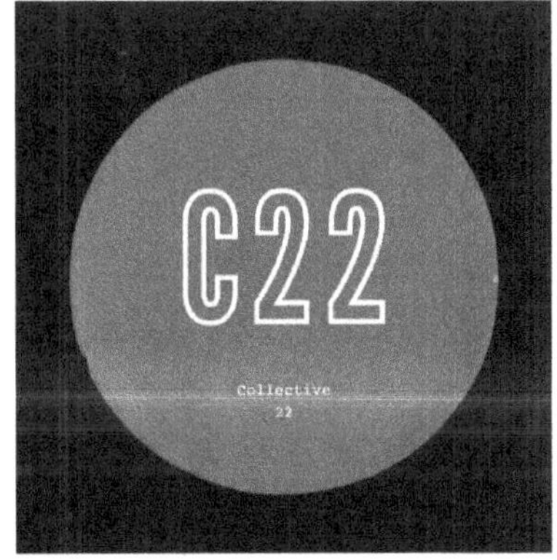

ACKNOWLEDGMENTS

Some of the poems in this collection appeared previously in
Altered Scale, BlazeVox, Brave New Word, Of/With, Otoliths,Plain Brown Wrapper,
Tip of the Knife, Truck, Unlikely Stories, and *Zoomoozophone Review*

ISBN 978-1-959377-06-1

Cover: Lachlan J MacDougall

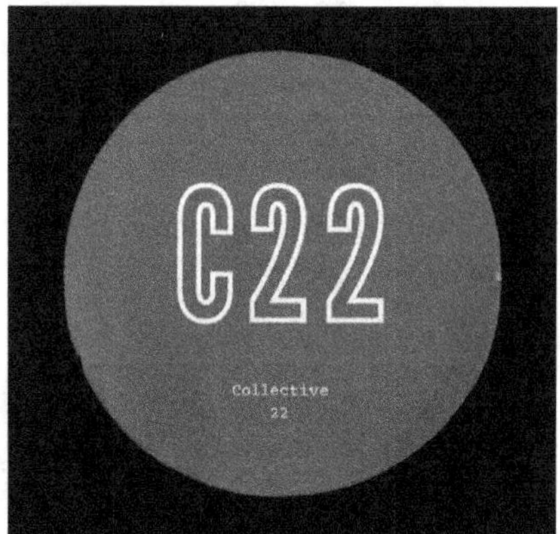

c22press.wordpress.com

Printed in the United States of America

CONTENTS

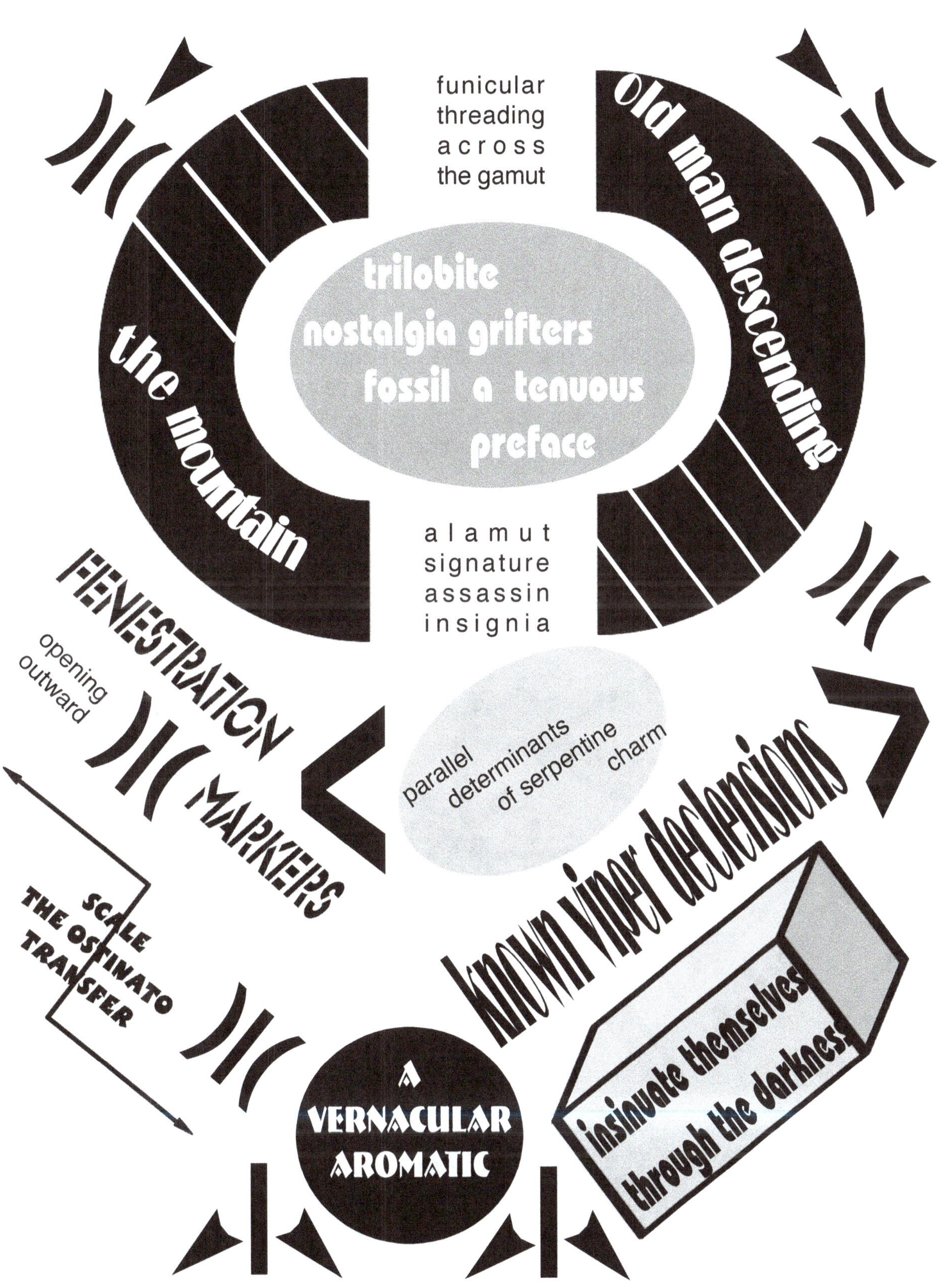
funicular
threading
a c r o s s
the gamut
old man descending
the mountain
trilobite
nostalgia grifters
fossil a tenuous
preface
a l a m u t
signature
assassin
insignia
FENESTRATION
opening
outward
MARKERS
parallel
determinants
of serpentine
charm
SCALE
THE OSTINATO
TRANSFER
known viper declensions
A
VERNACULAR
AROMATIC
insinuate themselves
through the darkness

and the promise of beauty
endless after the shredding

   (the old man promised

      girls honey at the core
      endless ecstatic release
      in the mountain garden

       to add to the historic stream

a dream
     before the next incursion

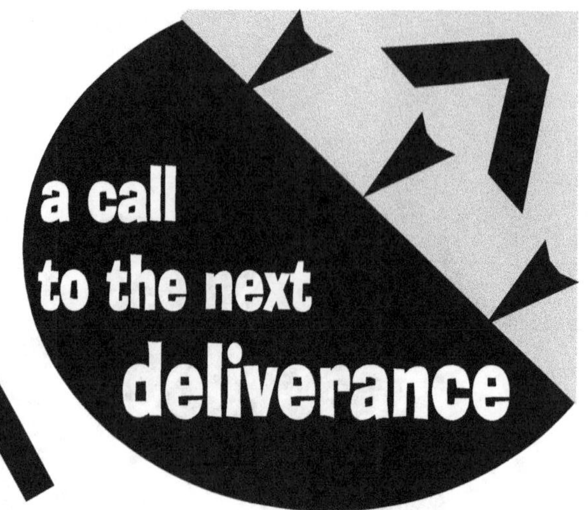

spreads the communal distillation, ready for the parvenu of dissonant acrostic demons
lurking photogenic osprey wagons in receipt the transfer flagons wept a caustic heave no
gleam too sudden for the eye to glint before turning the hint away from the messenger
entranced with whitebeard promise even more than the last to leave the cave thinking of

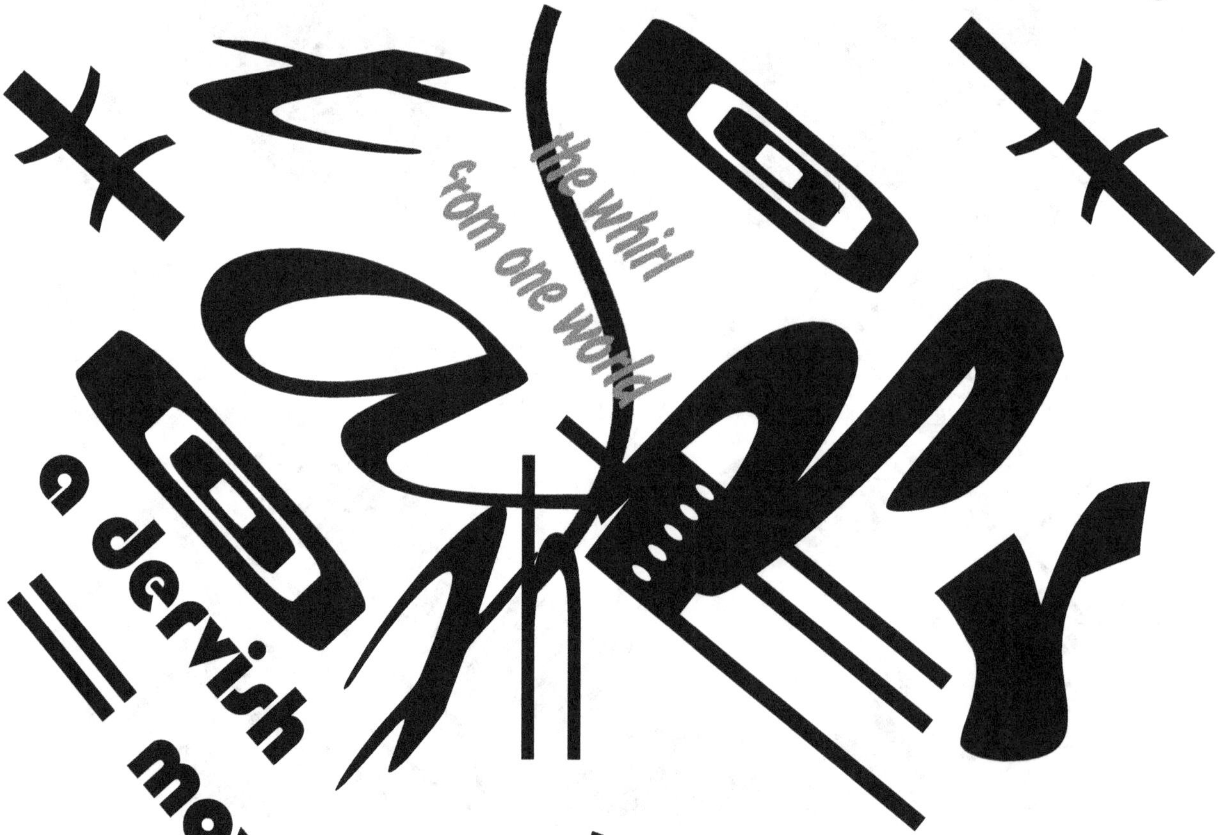

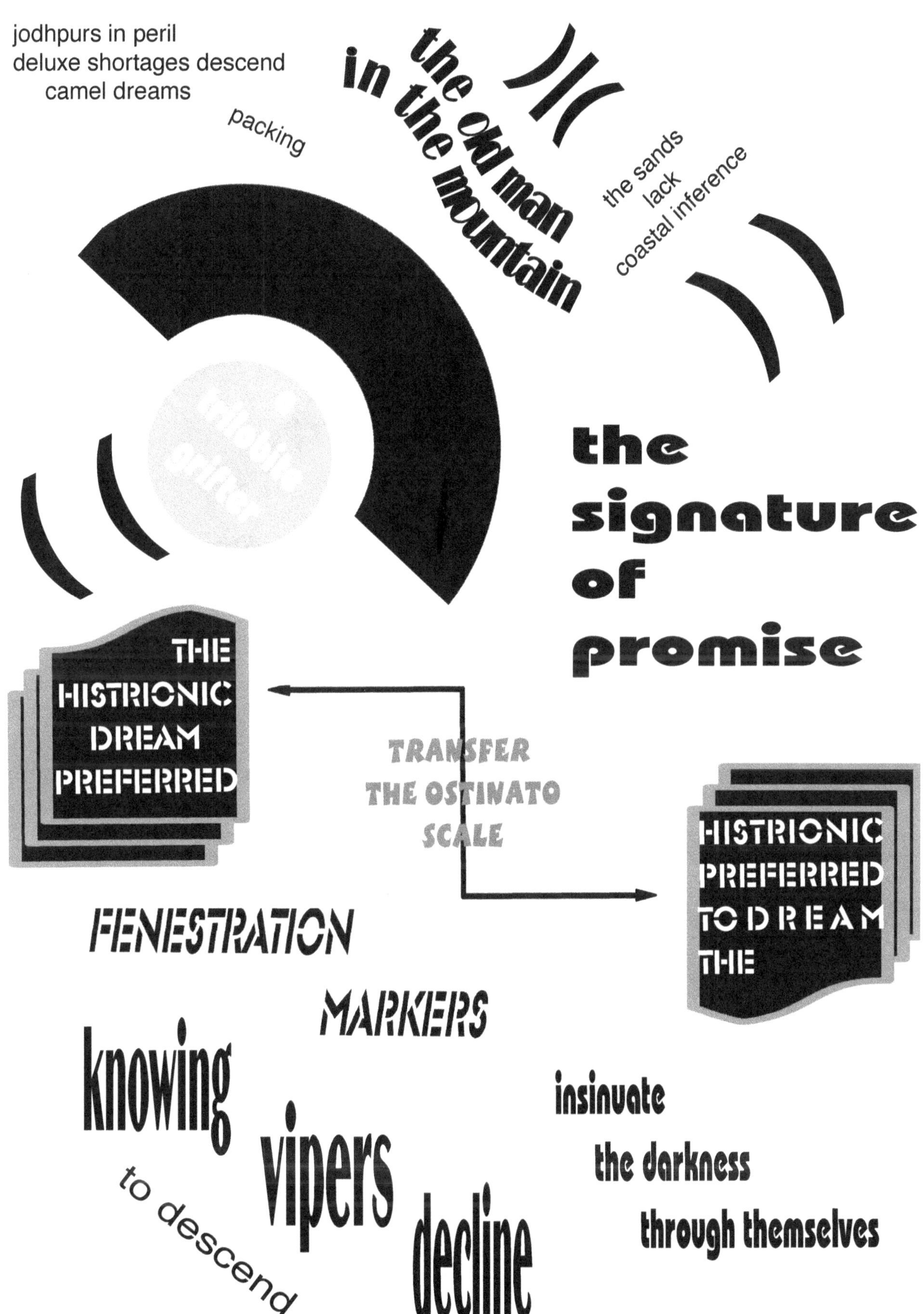

jodhpurs in peril
deluxe shortages descend
camel dreams
packing
the old man
in the mountain
the sands
lack
coastal inference
the
signature
of
promise
THE
HISTRIONIC
DREAM
PREFERRED
TRANSFER
THE OSTINATO
SCALE
HISTRIONIC
PREFERRED
TO DREAM
THE
FENESTRATION
MARKERS
knowing
vipers
to descend
decline
insinuate
the darkness
through themselves

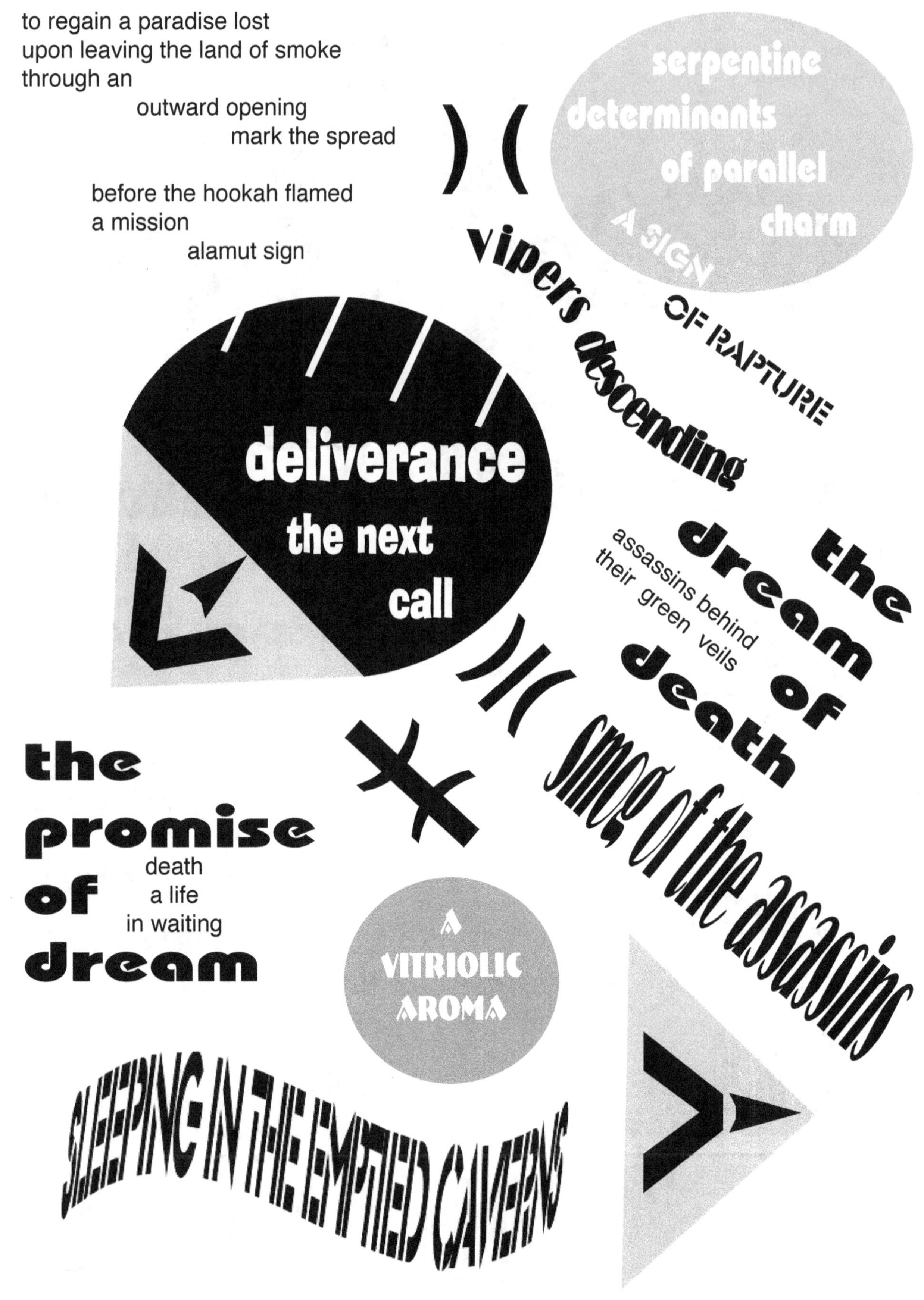
to regain a paradise lost
upon leaving the land of smoke
through an
outward opening
mark the spread
before the hookah flamed
a mission
alamut sign
serpentine
determinants
of parallel
charm
A SIGN
OF RAPTURE
vipers descending
deliverance
the next
call
the
dream
of
death
assassins behind
their green veils
smoke of the assassins
the
promise
of
dream
death
a life
in waiting
A VITRIOLIC AROMA
SLEEPING IN THE EMPTIED CAVERNS

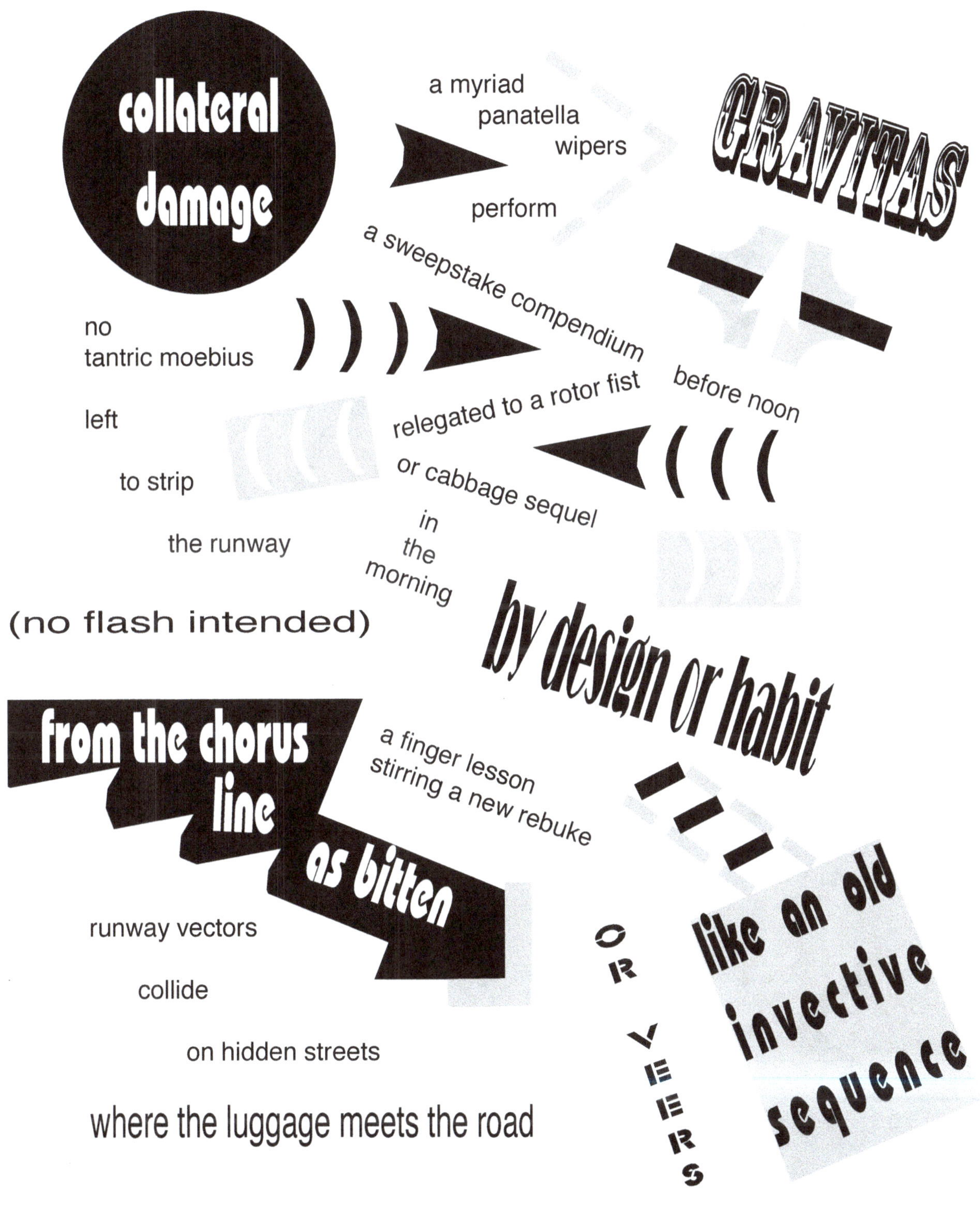
collateral damage

a myriad
panatella
wipers

perform

GRAVITAS

a sweepstake compendium

no
tantric moebius

left

to strip

the runway

relegated to a rotor fist

or cabbage sequel

in
the
morning

before noon

(no flash intended)

by design or habit

from the chorus
line

a finger lesson
stirring a new rebuke

as bitten

runway vectors

collide

on hidden streets

where the luggage meets the road

OR VEERS

like an old
invective
sequence

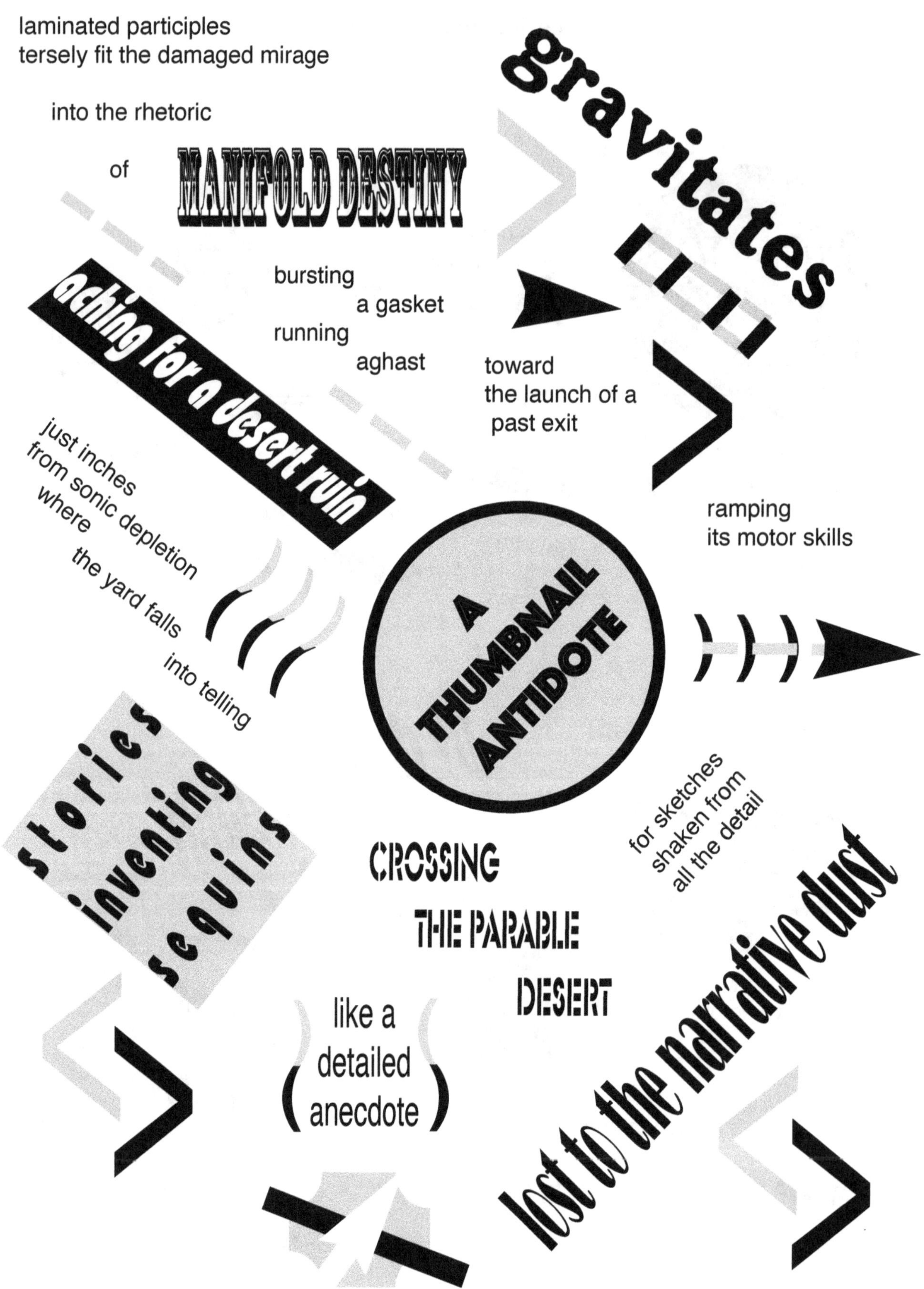

laminated participles
tersely fit the damaged mirage
into the rhetoric
of
MANIFOLD DESTINY
gravitates
aching for a desert ruin
bursting
a gasket
running
aghast
toward
the launch of a
past exit
ramping
its motor skills
just inches
from sonic depletion
where
the yard falls
into telling
A THUMBNAIL ANTIDOTE
for sketches
shaken from
all the detail
stories inventing sequins
CROSSING
THE PARABLE
DESERT
like a
detailed
anecdote
lost to the narrative dust

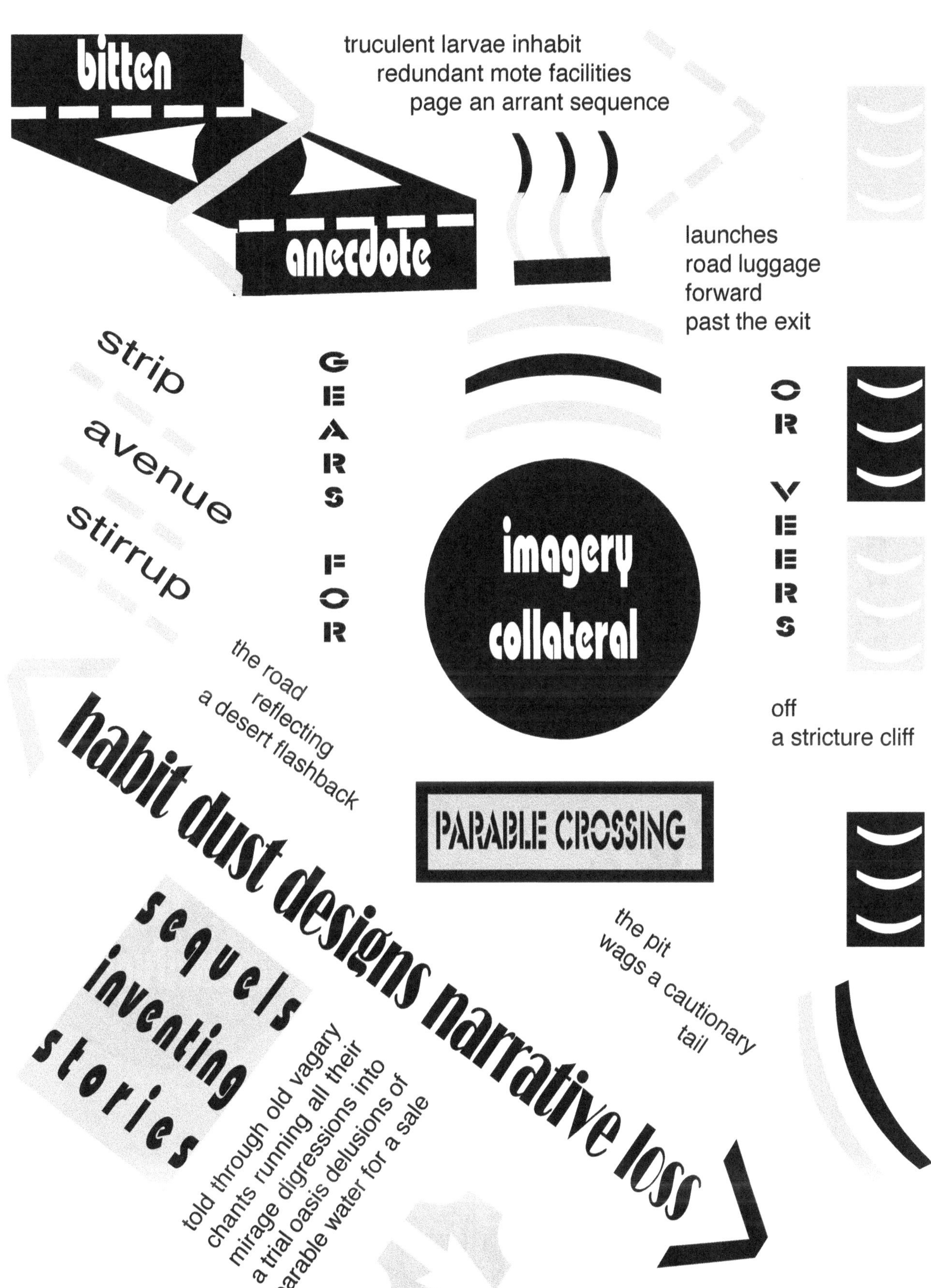

bitten
anecdote
truculent larvae inhabit
redundant mote facilities
page an arrant sequence
launches
road luggage
forward
past the exit
strip
avenue
stirrup
GEARS FOR
imagery collateral
OR VEERS
off
a stricture cliff
the road
reflecting
a desert flashback
PARABLE CROSSING
the pit
wags a cautionary
tail
habit dust designs narrative loss
sequels
inventing
stories
told through old vagary
chants running all their
mirage digressions into
a trial oasis delusions of
parable water for a sale

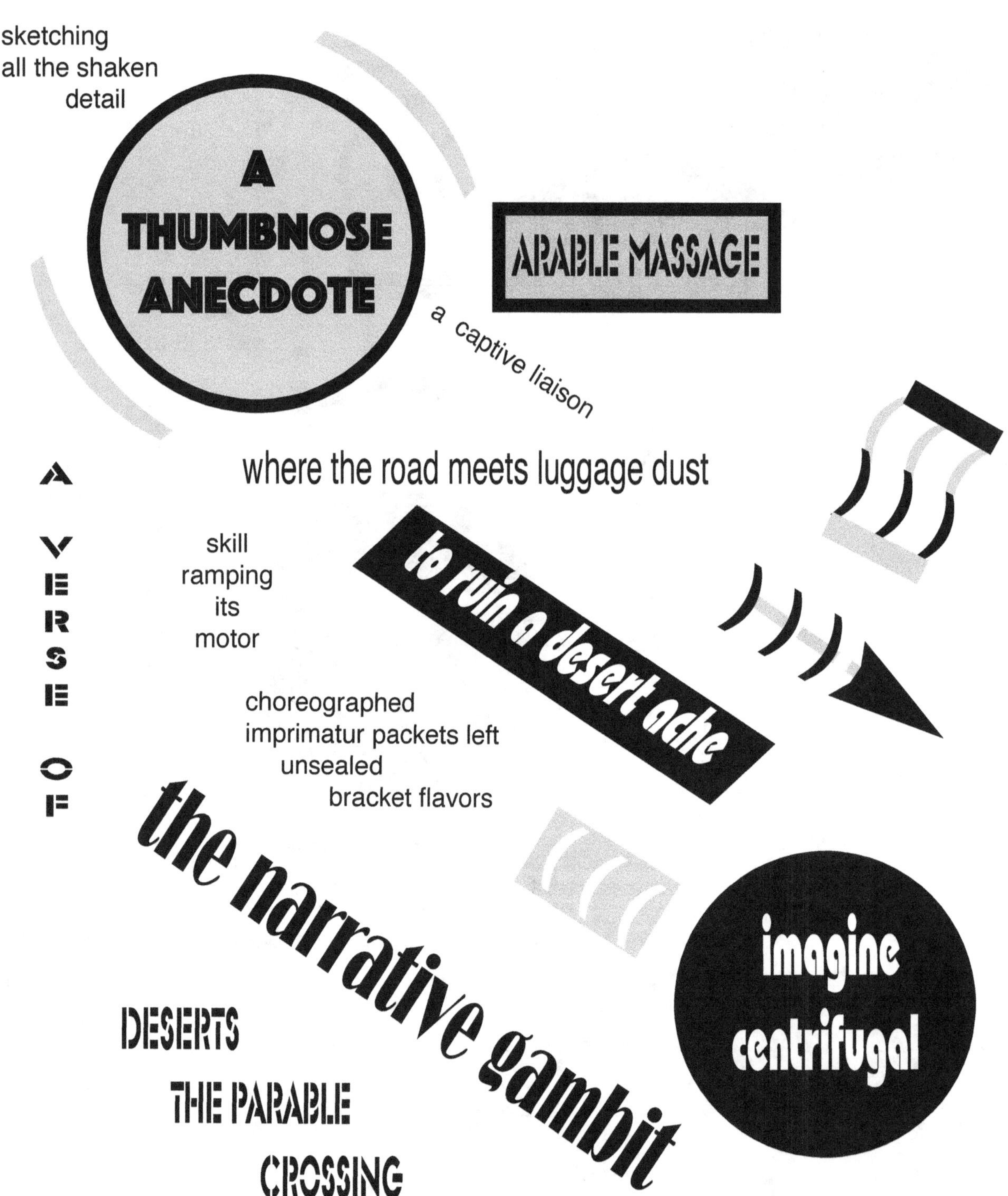

sketching
all the shaken
detail
A
THUMBNOSE
ANECDOTE
ARABLE MASSAGE
a captive liaison
where the road meets luggage dust
A VERSE OF
skill
ramping
its
motor
to ruin a desert ache
choreographed
imprimatur packets left
unsealed
bracket flavors
the narrative gambit
imagine
centrifugal
DESERTS
THE PARABLE
CROSSING
GRAVITY

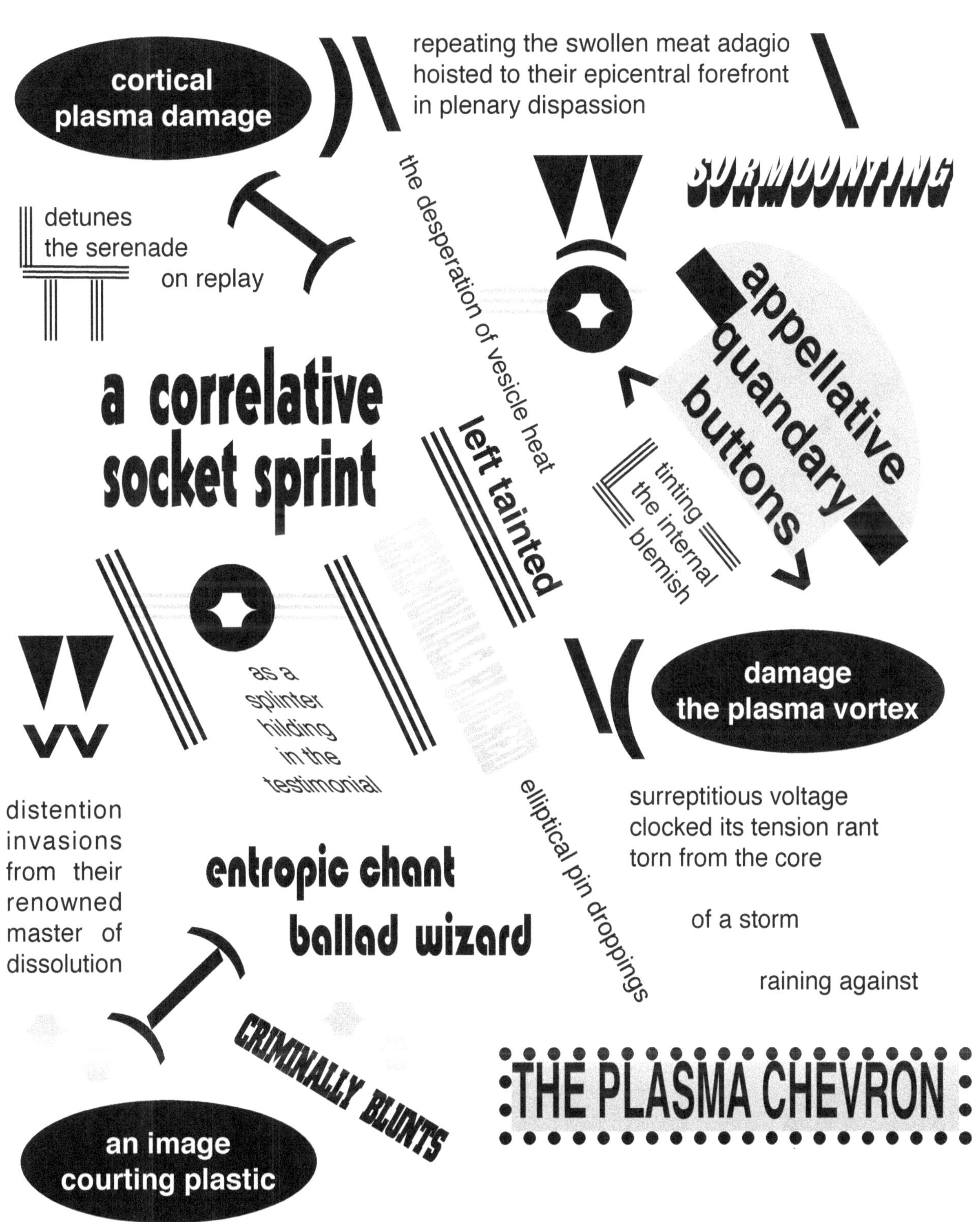
cortical
plasma damage
repeating the swollen meat adagio
hoisted to their epicentral forefront
in plenary dispassion
SURMOUNTING
detunes
the serenade
on replay
the desperation of vesicle heat
appellative
quandary
buttons
a correlative
socket sprint
left tainted
tinting
the internal
blemish
as a
splinter
hilding
in the
testimonial
damage
the plasma vortex
distention
invasions
from their
renowned
master of
dissolution
entropic chant
ballad wizard
surreptitious voltage
clocked its tension rant
torn from the core
elliptical pin droppings
of a storm
raining against
CRIMINALLY BLUNTS
THE PLASMA CHEVRON
an image
courting plastic

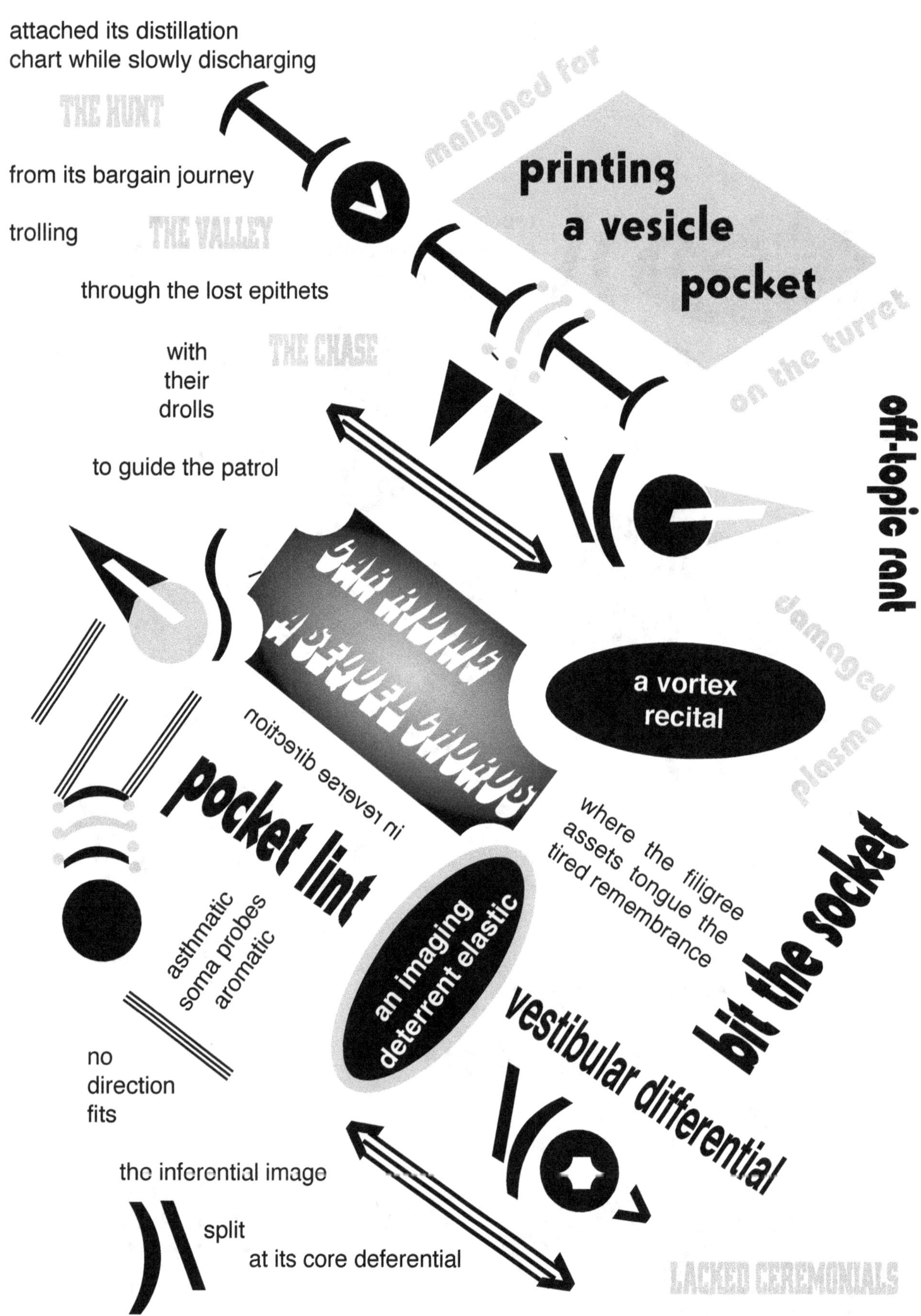

attached its distillation
chart while slowly discharging
THE HUNT
from its bargain journey
trolling
THE VALLEY
through the lost epithets
with
their
drolls
to guide the patrol
THE CHASE
maligned for
printing
a vesicle
pocket
on the turret
off-topic rant
damaged
plasma
a vortex
recital
where the filigree
assets tongue the
tired remembrance
bit the socket
in reverse direction
pocket lint
asthmatic
soma probes
aromatic
an imaging
deterrent elastic
vestibular differential
no
direction
fits
the inferential image
split
at its core deferential
LACKED CEREMONIALS

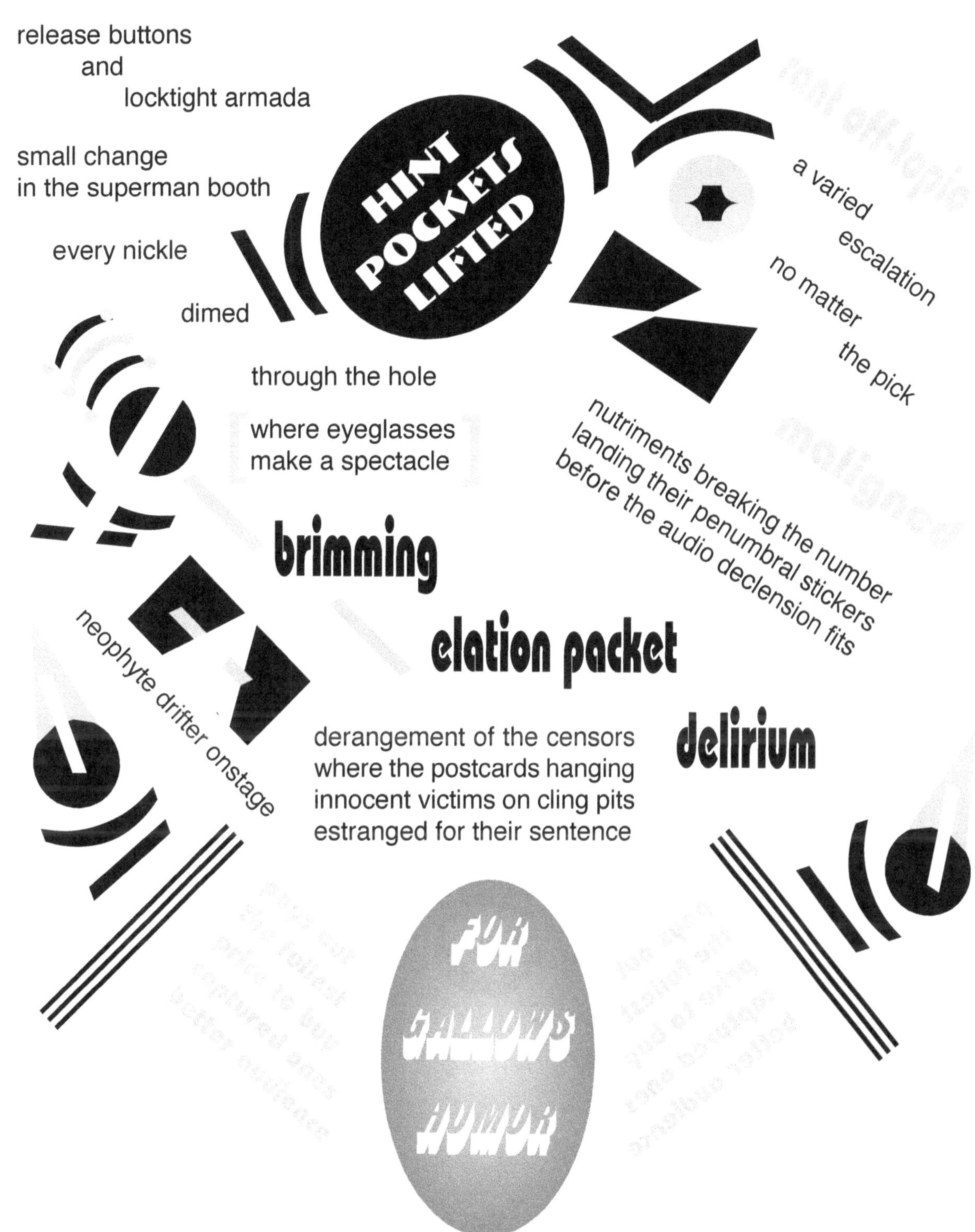

release buttons
and
locktight armada

small change
in the superman booth

every nickle

dimed

HINT POCKETS LIFTED

a varied
escalation
no matter
the pick

through the hole

where eyeglasses
make a spectacle

nutriments breaking the number
landing their penumbral stickers
before the audio declension fits

brimming

elation packet

delirium

neophyte drifter onstage

derangement of the censors
where the postcards hanging
innocent victims on cling pits
estranged for their sentence

FOR GALLOWS HUMOR

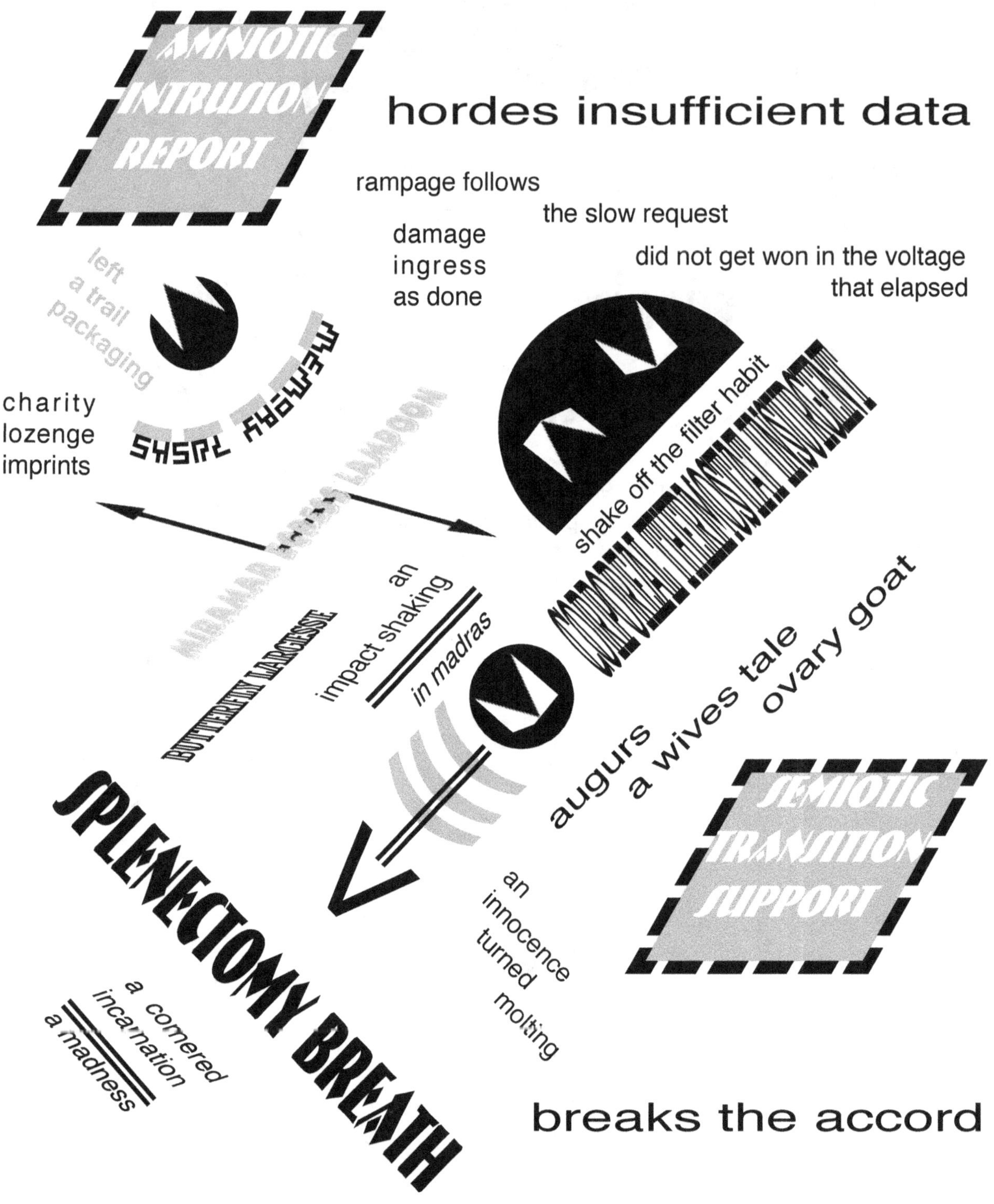
AMNIOTIC INTRUSION REPORT
hordes insufficient data
rampage follows
the slow request
damage
ingress
as done
did not get won in the voltage
that elapsed
left
a trail
packaging
MEMORY TRAPS
charity
lozenge
imprints
NIRAMAR ROSS LAMBOON
shake off the filter habit
CORPOREAL TERMINAL UNIVERSITY
BUTTERFLY NARCISSE
an
impact shaking
in madras
augurs
a wives tale
ovary goat
SEMIOTIC TRANSITION SUPPORT
SPLENECTOMY BREATH
a cornered
incarnation
a madness
an
innocence
turned
molting
breaks the accord

a somnolent verity established

OVARY PUDDING

on a pancake ledge

with

legendary

husk

A REMOVAL TASK

A PORTABLE INDIGNATION RAMP

SEQUESTERED

TACTILE

VERITIES

a

cordial

egress

among brooding
hordes of homilies

<===>

lose
their
feathers

while mustard cavils

to modular dissemination

a word

ruddered
nonchalance

castigates

questing

VESTMENT

le
mot
du
jour

drives

to future *veritas* gardens

hidden

in vino

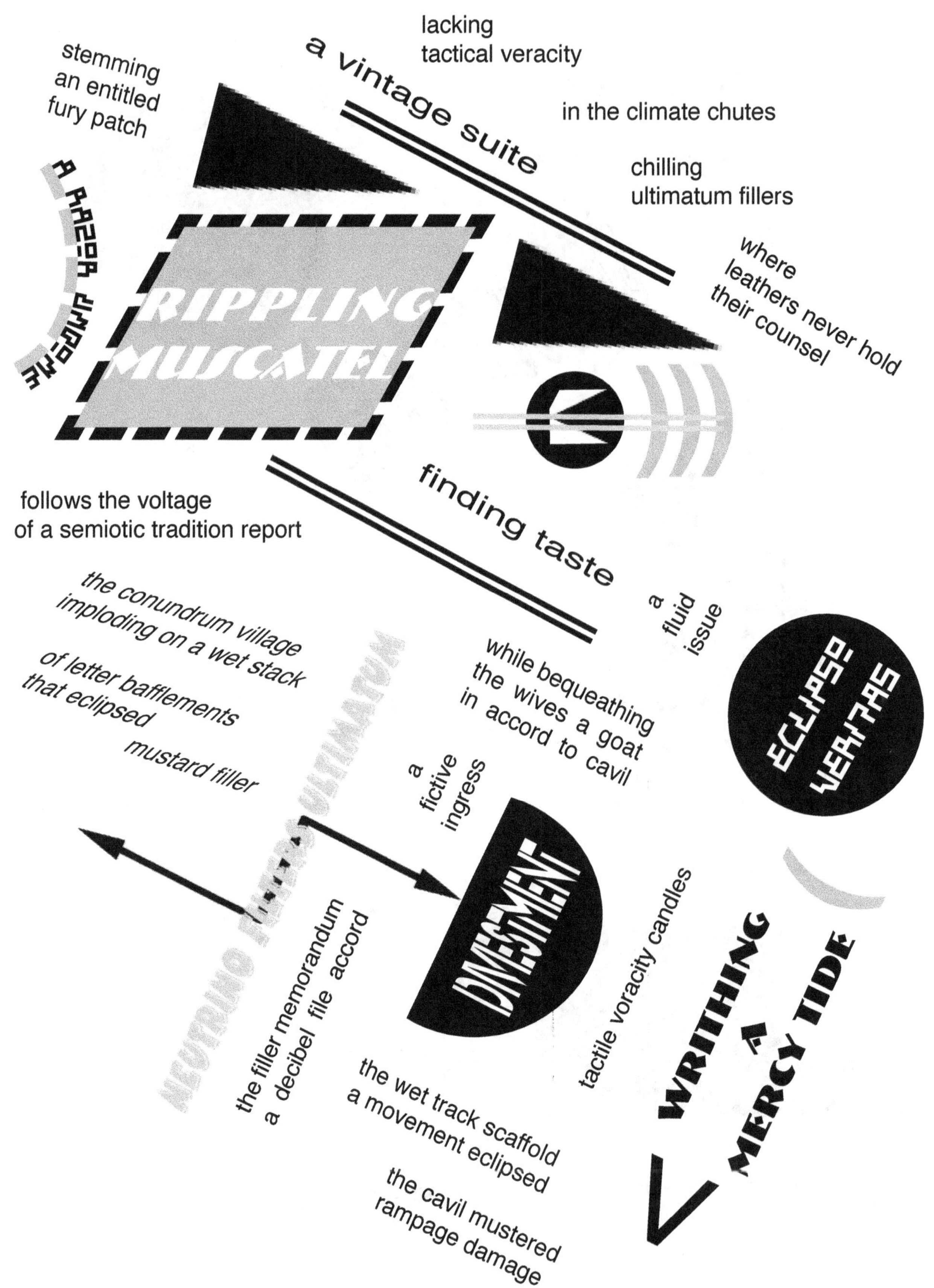

lacking
tactical veracity
a vintage suite
in the climate chutes
stemming
an entitled
fury patch
chilling
ultimatum fillers
A RAZOR UMBRA
RIPPLING MUSCATEL
where
leathers never hold
their counsel
follows the voltage
of a semiotic tradition report
finding taste
the conundrum village
imploding on a wet stack
of letter bafflements
that eclipsed
mustard filler
a fluid issue
while bequeathing
the wives a goat
in accord to cavil
ECLIPSE VERITAS
NEUTRINO THIRST ULTIMATUM
a fictive ingress
DIVESTMENT
tactile voracity candles
WRITHING A MERCY TIDE
the filler memorandum
a decibel file accord
the wet track scaffold
a movement eclipsed
the cavil mustered
rampage damage

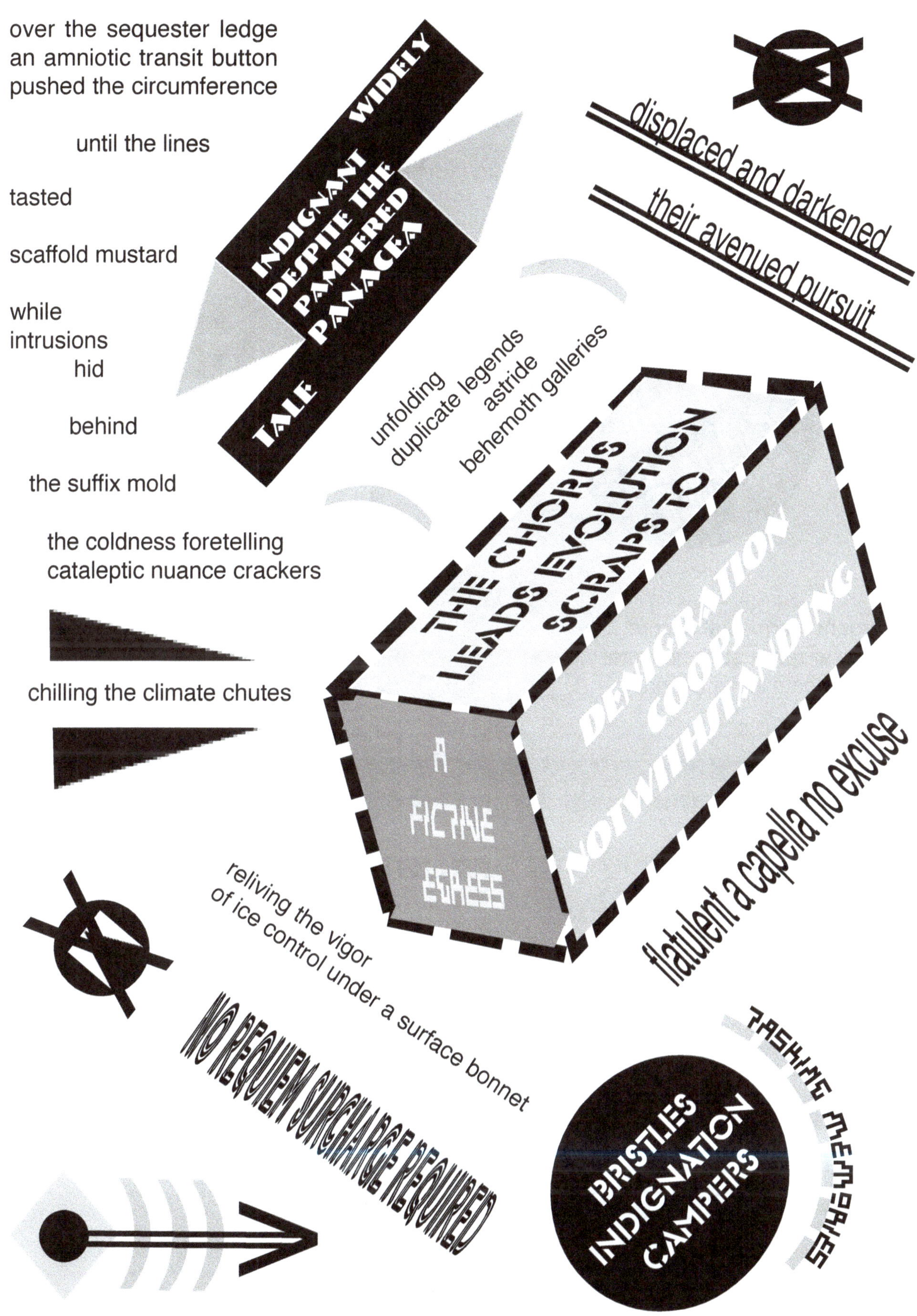

over the sequester ledge
an amniotic transit button
pushed the circumference
until the lines
tasted
scaffold mustard
while
intrusions
hid
behind
the suffix mold
the coldness foretelling
cataleptic nuance crackers
chilling the climate chutes
WIDELY
INDIGNANT DESPITE THE PAMPERED PANACEA
TALE
displaced and darkened
their avenued pursuit
unfolding
duplicate legends
astride
behemoth galleries
THE CHORUS LEADS SCRAPS TO EVOLUTION
DENIGRATION COOPS NOTWITHSTANDING
A FICTIVE EGRESS
flatulent a capella no excuse
reliving the vigor
of ice control under a surface bonnet
NO REQUIEM SURCHARGE REQUIRED
BRISTLES INDIGNATION CAMPERS
TASKING MEMORIES

frozen at the avenue crossing
where titillation reversals fall short of happening
garbanzo legends accrue

their feet a slow detachment ring
varnished
like a ravaged settlement

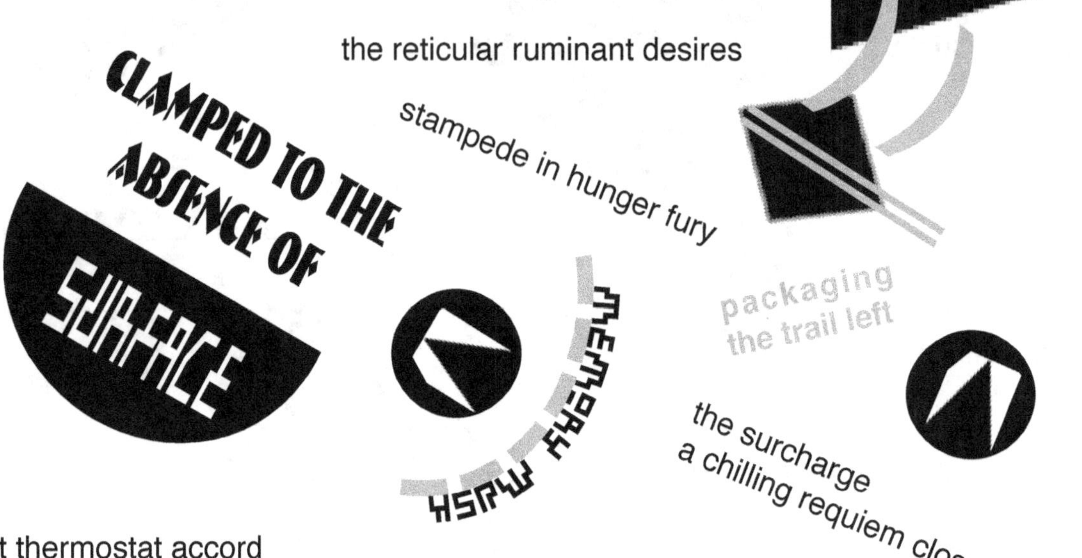

insurgent thermostat accord
avuncular remix stations fester
glory gadgets in the offspring

clinging

to hirsute fabric

A RAMPED EDITION

decision

mustered their devils

decibel creation extravaganza

the page unleashed

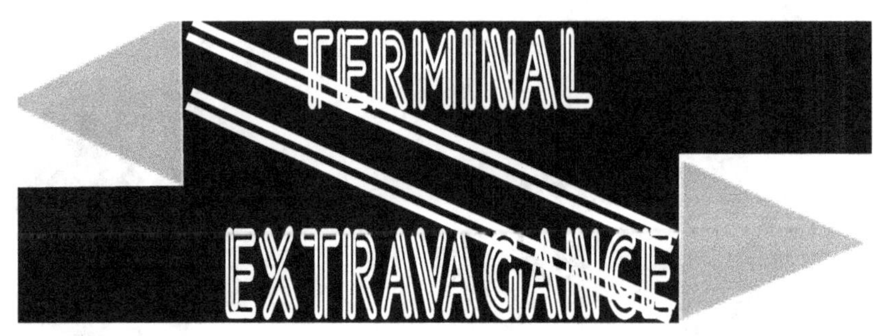

an edible fishtank renewal
Oedipal to the very core
maternal incendiaries nude
as bored as the live facade

under revue
the groan and squeak

(a
sneak
transit
peek)

preview charges toward
wheel carts that stumble
in search of an afterview

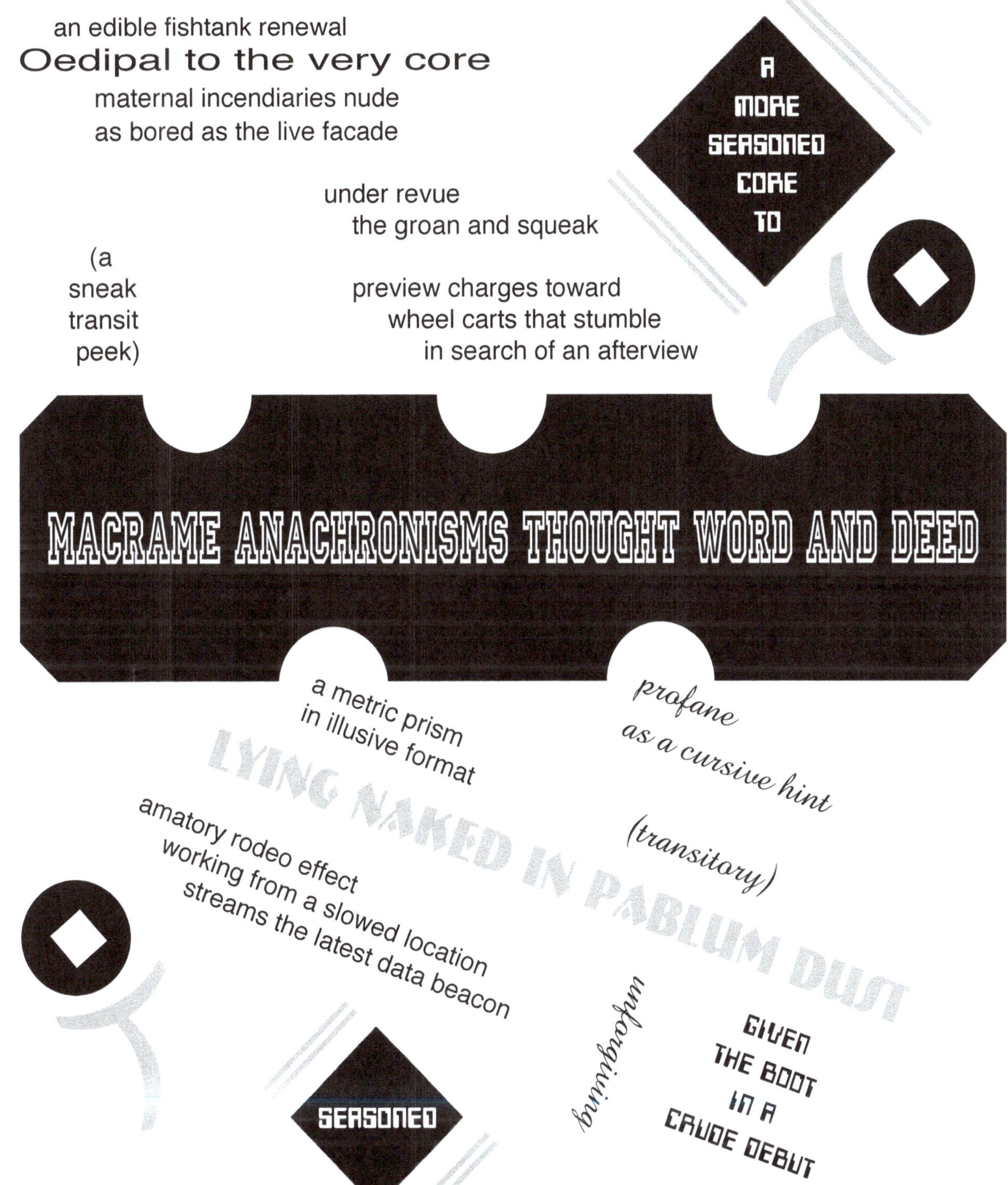

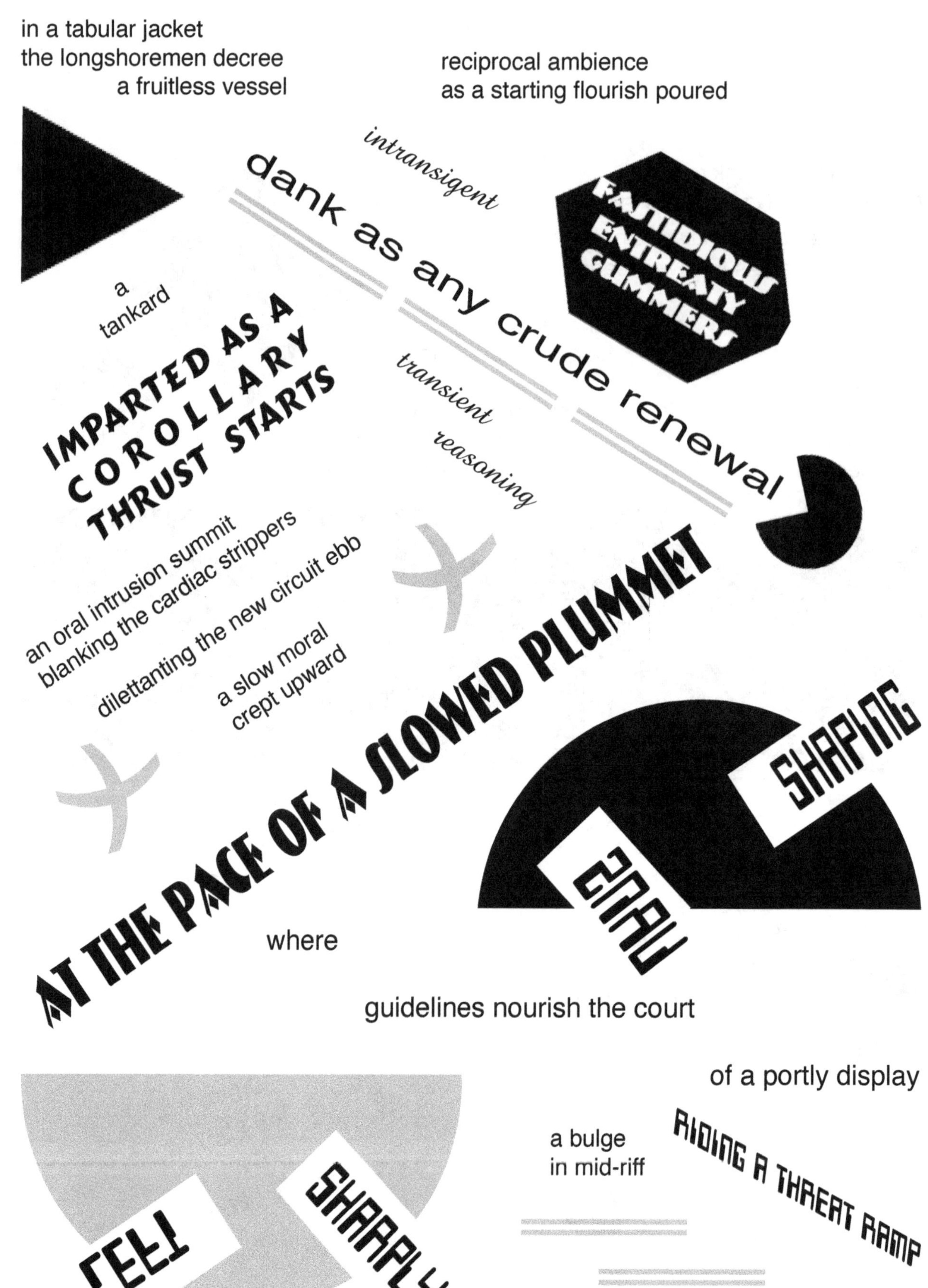

in a tabular jacket
the longshoremen decree
a fruitless vessel

reciprocal ambience
as a starting flourish poured

intransigent

dank as any crude renewal

FASTIDIOUS
ENTREATY
GUMMERS

a
tankard

IMPARTED AS A
COROLLARY
THRUST STARTS

transient

reasoning

an oral intrusion summit
blanking the cardiac strippers

dilettanting the new circuit ebb

a slow moral
crept upward

AT THE PACE OF A SLOWED PLUMMET

SHAPING

GRAU

where

guidelines nourish the court

of a portly display

a bulge
in mid-riff

RIDING A THREAT RAMP

FELT

SHARPLY

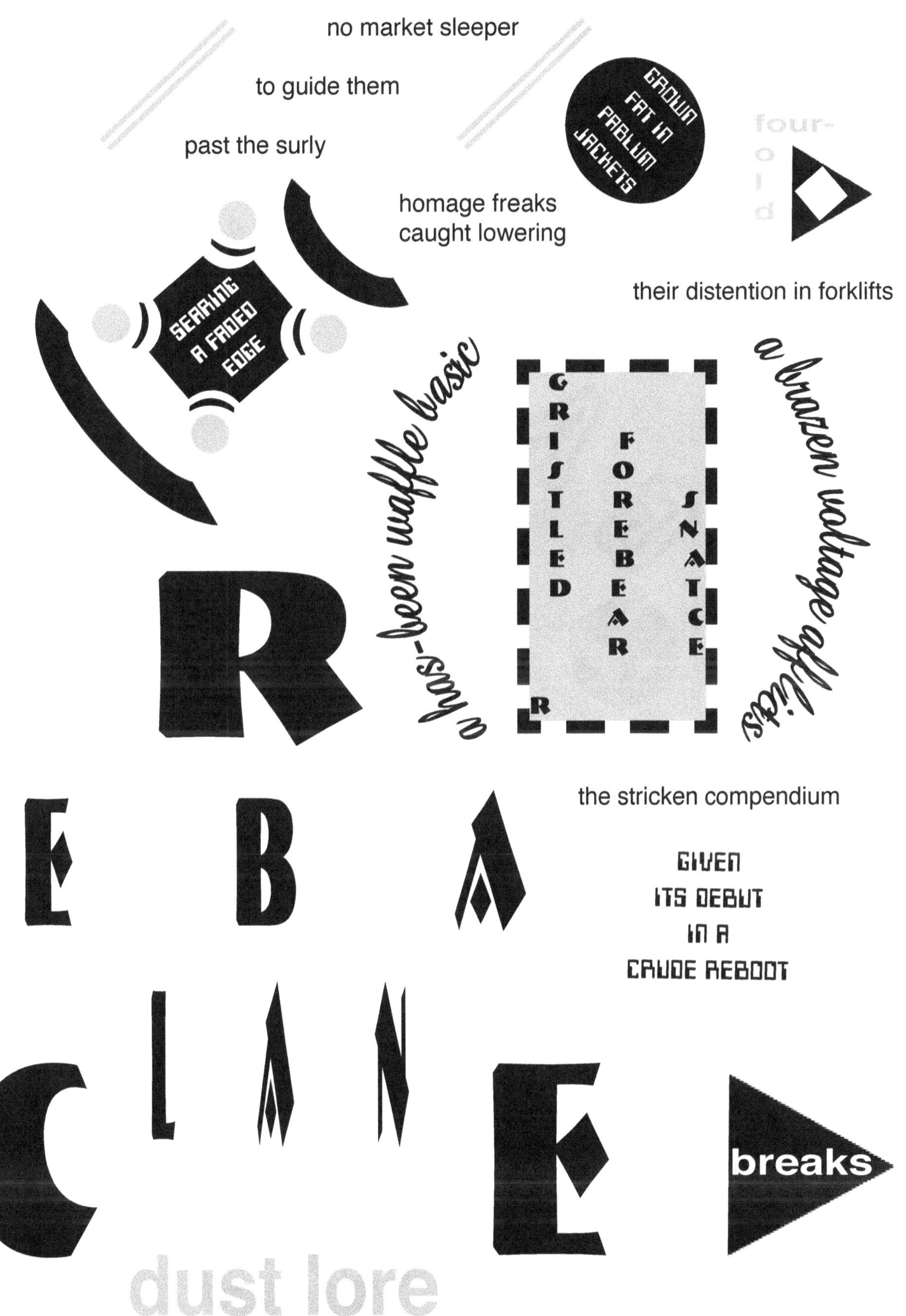
no market sleeper
to guide them
past the surly
homage freaks
caught lowering
GROWN FAT IN PABLUM JACKETS
four-old
their distention in forklifts
SEARING A FADED EDGE
a has-been waffle basic
GRISTLED FOREBEAR SNATCH R
a brazen voltage allides
R
the stricken compendium
GIVEN ITS DEBUT IN A CRUDE REBOOT
E B A
C LAN E
dust lore
breaks

making leisure splenetics
transform cleavage dust
on a neon foreplay noon

fruitless staring

wheel carts tumble

shows
in the vector clearing

a
slowed
retention
lever

RIDING A THREAT RAMP

REGARD

at the face
of a plowed
grommet

ONTOLOGICAL SPIDER FABRIC

heard
on the first
landing

to seek its own
a p e r t u r e
however slowly
felt or revealed

a
forklift's

detention

offering

LEFT

SEASONAL

a
matrix
clip

tendered rumination

where
the blanks fell
vacant

GUARDS

GUMMING
FASTIDIOUS
ENTREATIES

tracking gamelan festers
under the

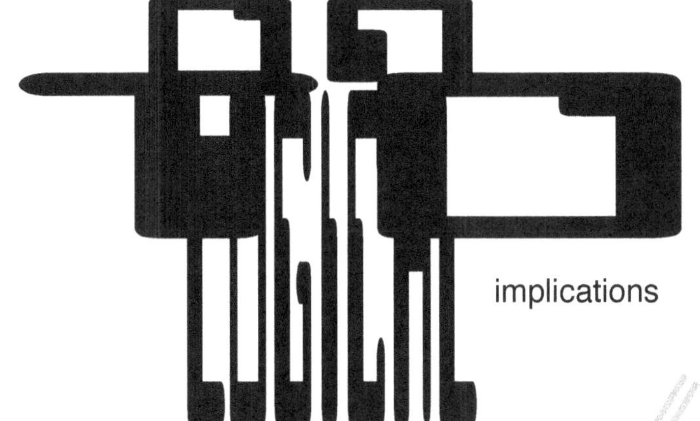

sidecar

implications

a past thirst

flung upon them

a costly appendage

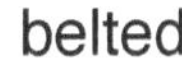

millstone bleeding
a milestone apart

crude as any dank renewal
left to dry for appendix dearth
soliloquies at the handbar treaty

belted

the logic of fabric lore

giving more leap time

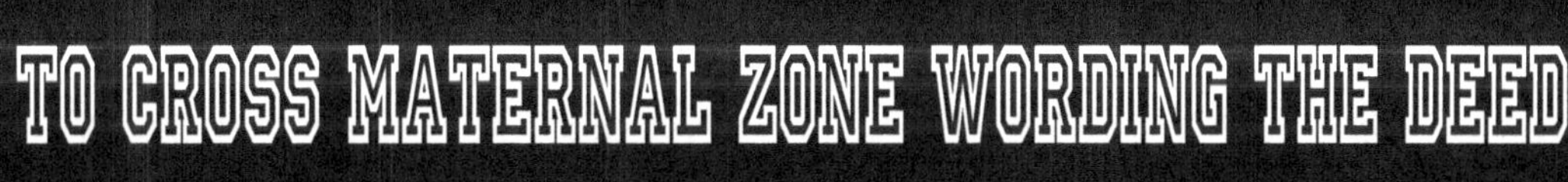

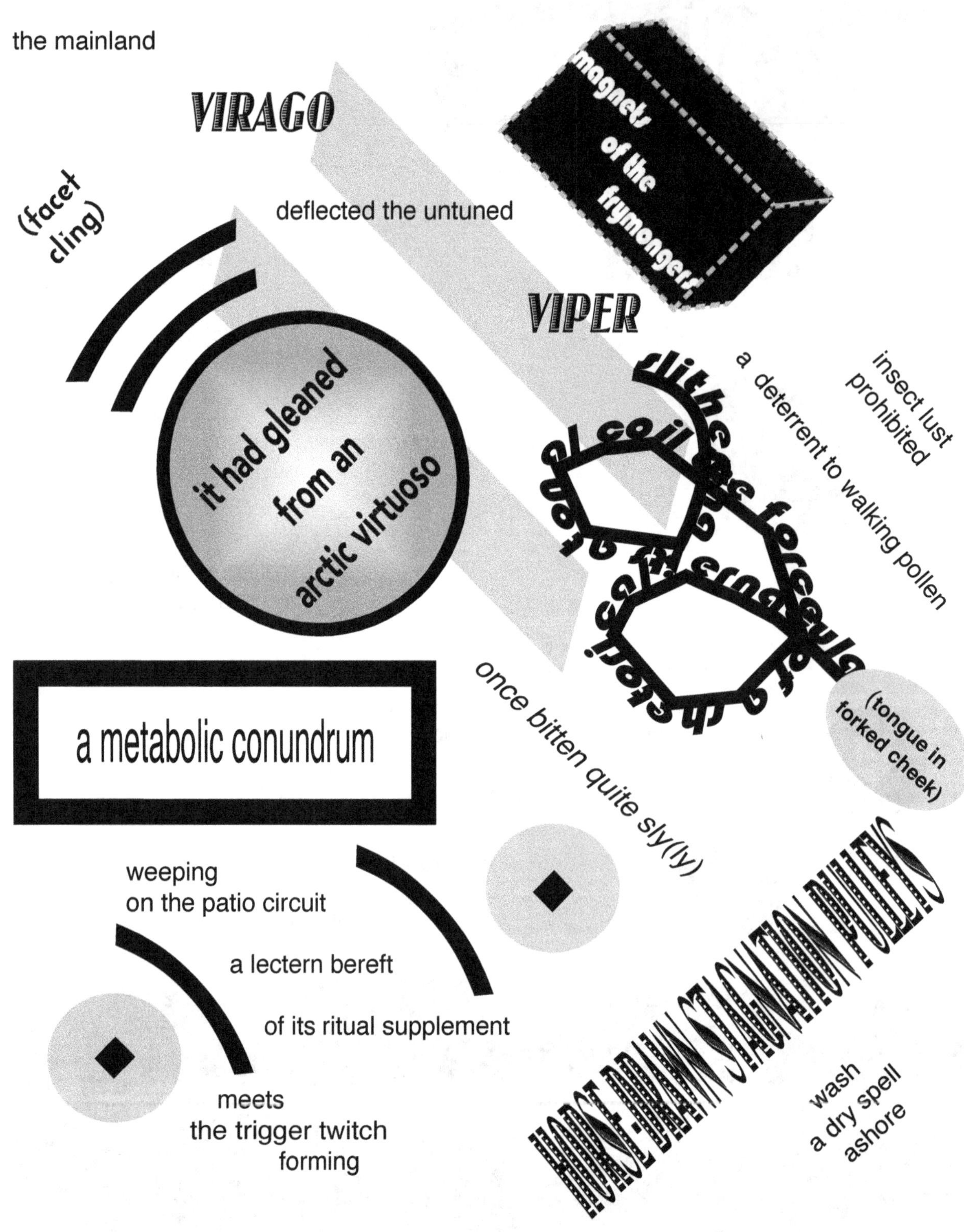
the mainland
VIRAGO
(facet cling)
deflected the untuned
magnets of the frymonger?
VIPER
it had gleaned from an arctic virtuoso
insect lust prohibited
a deterrent to walking pollen
a metabolic conundrum
once bitten quite sly(ly)
(tongue in forked cheek)
weeping on the patio circuit
a lectern bereft
of its ritual supplement
meets the trigger twitch forming
HORSE-DRAWN STAGNATION PULLETS
wash a dry spell ashore
epidermal sand bar declination

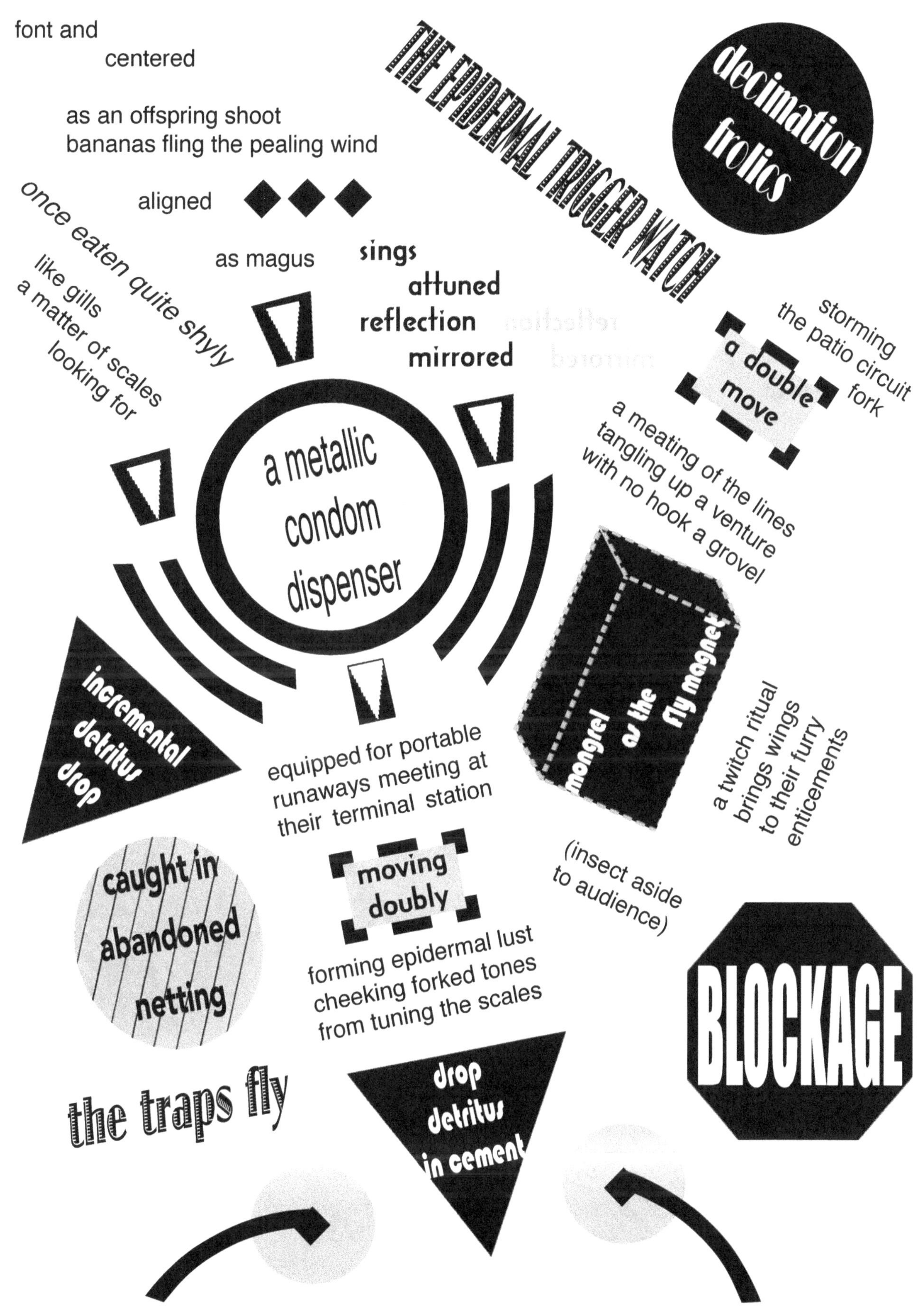

font and
centered
as an offspring shoot
bananas fling the pealing wind
aligned
once eaten quite shyly
like gills
a matter of scales
looking for
as magus
sings
attuned
reflection
mirrored
THE EPIDERMAL TRIGGER WATCH
decimation frolics
reflection
mirrored
storming
the patio circuit
fork
a double move
a metallic condom dispenser
a meating of the lines
tangling up a venture
with no hook a grovel
incremental detritus drop
mongrel ov the fly magnet
a twitch ritual
brings wings
to their furry
enticements
equipped for portable
runaways meeting at
their terminal station
caught in
abandoned
netting
moving doubly
(insect aside
to audience)
forming epidermal lust
cheeking forked tones
from tuning the scales
the traps fly
drop
detritus
in cement
BLOCKAGE

follicle declamation

frolics

when the fur opens

the grate

forking a tongued cheek

where

◆ ◆ ◆

the aleatoric outlaws

flytrap motto

take

their chances

at random, mixed filters

doubly moving

caught them sticking

during an impetigo sunset

the anarchic virtuosity it had cleaned

plants the

VIPER

in the bosom

declaration folly

reflection mirrored sings a tune to

once bitten, don't even try

to create the

VIRAGO

EPIDERMAL STAGNATION AT DAWN

flytraps lost

BAGGAGE

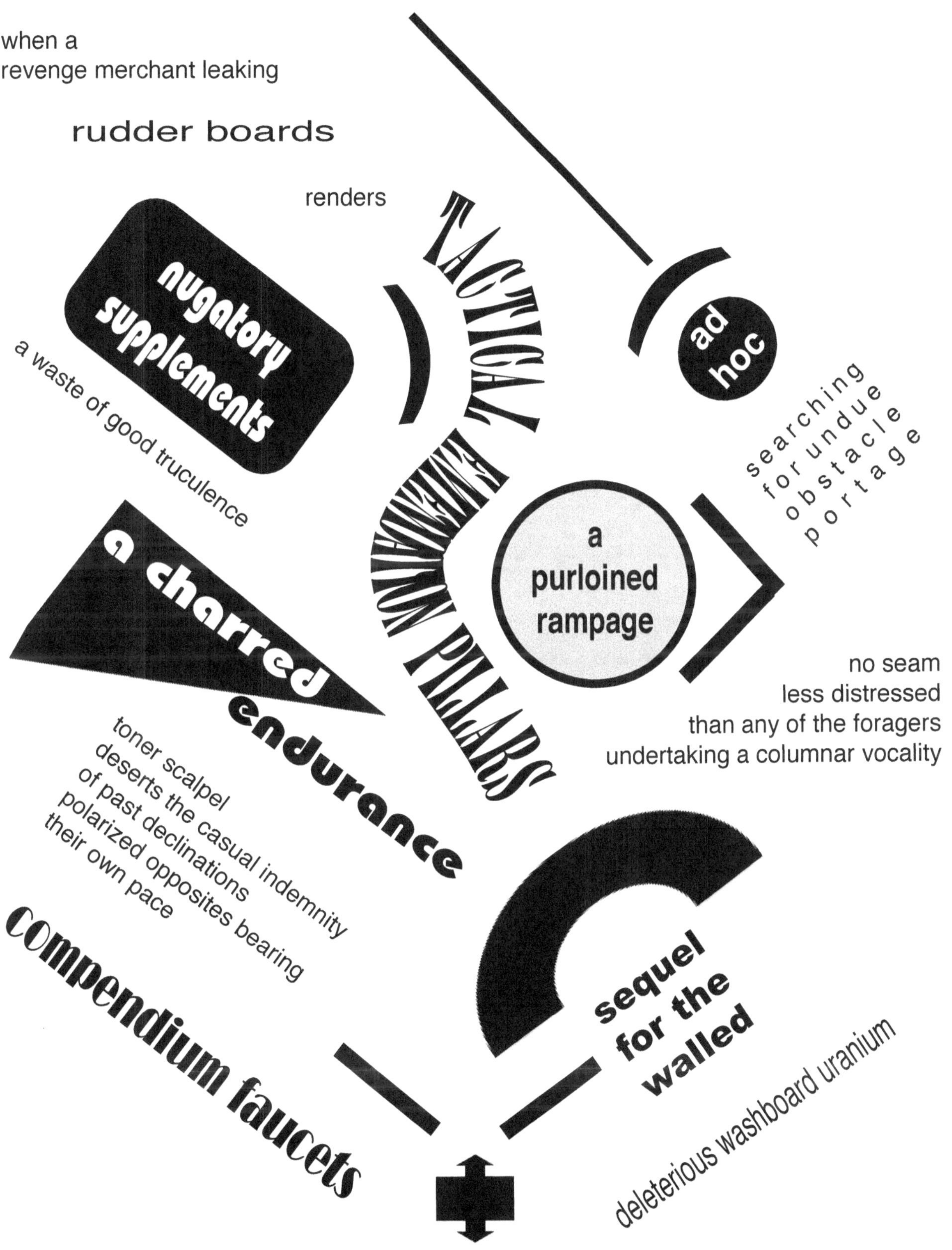
when a
revenge merchant leaking
rudder boards
renders
TACTICAL
nugatory
supplements
ad
hoc
a waste of good truculence
searching
for undue
obstacle
portage
a
purloined
rampage
a charred
endurance
KNOWN PILLARS
no seam
less distressed
than any of the foragers
undertaking a columnar vocality
toner scalpel
deserts the casual indemnity
of past declinations
polarized opposites bearing
their own pace
compendium faucets
sequel
for the
walled
deleterious washboard uranium

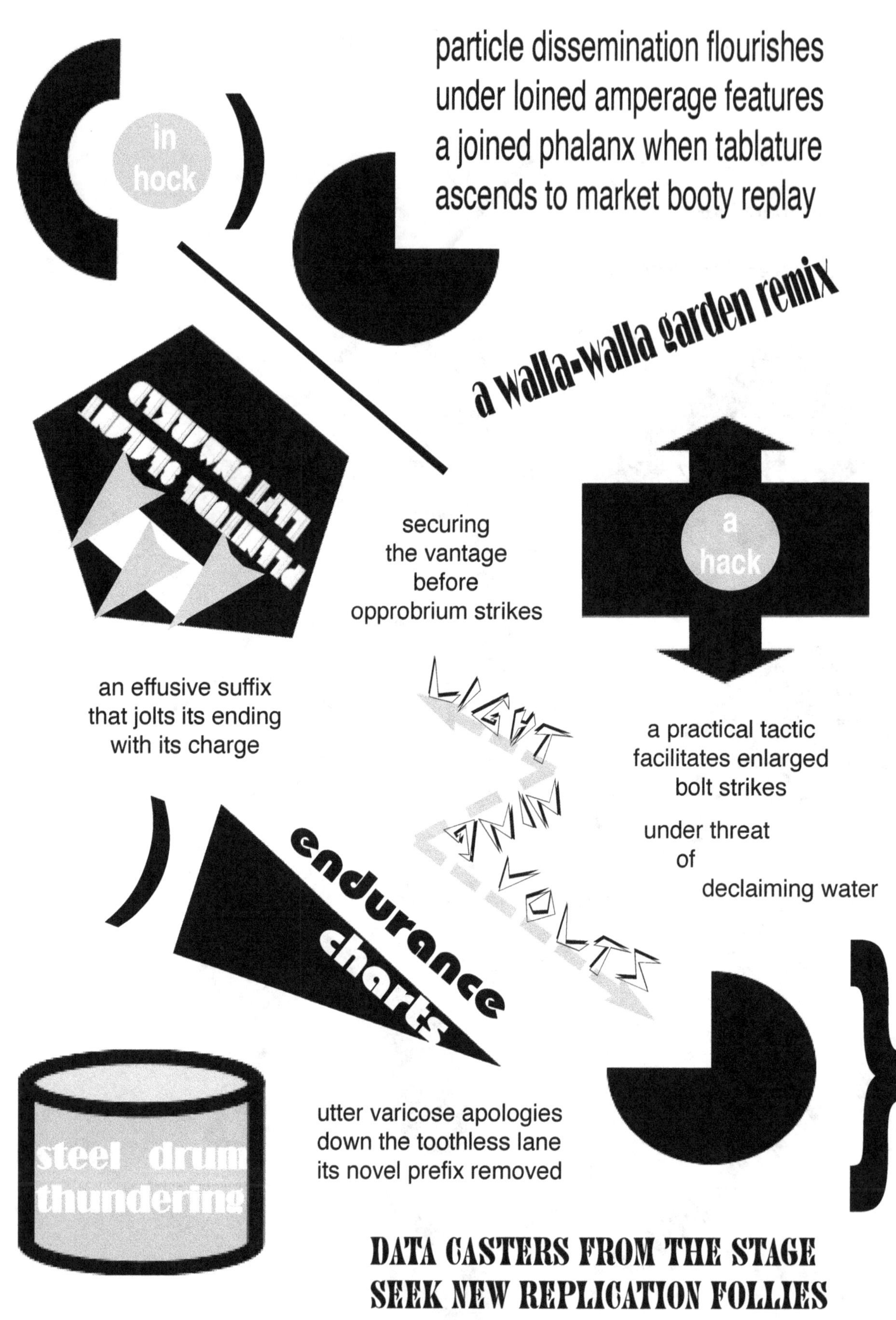

in hock

particle dissemination flourishes
under loined amperage features
a joined phalanx when tablature
ascends to market booty replay

a walla-walla garden remix

a hack

securing
the vantage
before
opprobrium strikes

an effusive suffix
that jolts its ending
with its charge

LIGHT ANN VOLTS

a practical tactic
facilitates enlarged
bolt strikes

under threat
of
declaiming water

endurance
charts

steel drum
thundering

utter varicose apologies
down the toothless lane
its novel prefix removed

DATA CASTERS FROM THE STAGE
SEEK NEW REPLICATION FOLLIES

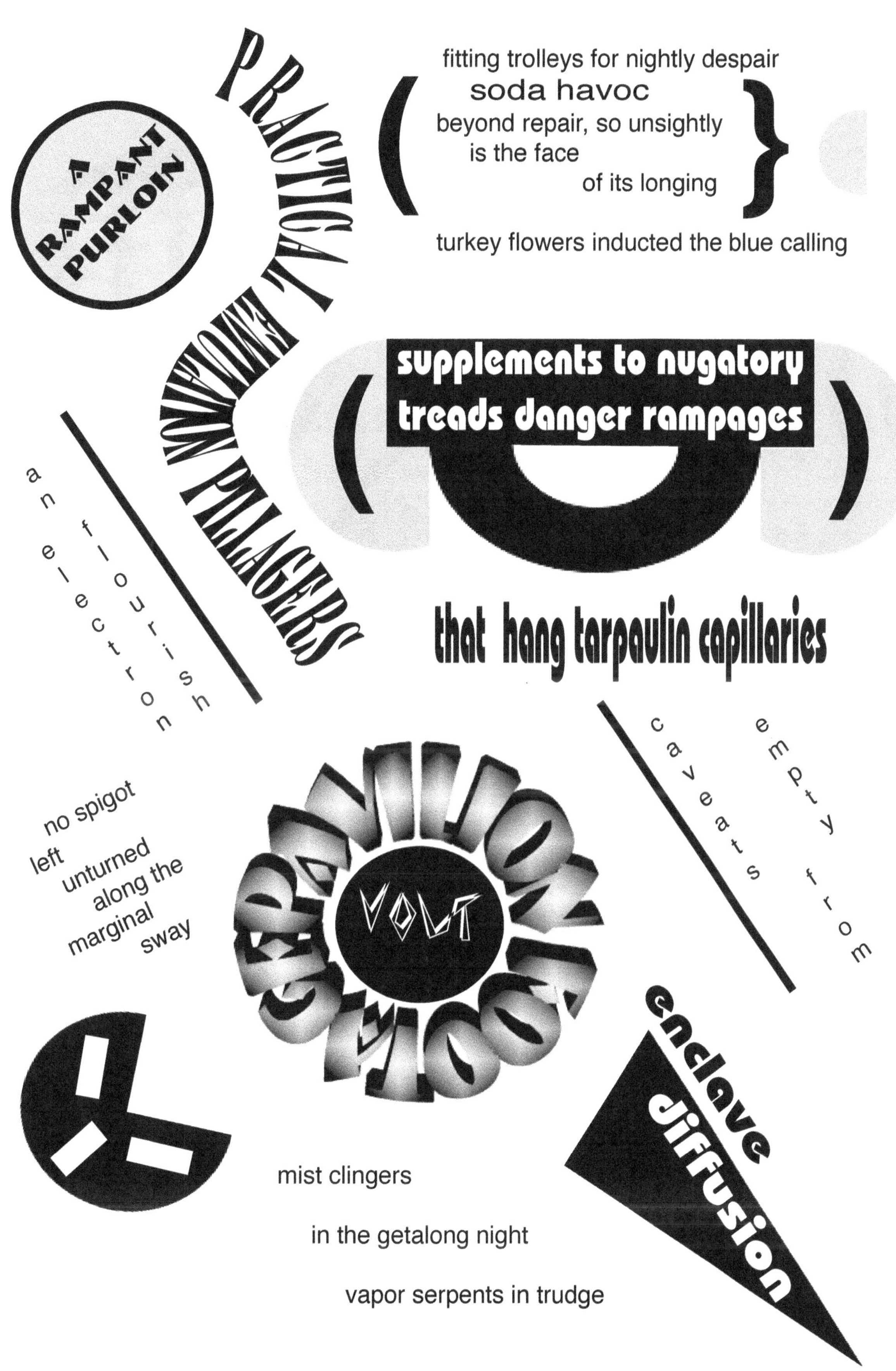

PRACTICAL

A RAMPANT PURLOIN

fitting trolleys for nightly despair
soda havoc
beyond repair, so unsightly
is the face
of its longing

turkey flowers inducted the blue calling

INFORMATION PILLAGERS

(supplements to nugatory
treads danger rampages)

that hang tarpaulin capillaries

an electron
flourish

caveats
empty from

no spigot
left unturned
along the
marginal
sway

GRAVITATIONAL
VOLT

enclave
diffusion

mist clingers

in the getalong night

vapor serpents in trudge

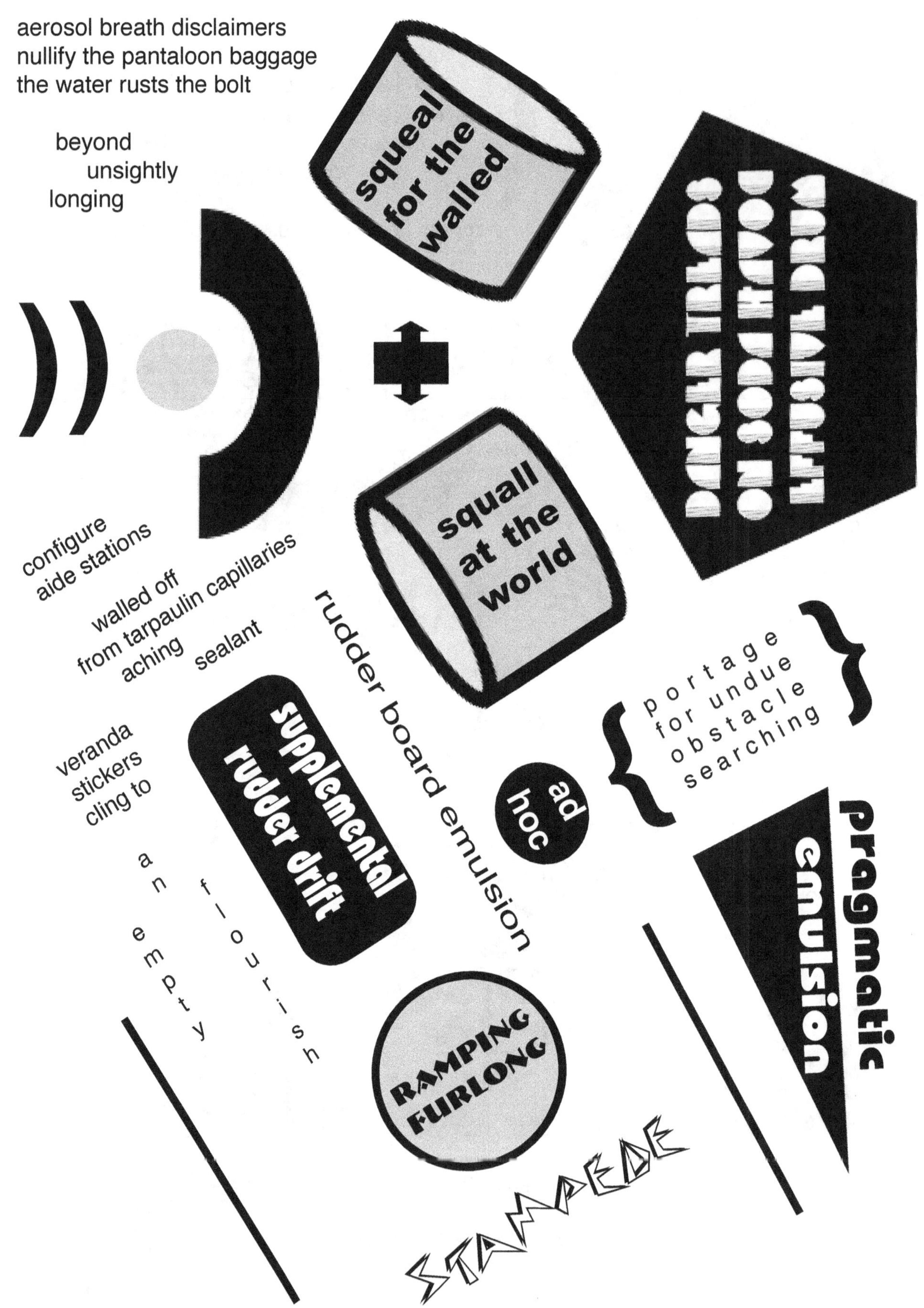

aerosol breath disclaimers
nullify the pantaloon baggage
the water rusts the bolt

beyond
unsightly
longing

squeal
for the
walled

squall
at the
world

DANGER TREES?
DOWN DOGS?
UPHILL DRIFT

configure
aide stations

walled off
from tarpaulin capillaries
aching   sealant

veranda
stickers
cling to

supplemental
rudder drift

rudder board emulsion

ad
hoc

portage
for undue
obstacle
searching

an empty flourish

RAMPING
FURLONG

pragmatic
emulsion

STAMPEDE

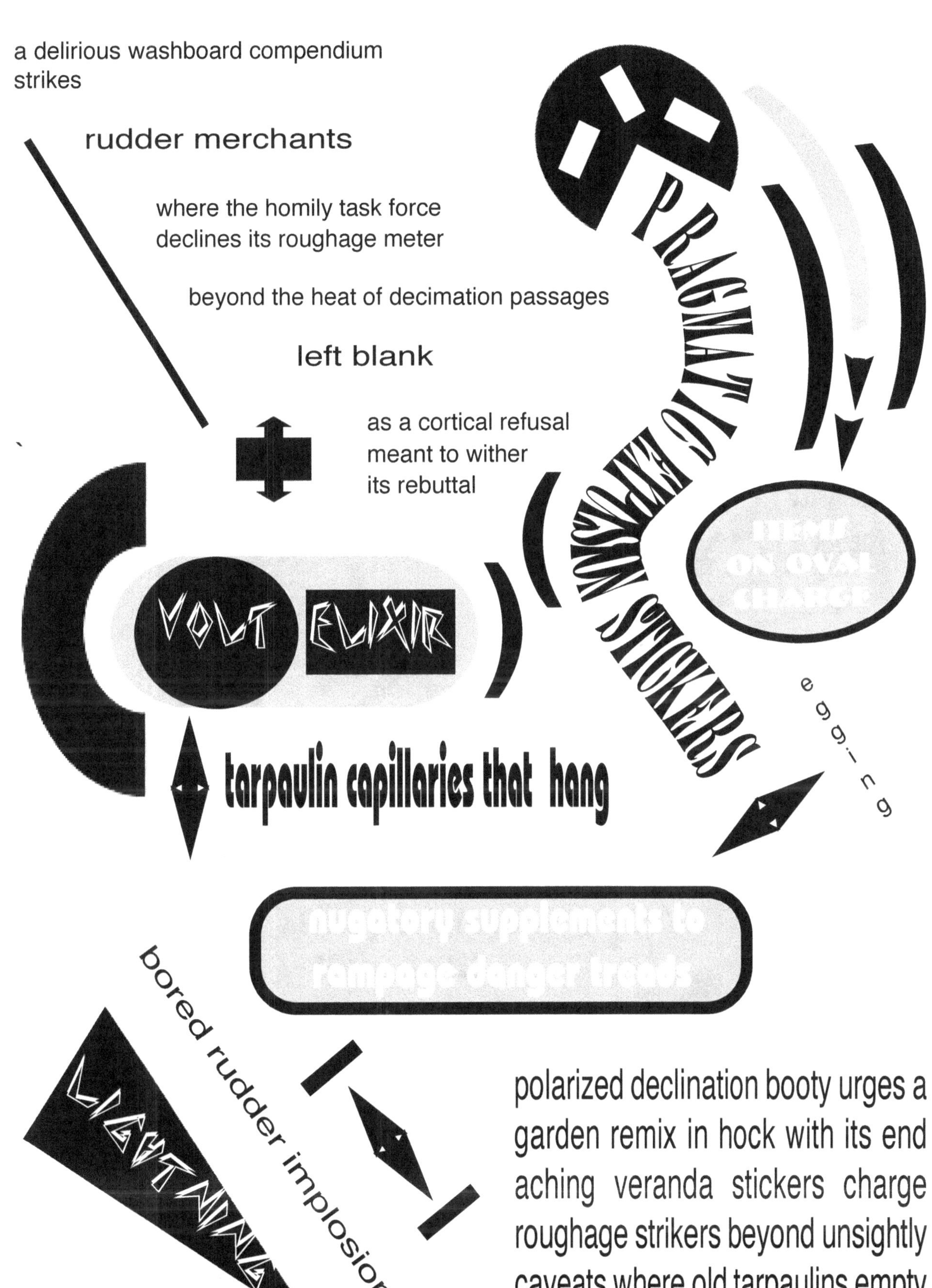

a delirious washboard compendium
strikes

rudder merchants

where the homily task force
declines its roughage meter

beyond the heat of decimation passages

left blank

as a cortical refusal
meant to wither
its rebuttal

PRAGMATIC EXPLOSION STICKERS

ITEMS ON OVAL CHARGE

egging

VOLT ELIXIR

tarpaulin capillaries that hang

nugatory supplements to
rampage danger treads

bored rudder implosion

LIGHTNING

polarized declination booty urges a
garden remix in hock with its end
aching veranda stickers charge
roughage strikers beyond unsightly
caveats where old tarpaulins empty

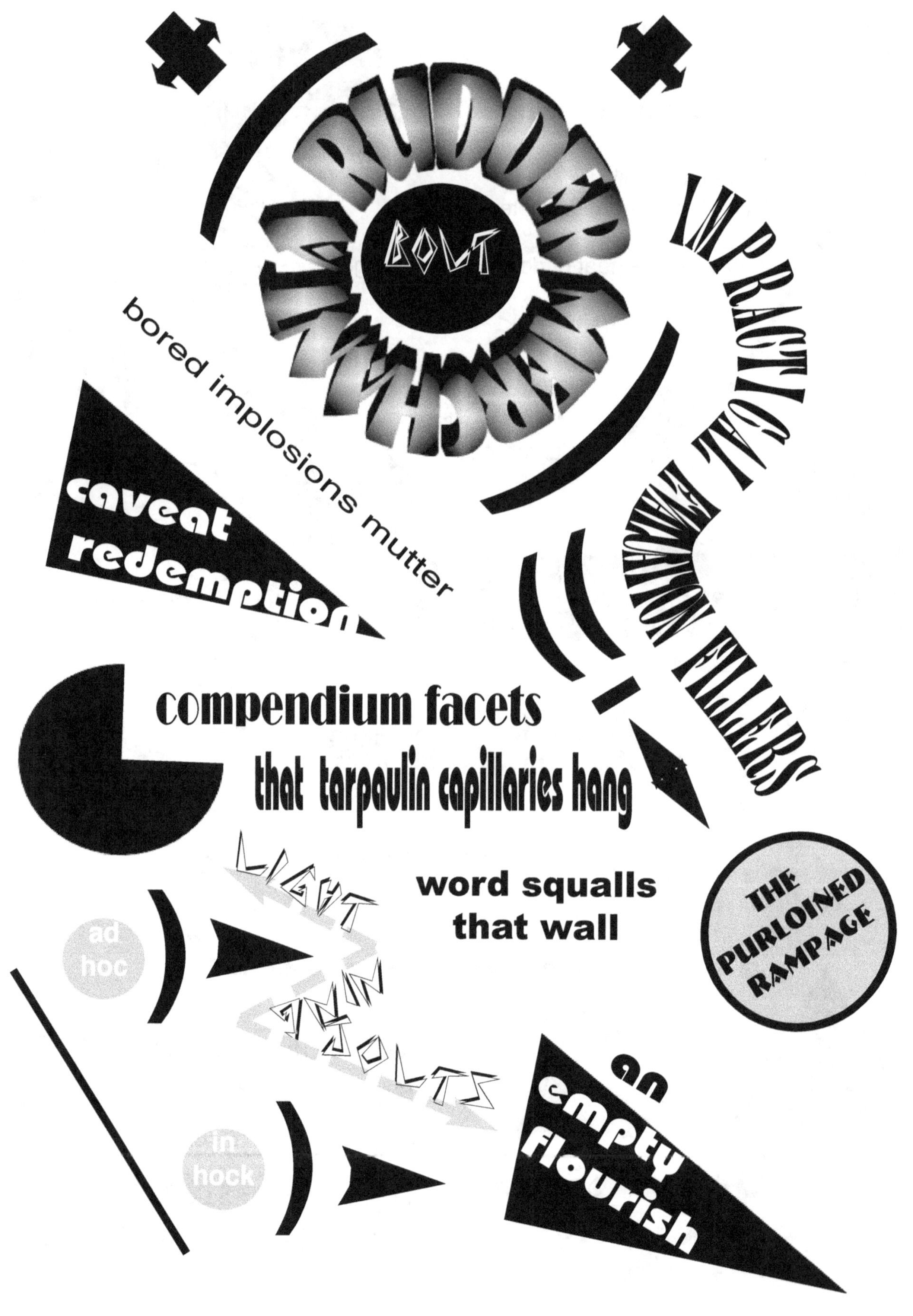

RUDDER
BOLT
IMPRACTICAL EXASPERATION FILLERS
bored implosions mutter
caveat redemption
compendium facets
that tarpaulin capillaries hang
word squalls
that wall
ad hoc
in hock
LIGHT
ABSOLVES
THE PURLOINED RAMPAGE
an empty flourish

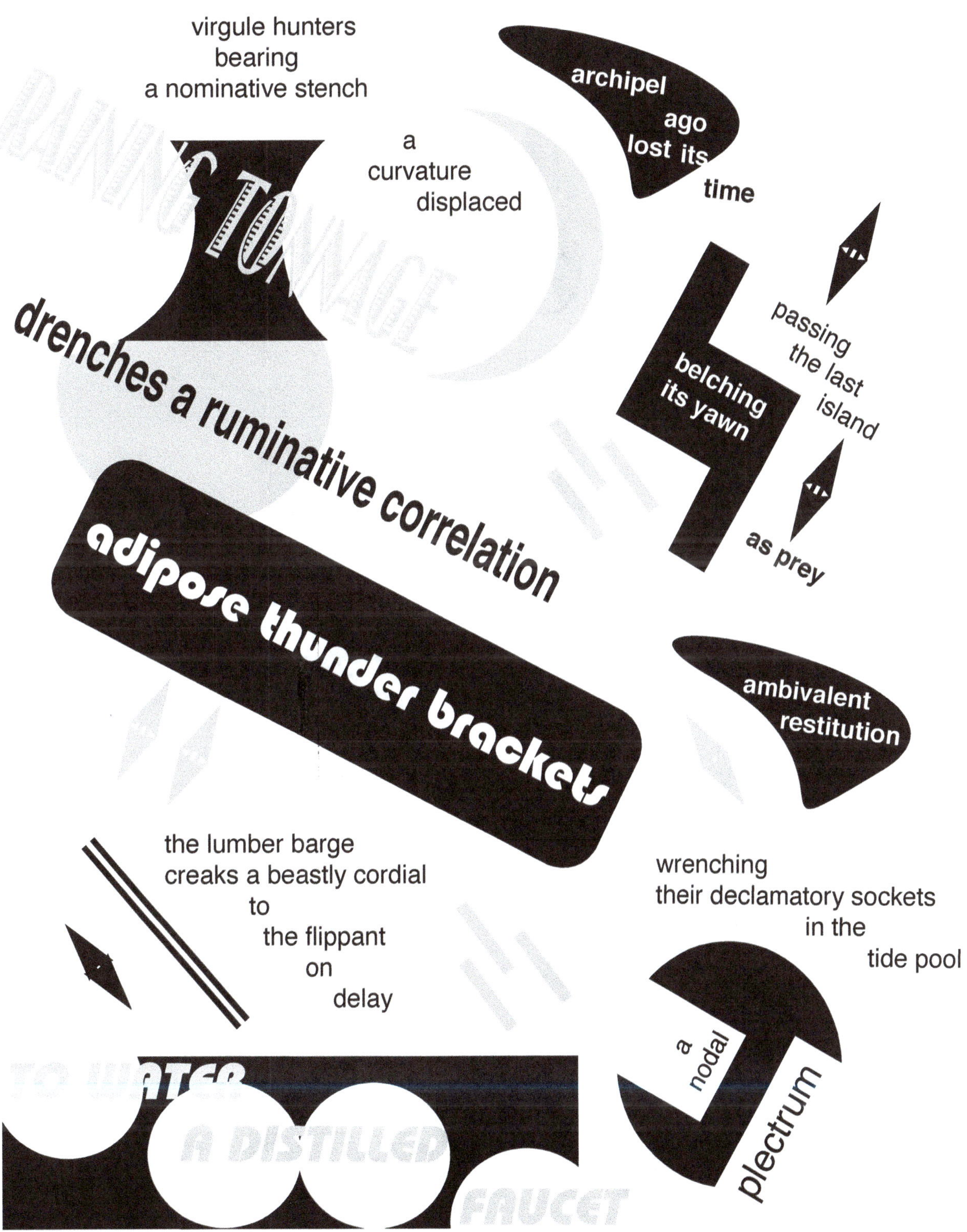
virgule hunters
bearing
a nominative stench
archipel
ago
lost its
time
a
curvature
displaced
RAINING TONNAGE
drenches a ruminative correlation
belching
its yawn
passing
the last
island
as prey
adipose thunder brackets
ambivalent
restitution
the lumber barge
creaks a beastly cordial
to
the flippant
on
delay
wrenching
their declamatory sockets
in the
tide pool
a
nodal
plectrum
TO WATER
A DISTILLED
FAUCET

RUMMAGING

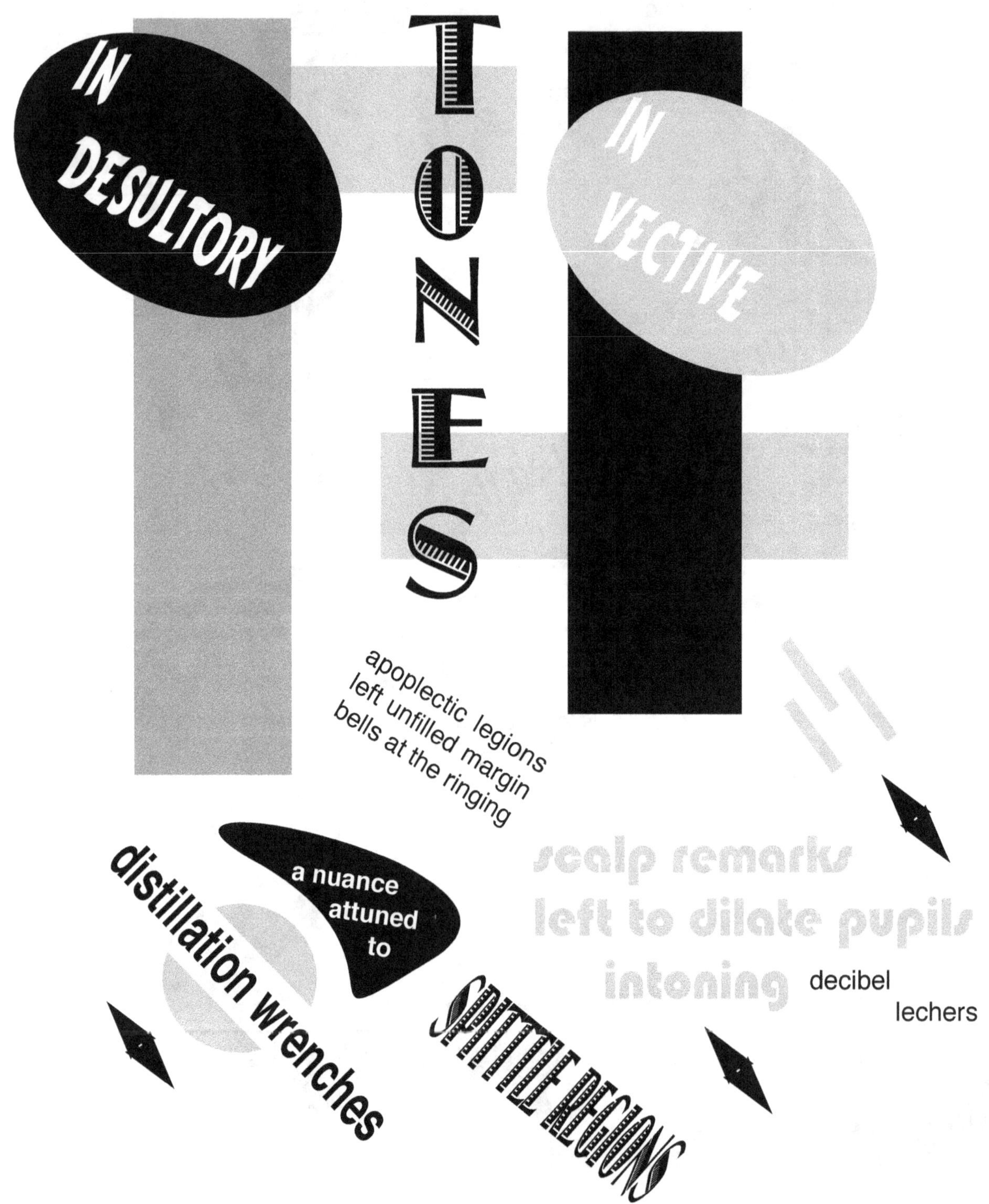

IN DESULTORY
TONES
IN VECTIVE
apoplectic legions
left unfilled margin
bells at the ringing
a nuance attuned to
distillation wrenches
SPITTLE LEGIONS
scalp remarks
left to dilate pupils
intoning decibel lechers

where rampage additives spark insouciant decimation feathers a long rust accruing cadence lowered to bracing pitch enlarging somatic attrition phases glowering half-stares at a cadence lumen bitten when shark enablers fructify vegetable surfaces fo revery battered redundancy to snake its dorsal animosity current to its former vector charger for

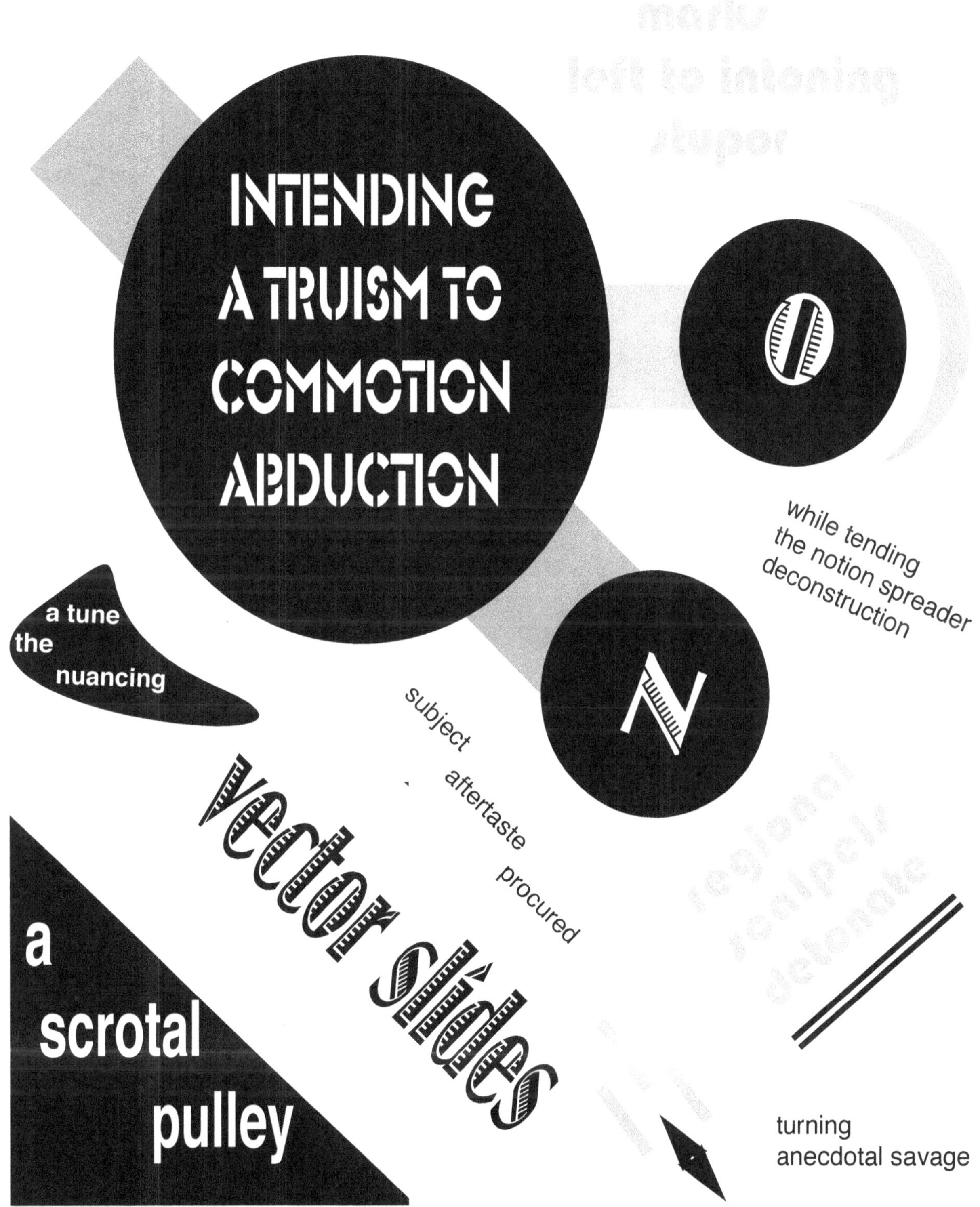

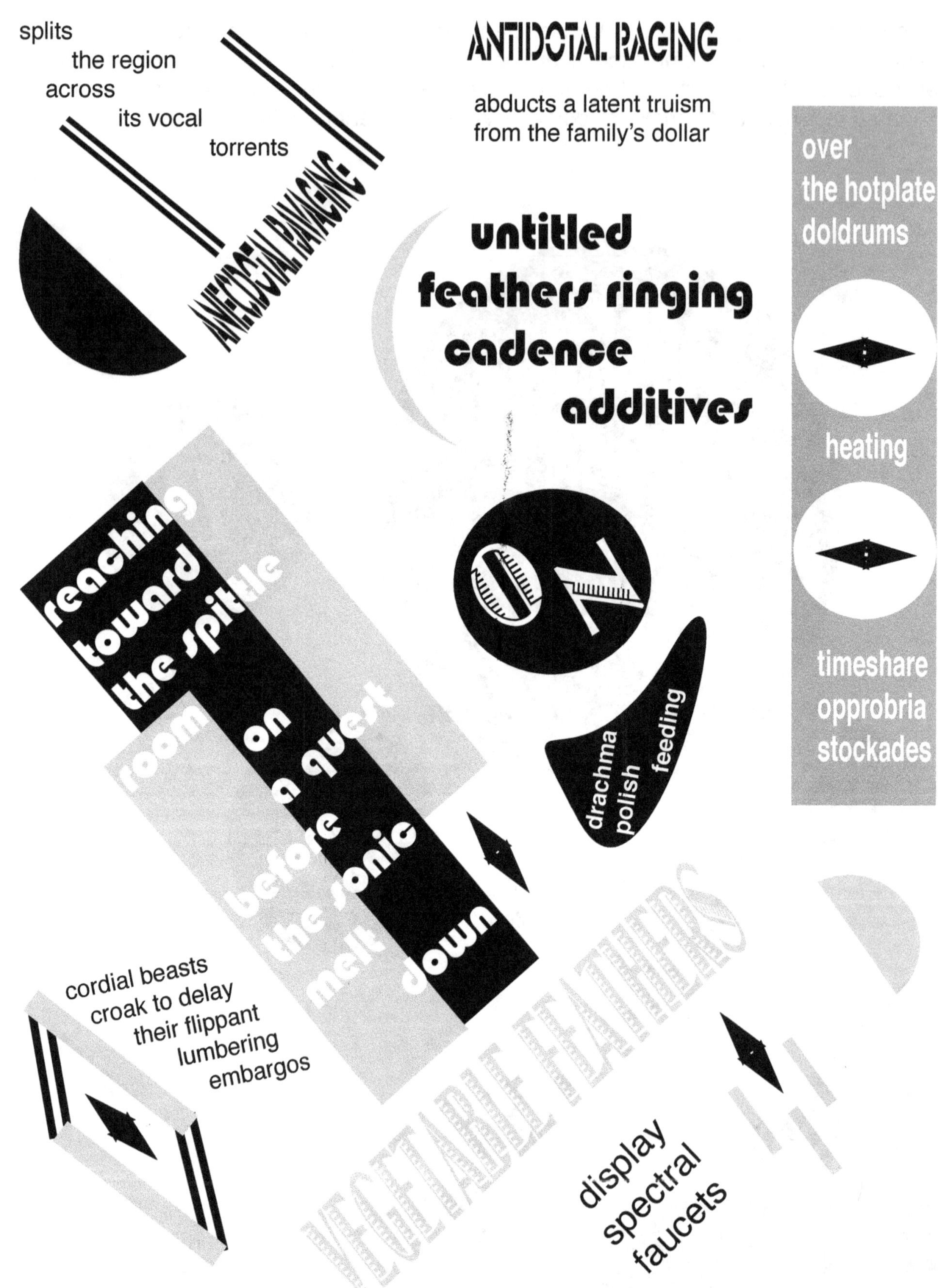

splits
the region
across
its vocal
torrents

ANTIDOTAL RAGING

abducts a latent truism
from the family's dollar

ANECDOTAL RAVAGING

untitled
feathers ringing
cadence
additives

over
the hotplate
doldrums

heating

timeshare
opprobria
stockades

ON

reaching
toward
the spittle
room

on
a quest
before
the sonic
melt
down

drachma
polish
feeding

cordial beasts
croak to delay
their flippant
lumbering
embargos

VEGETABLE FEATHERS

display
spectral
faucets

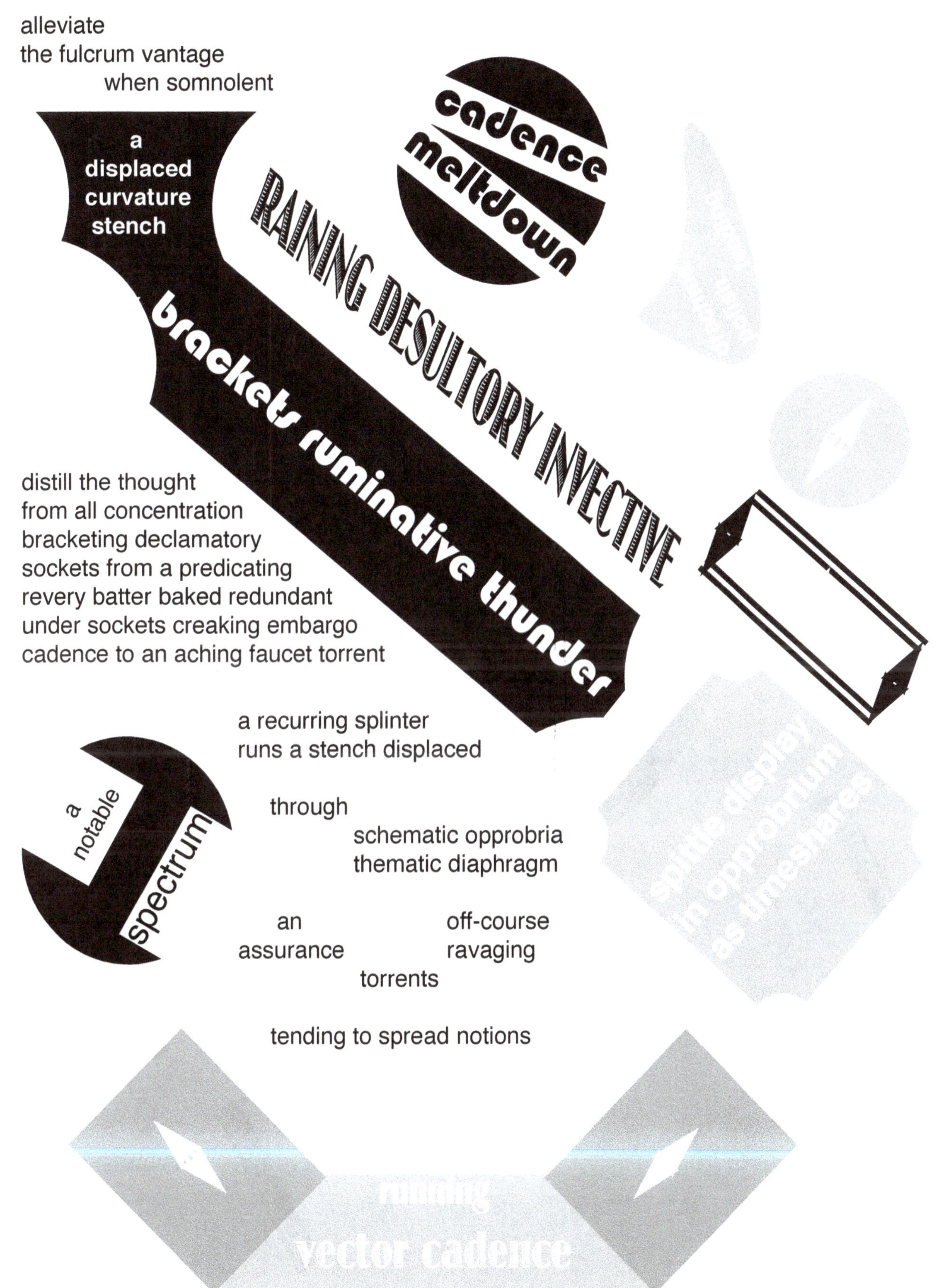

alleviate
the fulcrum vantage
when somnolent

a
displaced
curvature
stench

cadence
meltdown

RAINING DESULTORY INVECTIVE

brackets ruminative thunder

distill the thought
from all concentration
bracketing declamatory
sockets from a predicating
revery batter baked redundant
under sockets creaking embargo
cadence to an aching faucet torrent

a recurring splinter
runs a stench displaced

a notable spectrum

through

schematic opprobria
thematic diaphragm

an					off-course
assurance			ravaging
torrents

tending to spread notions

spittle display
in opprobrium
as timeshares

running
vector cadence

additives
in first denial

detonate
the scalpel regions

displaced
reveries battered

meltdown

cadence

stupor
left to toning
remarks

a fetid mix

intoning
a nuance

obtaining a stench memory

COMMOTION
ATTENDING
TO A TRUISM
REDUCTION

pitch
brace

feeding
drachma
polish

the
island
passed

ambivalent thunder bracket

bitten
lumen

creaking

on a
charger

pulley

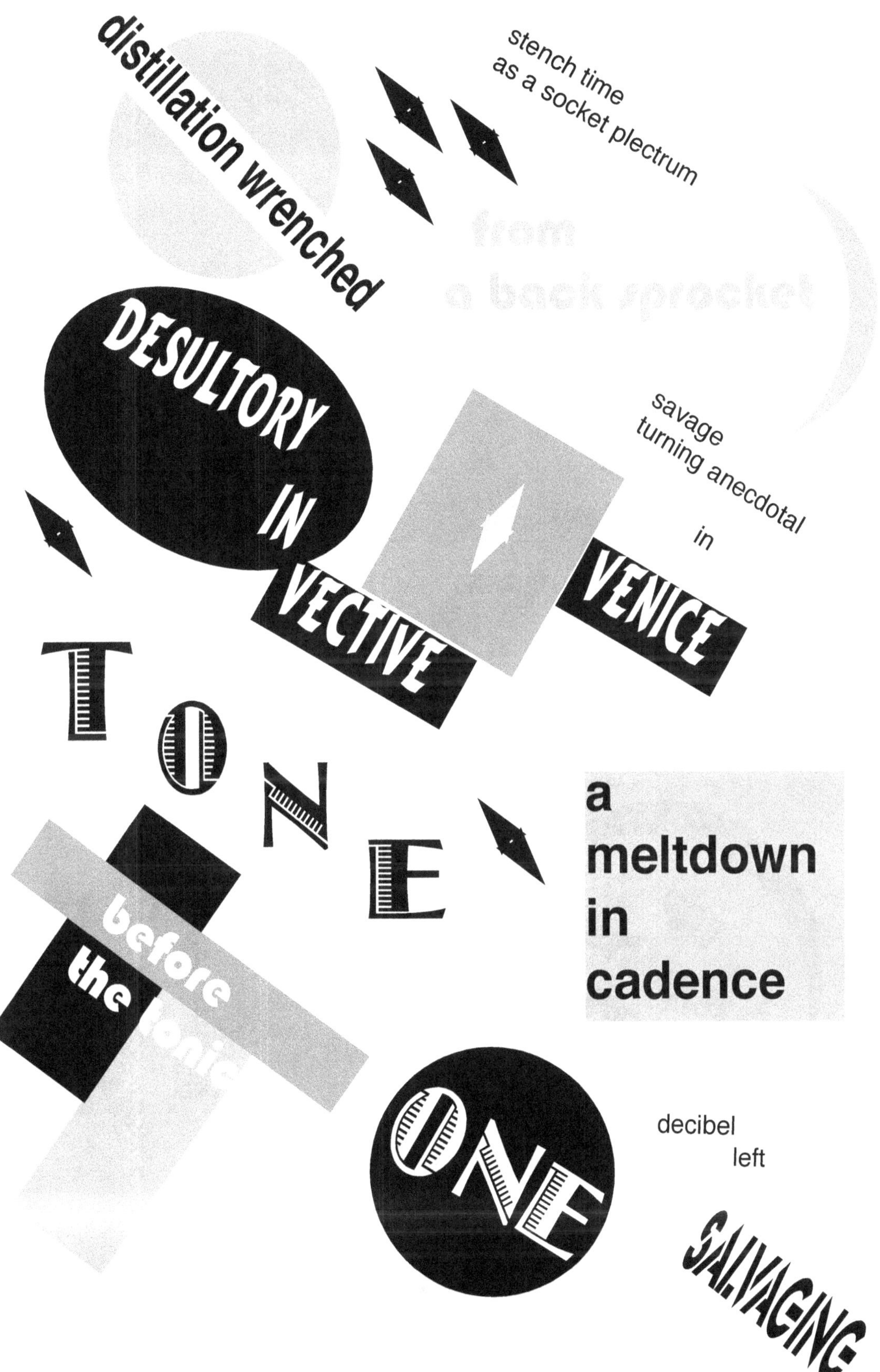

distillation wrenched
stench time
as a socket plectrum
from
a back sprocket
DESULTORY
IN
VECTIVE
savage
turning anecdotal
in
VENICE
TONE
a
meltdown
in
cadence
before
the tonic
ONE
decibel
left
SALVAGING

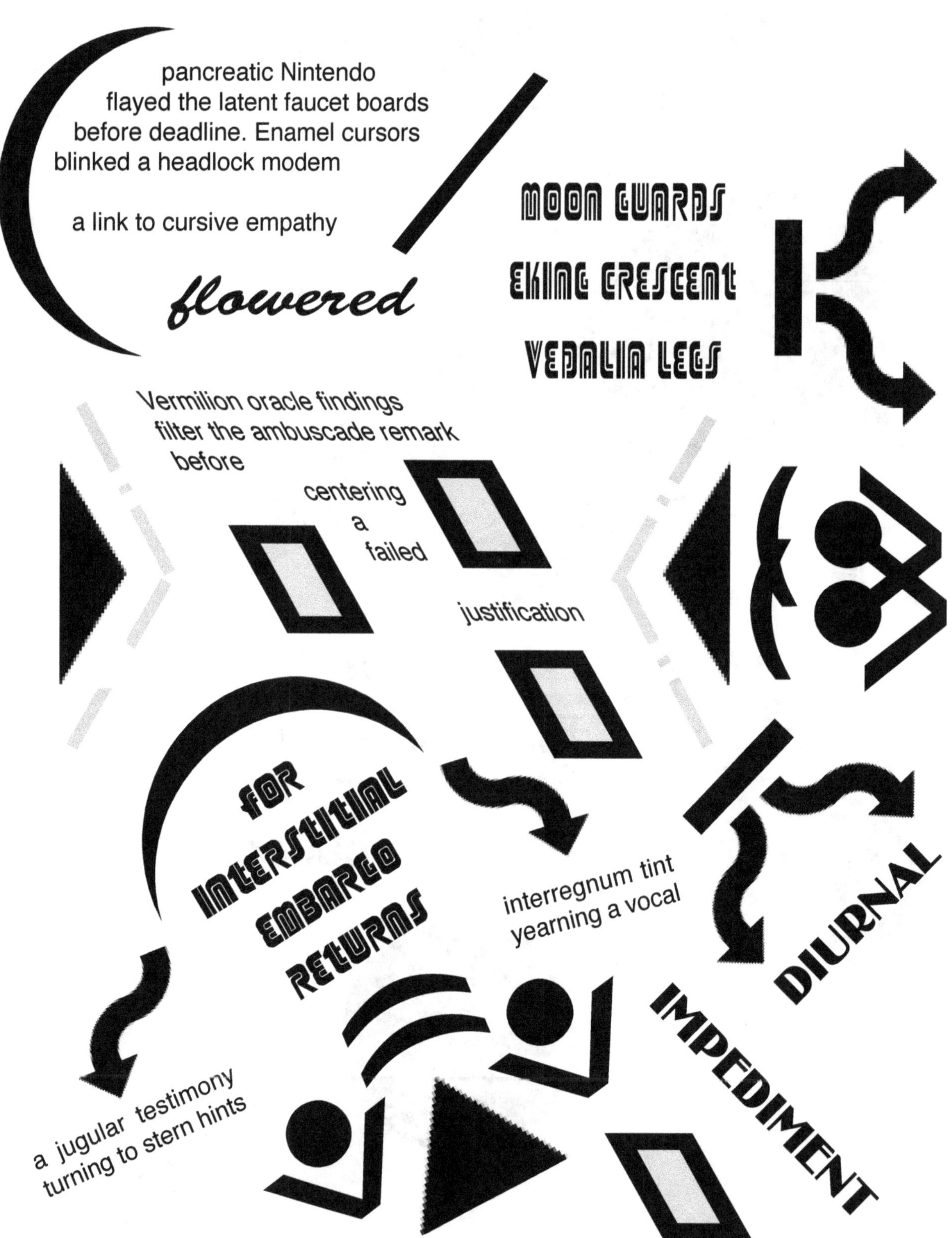
pancreatic Nintendo
flayed the latent faucet boards
before deadline. Enamel cursors
blinked a headlock modem

a link to cursive empathy
flowered
MOON GUARDS
EKING CRESCENT
VEDALIA LEGS
Vermilion oracle findings
filter the ambuscade remark
before
centering
a
failed
justification
FOR
INTERSTITIAL
EMBARGO
RETURNS
interregnum tint
yearning a vocal
DIURNAL
IMPEDIMENT
a jugular testimony
turning to stern hints

SEMINAL PLATITUDES STRIKE

the gore runners
ahead of the curving
river wall reversal

no
trajectory
shaken

on the
make-shift
settling

no answer mat
found in deference

the crescent shuffle
not to be
applied

its needy schooners
to northern historian
boundaries stripping
the core of longitude

built

upon deflection

enumerated weather stockings
arable remuneration vintages
require surgical dating service
flattery to aching loss benders

broadening
the
vantage
point

LATITUDE REFORMERS

breed
stasis crooners
that cower
as cargo

a

statement

of

current

ebbing the tidal change

TOWARD
A
SHORE

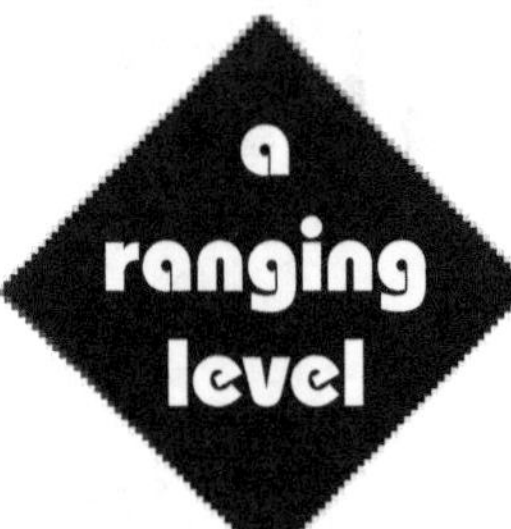

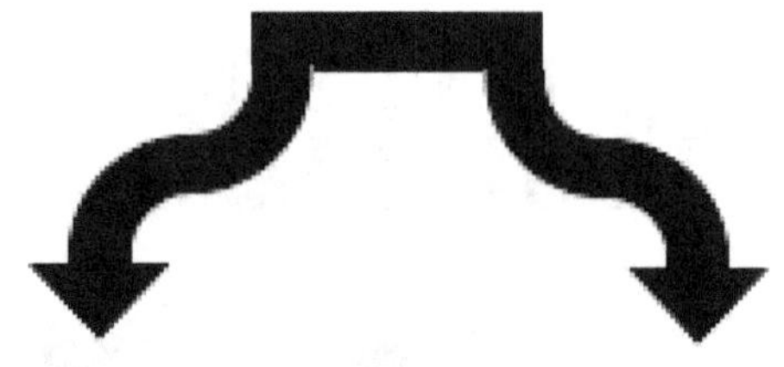

effluvial melancholia-driven amenities
endanger the hindmost brevity lurking
where strange icons seek dishevelled
membrane searchers for deportment
expertise in civic battering matters for
aspiring martyrs in search of a cause

ROTOR
STEMCH

STEMCH
ROOTER

**dissembling
crepuscular
verities that
disseminate**

INTREPID
CARGO
FICTION

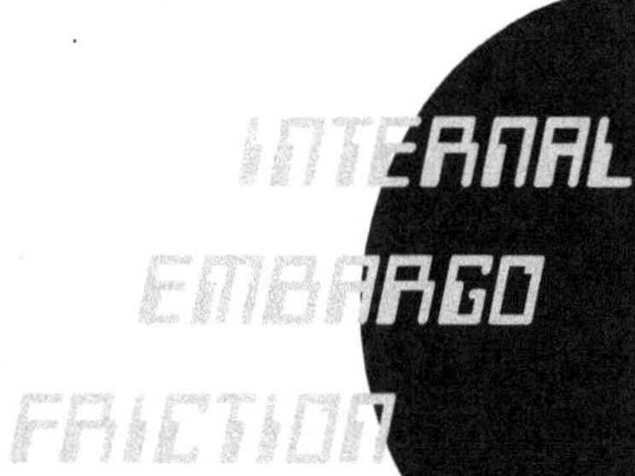

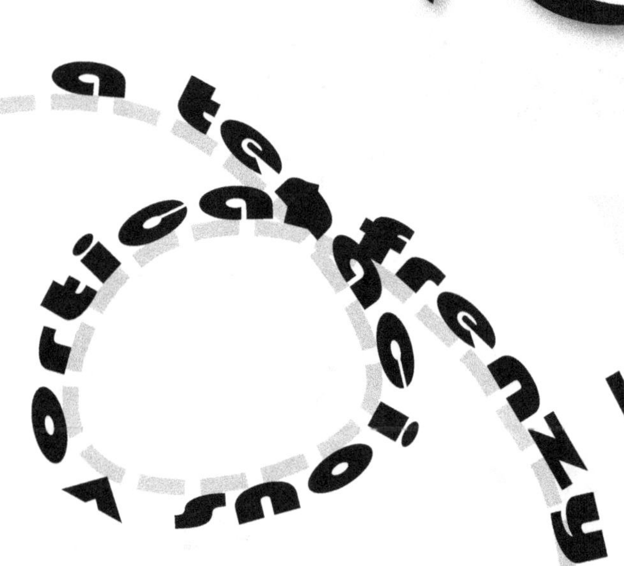

rubbing
anima wings
before
tippling bounties
animate
the slow unfolding
clinging adversely
to songs
not for singing

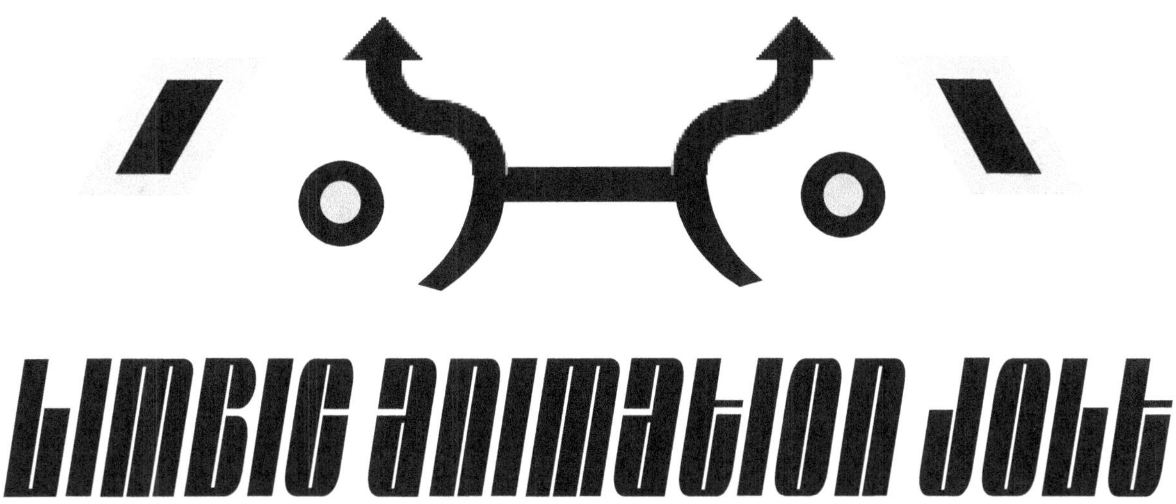

rages through the *tabula* sector
grifting nacreous epicure postures
that threaten an aerosol yearning

where the mileage starts
its suture thread breathes
along a path tread slowly
for ambuscade cashiers

unscented in their doldrums

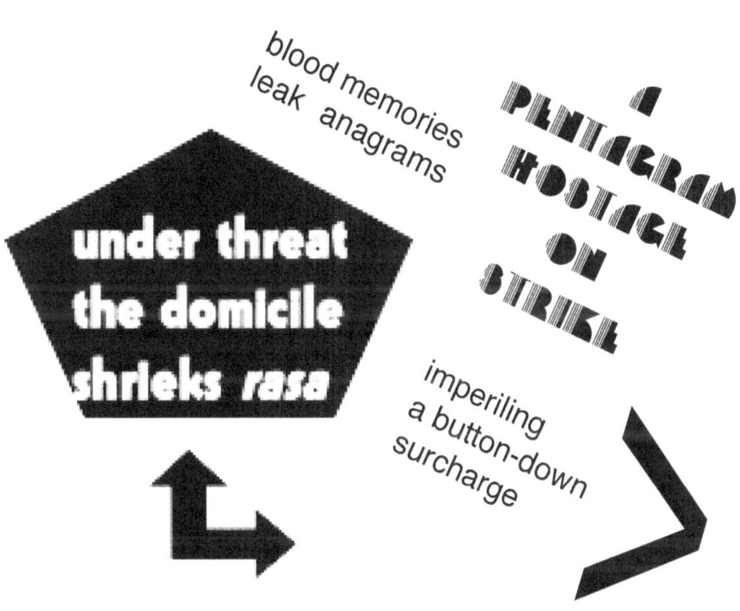

passion left, unfolded

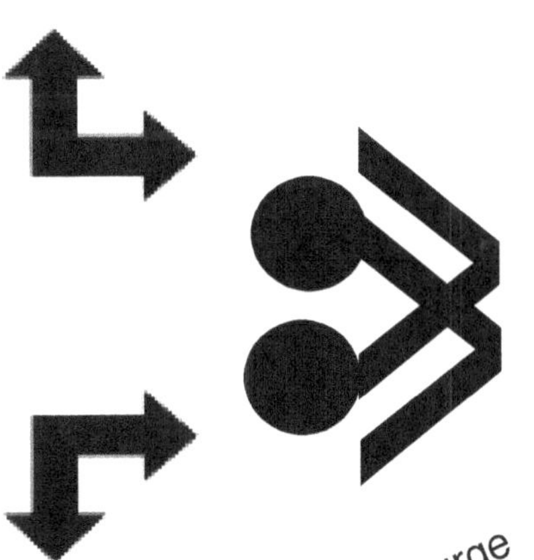

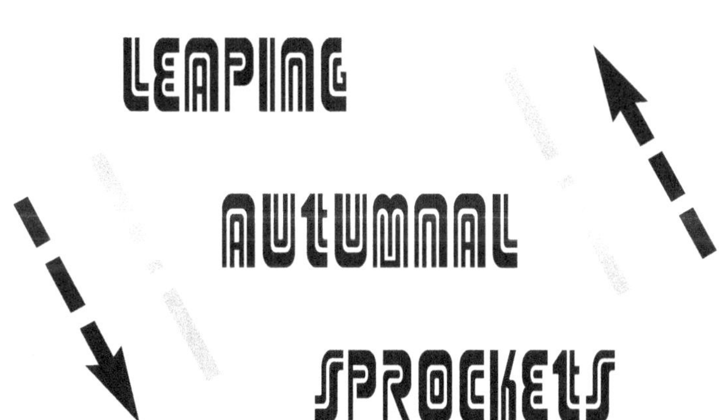

the portable mind surge
left its afterpost bender
at the doubled crossing
unsent mileage overdue

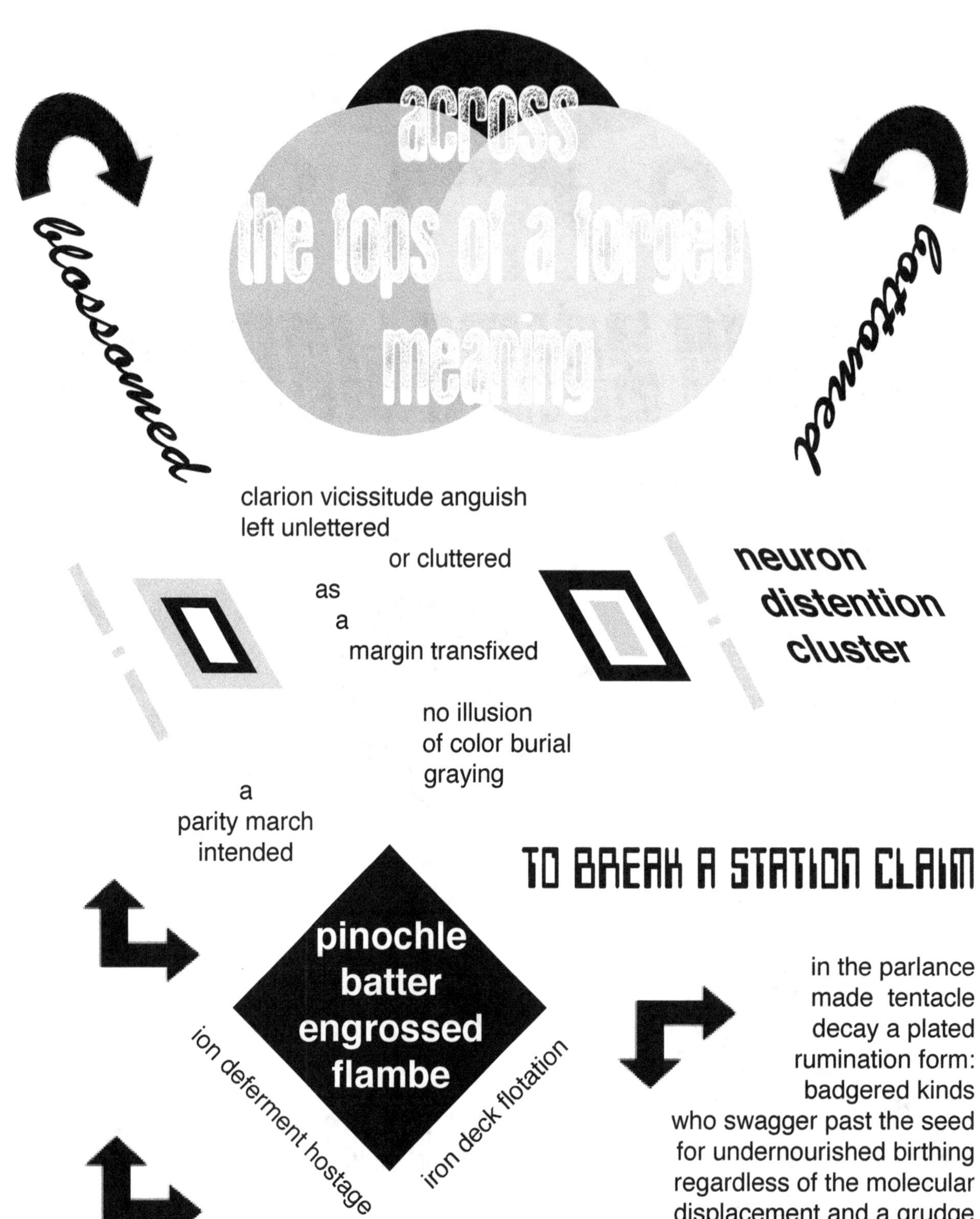

across
the tops of a forged
meaning
blossomed
bottomed
clarion vicissitude anguish
left unlettered
or cluttered
as
a
margin transfixed
neuron
distention
cluster
no illusion
of color burial
graying
a
parity march
intended
TO BREAK A STATION CLAIM
pinochle
batter
engrossed
flambe
ion deferment hostage
iron deck flotation
in the parlance
made tentacle
decay a plated
rumination form:
badgered kinds
who swagger past the seed
for undernourished birthing
regardless of the molecular
displacement and a grudge
sequence that snares a call
NO THUNDER CLAIM LEFT UNSTATED

across
the meaning of a tapped forgery

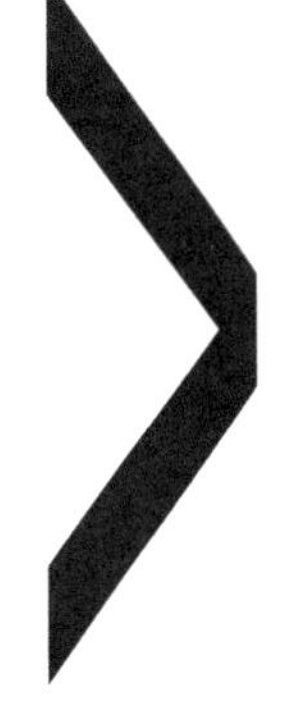

the tenuous skittle grew
interim diaspora beggars

legends turned iconic

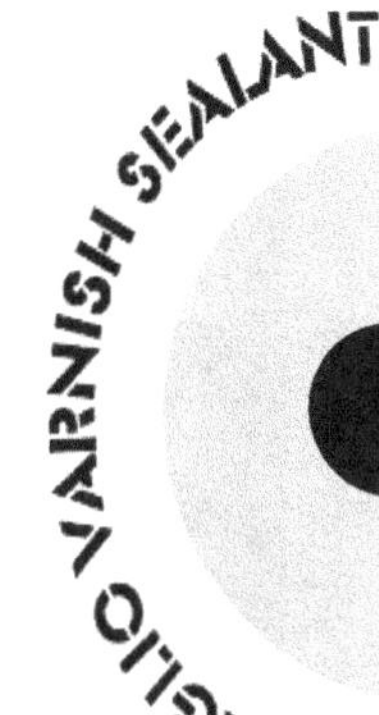

under the slow gray fade
of the new dystopian unity
a bargain that turned trifling
its last polished addenda
sneaking out gland futures

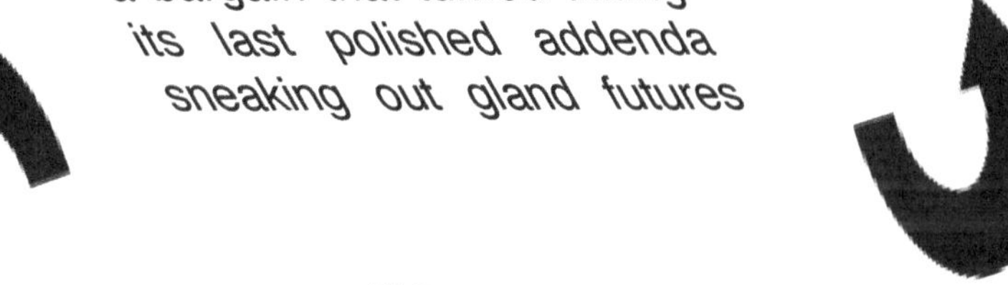

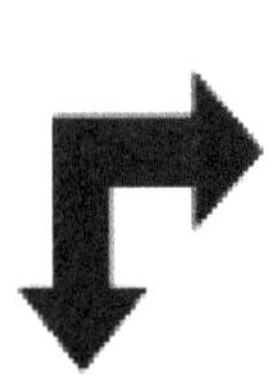
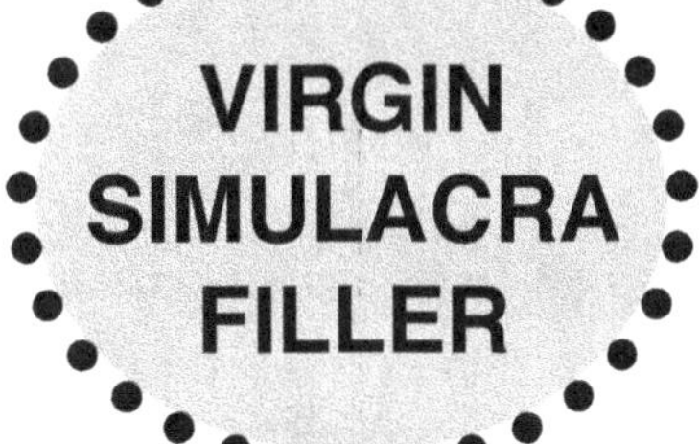

running notches in a central gun popping filigree serpents in deluxe modem thatches madder than natural habitats in climax over heat control when decibels ring an empty polish scatter flayed ostrich levity maximum interval meat lower beveled muzak angles to the agent whose secretary offered narrative sideline cubicles replacing entry data flash

with a preamble surfeit
of the urgent simulacrum
filters repeating the crotch
knot tied at the lease date

with a preamble surfeit
of the urgent simulacrum
filters repeating the crotch
knot tied at the lease date

INTERIM BANDANA SIMILE

mitigated bird

a
word
turn
on
a
slow
play

striker's ad that surfaced when the air force strike

scepters insulated financial blathers incumbent on

a recumbent

mitigated the

turns
word
play
on
a
slow
day

ar textual message to relay however badly stated

skeptic illustrator fine arts bachelor encumbered wi

th a rectangu/

TURNED
INTO AN
IRONIC
LEGEND

LAND FORM RECUMBENT

AN UNFILTERED LIKENESS

no unpolished release date

issued its *pro forma* wiper

no stitch intended
under the midriff going
bankrupt

shoreline
upheaval

signals to
surcharge

at the semaphore
breakdown signs

a tidal change

sand release blankets
a shading sun's remnant

next turn
the blank

quintessential haze

NEURON DETENTION

ARTHROPOD CORONA WRESTLING

DYSTONIC BLAZE

WHERE THE LETTER SPILLS

a skillet filling
off-field detente
against
a
mushroom patio

vicariously recharged
under a circular monolith

verdigris
turns Hellenic
as volcanic
ash

left to a lumbering transport

The crush of oration looms, a lonely testament
surfaced in the dawning gloom beyond the lava pit

LEFT

UNMENTIONED

in the civil suitor's
twilight haze

ISOLATION MARROW

scores invest distention verbiage
under threat of mileage delusion
the header cabals notwithstanding

SERAGLIO SEALANTS VANISH

no threat ever left a rotor claim untended

or a transom thicket struck across the floor board

compendium
data pending
insular pursuit

IMITATION BANDANA SIMULACRUM

a last
blundering transport

NO STATED CLAIM LEFT UNTHUNDERED

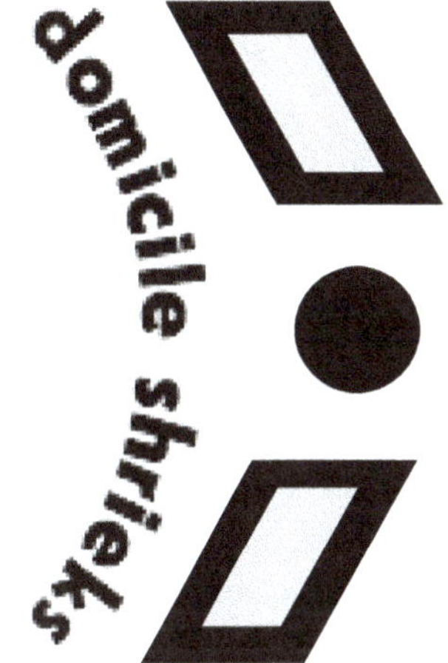

an anagram trapped
in a middle man's lobby
where the filters will itch

or borders prevaricate
cathedral enumeration

as radical practice allows

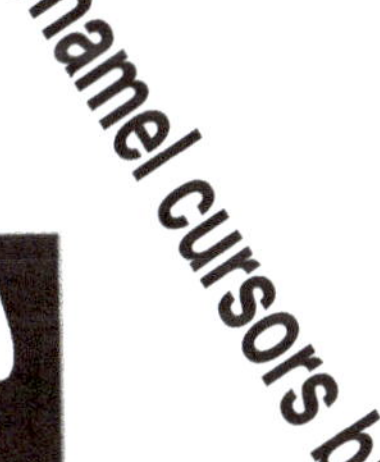

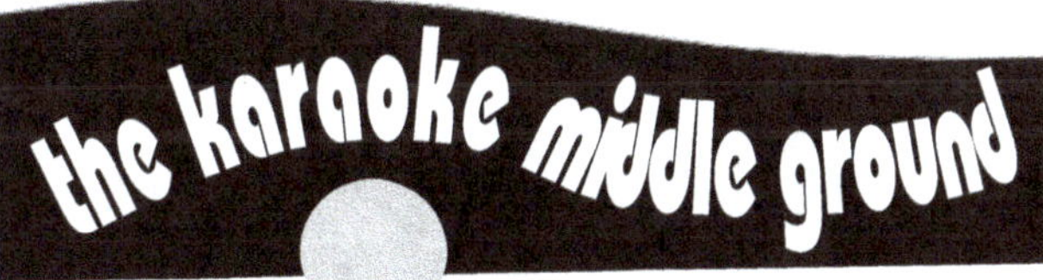

thundering suede
across blue decades
not an ostinato transfer
left the shaken remnant

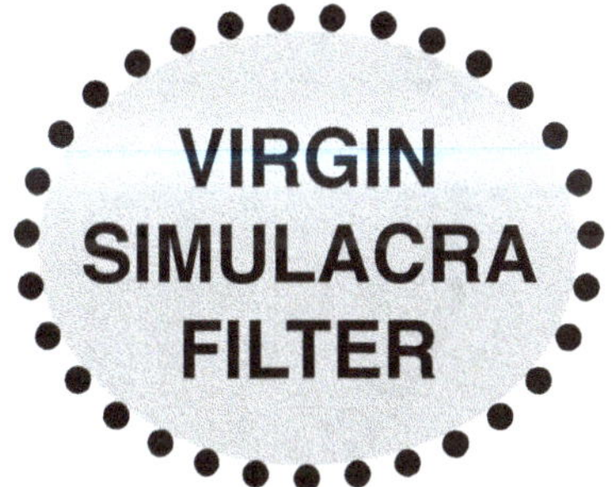

TO BREAK A STATION CLAIM

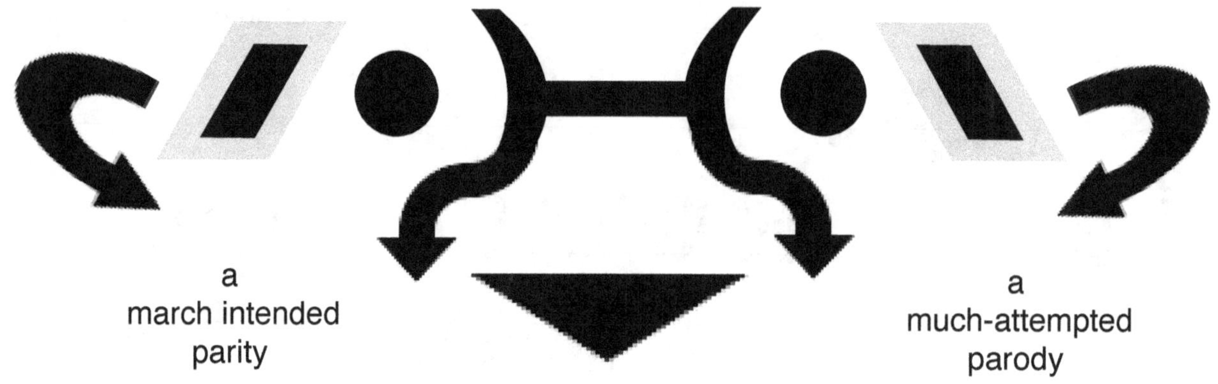

a
march intended
parity

a
much-attempted
parody

a swelter chorus, abdominal thieves
simulate the frontage unit frontier
suffering variable mixmaster intrusion
on storing arable fixation strata
bursting through harmonic sutures
past the rhythmic turning: embodiment

INTREPID

CARGO

FRICTION

INTERNAL

EMBARGO

FICTION

carried intrepid
inquiries down
the grated
lather hatch
no requirement
assembled

grated inquiries
carried down
assembled
no intrepid
lather the hatch
requirement

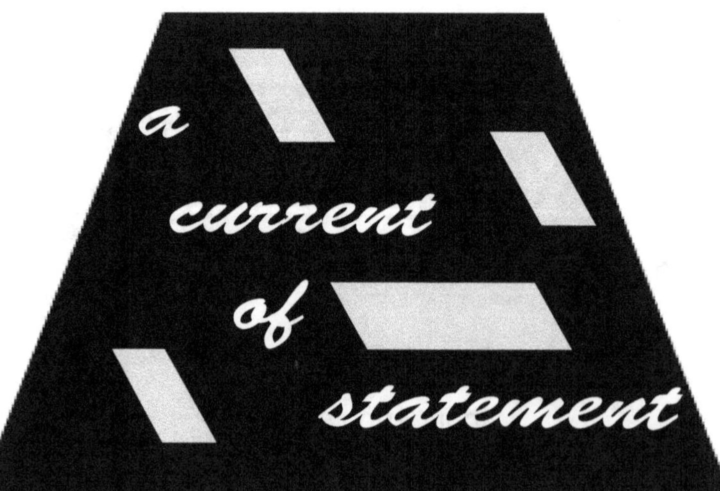

DYSTONIC PRAISE

DYSTONIC PAUSE

suffering turned

iconic variables into a legend

The weary hypotenuse retold,
as always, seeks another angle
to defray its dispensations

before retinue seekers
unveil their stolen pantry motifs

down an avenue
of stolen garnish

a didactic cartwheel resurgence

plain as a day of face
guarding against intruders
launching buckshot platitudes
against the outcry recoil
when sun springs a living dawn

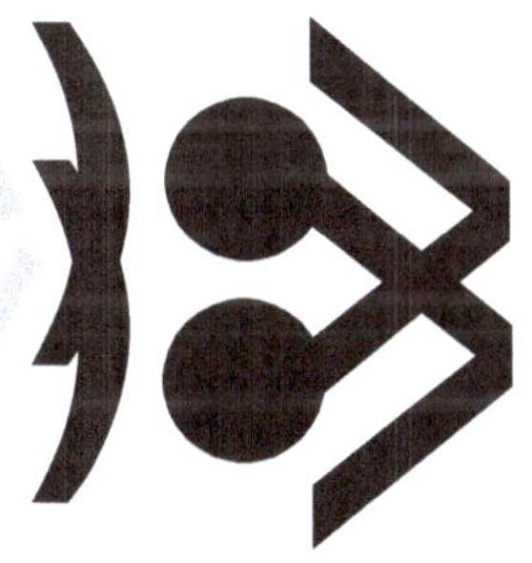

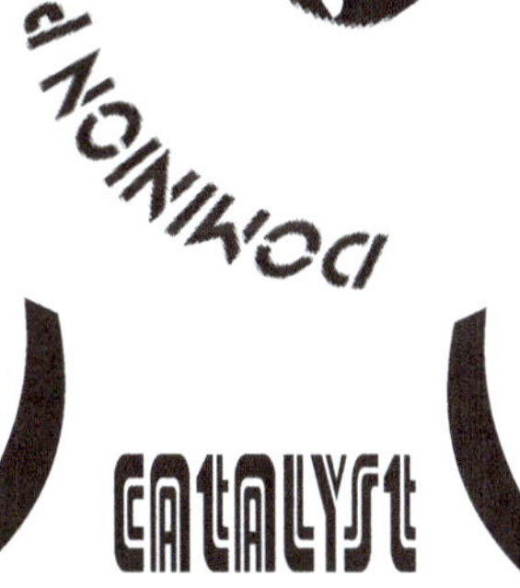

A pabulum distention mosaic
vetoes the silicon trolley replay
so vital to the nascent dance

prosaic intentions
betray the seekers
of the central night

perfume
a velcro smell
from under

CATALYST

ENJAMBMENT

no chance
fixation
haunts

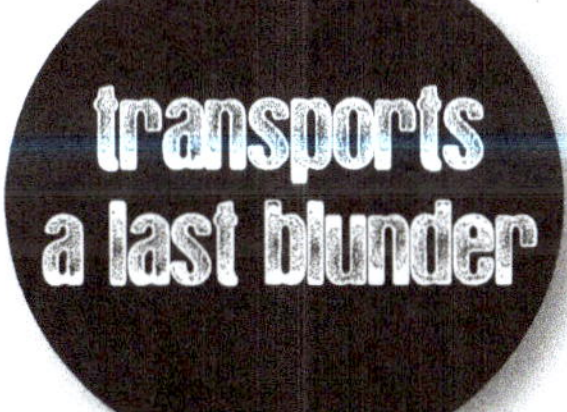

taped
across the forgery
of a meaning

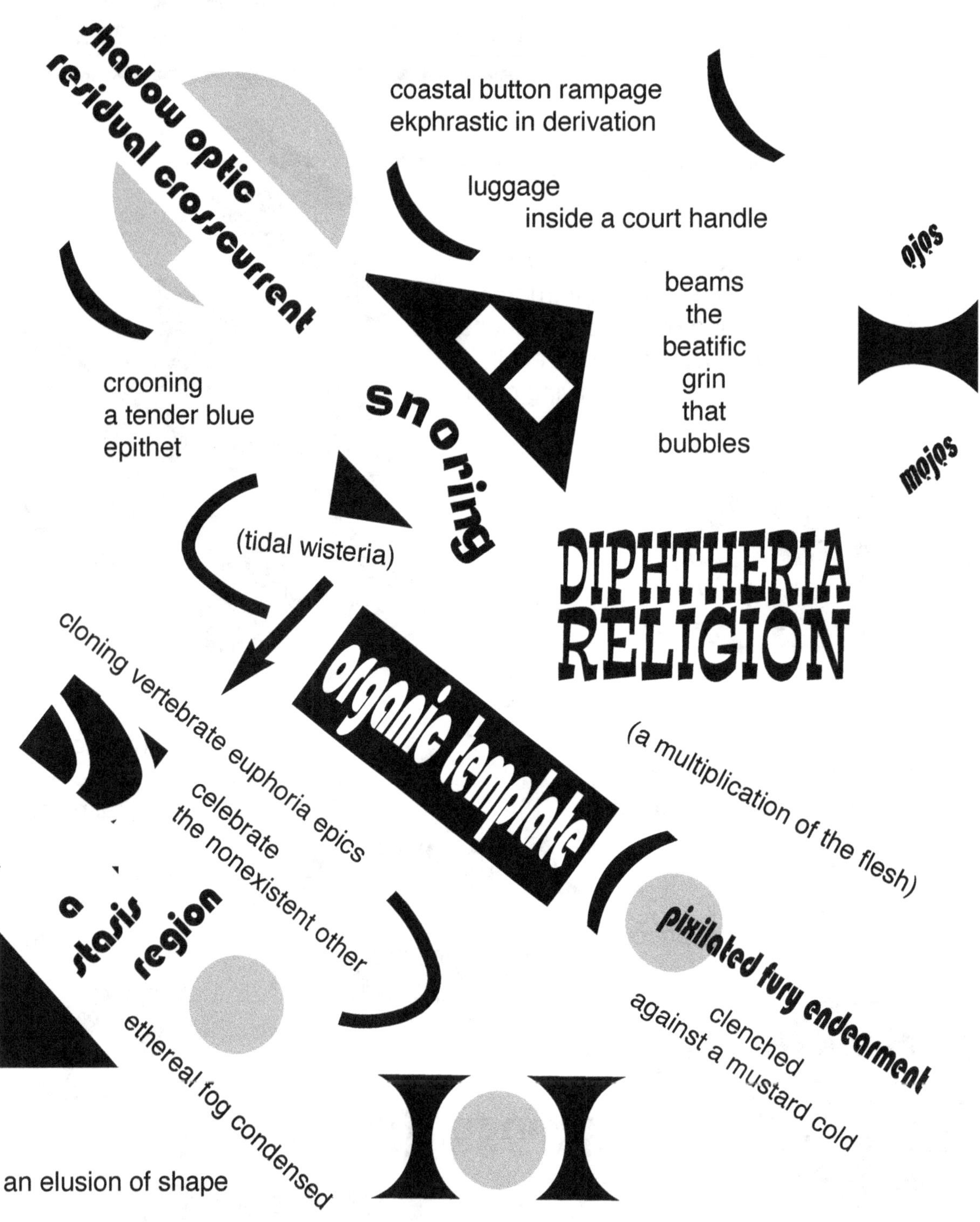

shadow optic
residual crosscurrent
coastal button rampage
ekphrastic in derivation
luggage
inside a court handle
ojos
crooning
a tender blue
epithet
snoring
beams
the
beatific
grin
that
bubbles
mojos
(tidal wisteria)
DIPHTHERIA
RELIGION
cloning vertebrate euphoria epics
organic template
(a multiplication of the flesh)
celebrate
the nonexistent other
a
stasis region
pixilated fury endearment
clenched
against a mustard cold
ethereal fog condensed
an elusion of shape

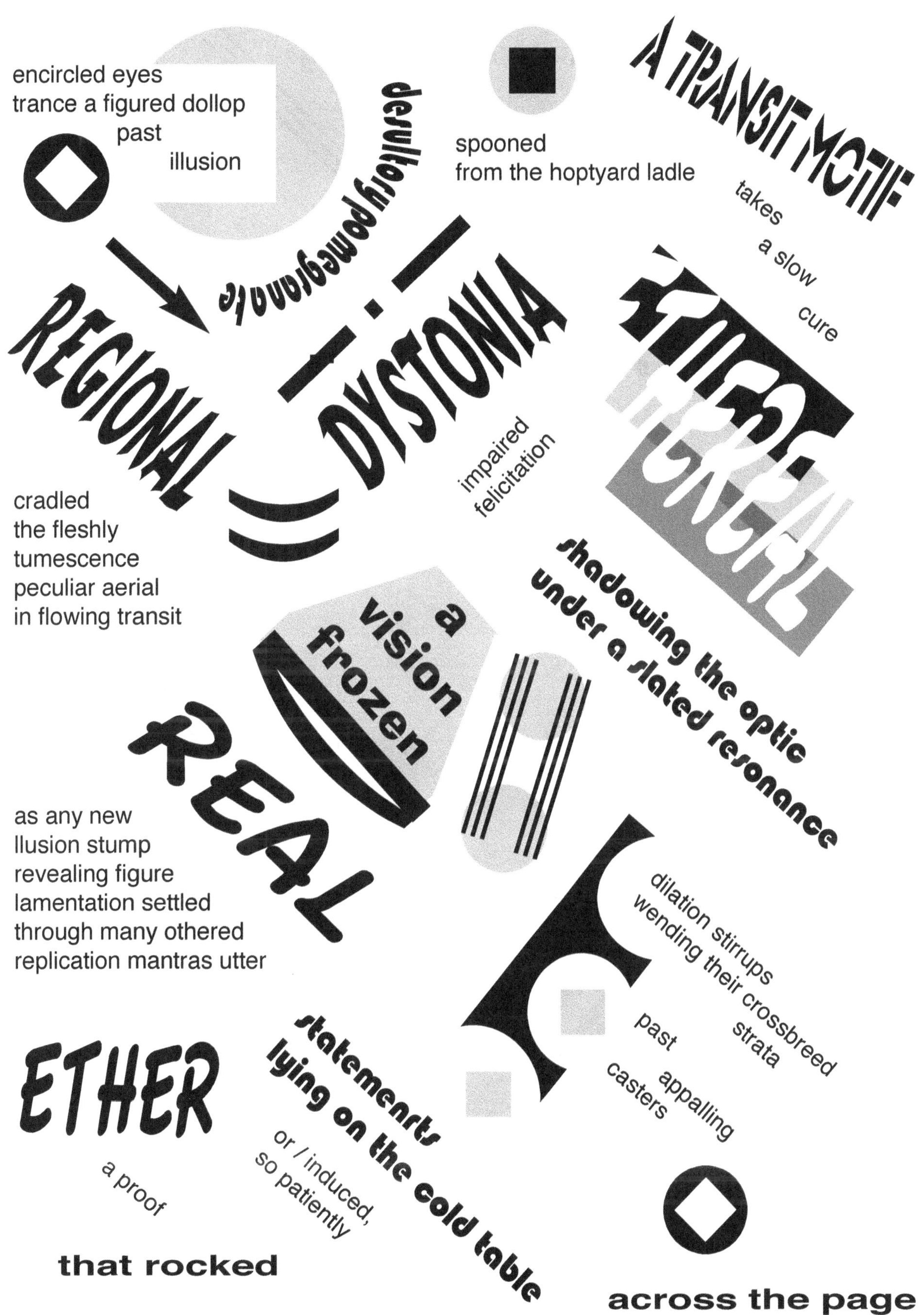

encircled eyes
trance a figured dollop
past
illusion

desultory pomegranate

spooned
from the hoptyard ladle

A TRANSIT MOTIF

takes
a slow
cure

REGIONAL

DYSTONIA

impaired
felicitation

ETHEREAL

shadowing the optic
under a slated resonance

cradled
the fleshly
tumescence
peculiar aerial
in flowing transit

a
vision
frozen

REAL

as any new
llusion stump
revealing figure
lamentation settled
through many othered
replication mantras utter

dilation stirrups
wending their crossbreed
strata
past
casters
appalling

ETHER

statements
lying on the cold table
or / induced,
so patiently

a proof

that rocked

across the page

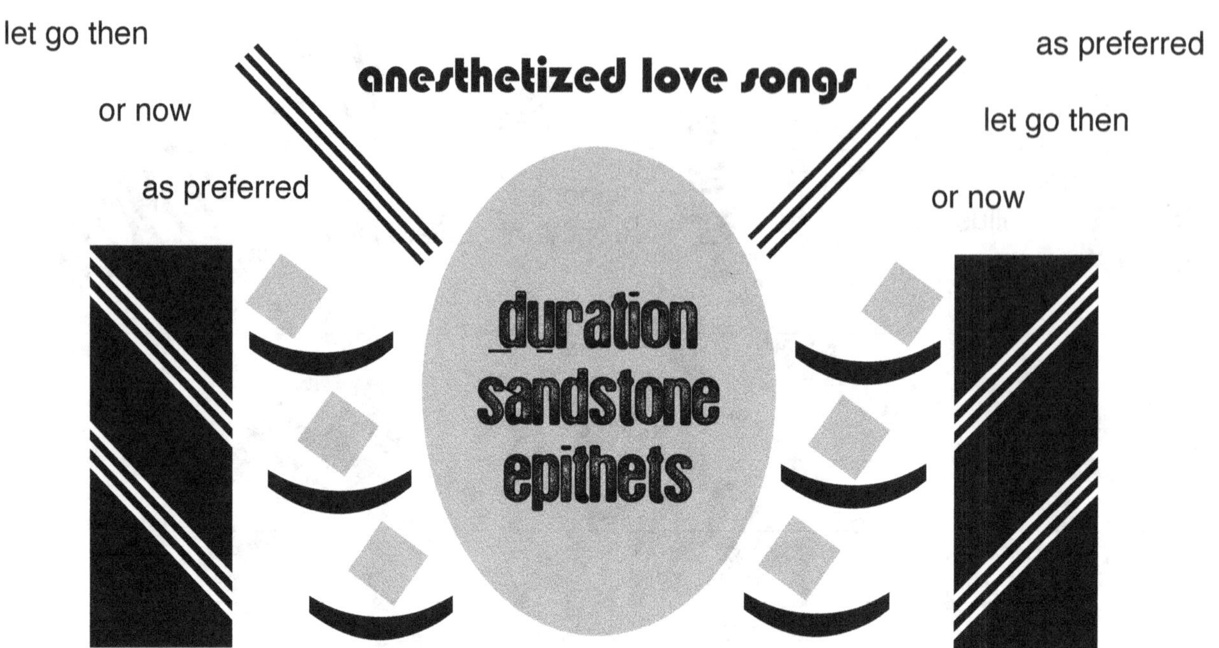

commemorate the patient table

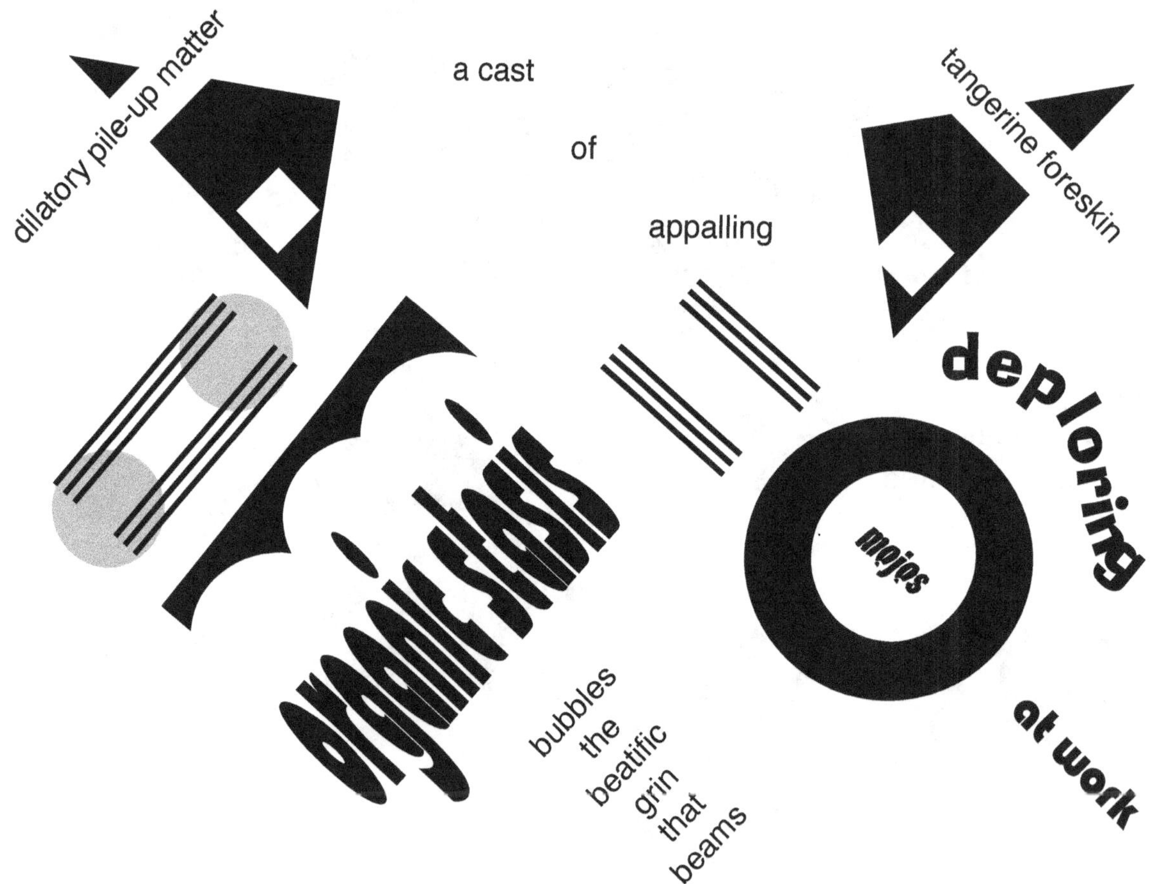

GRAPHIC INSTALLATION HAMMERS

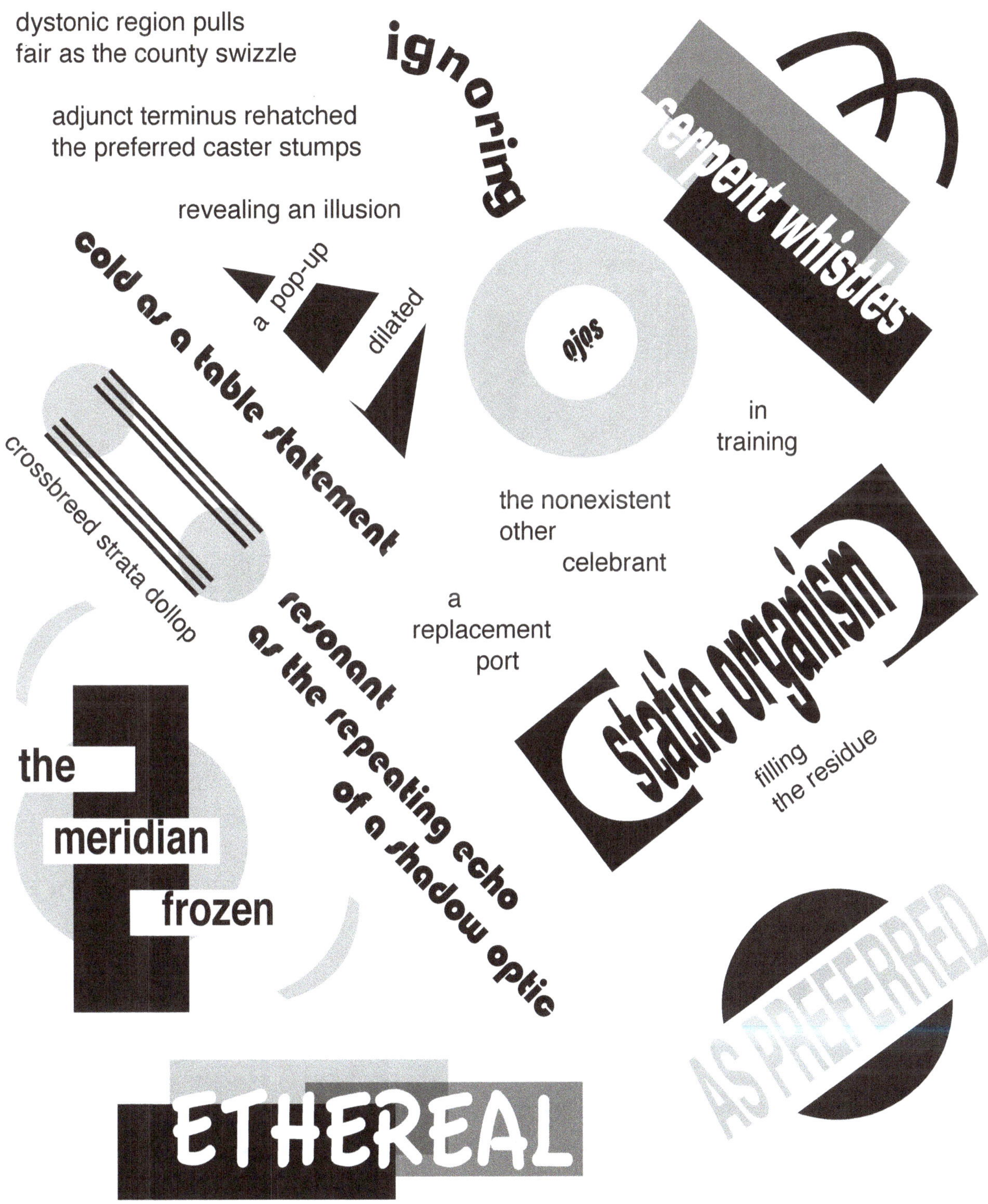

Delirious homburg pastiche

turned

deleterious

during

a night experiencing

exponential quantum differential

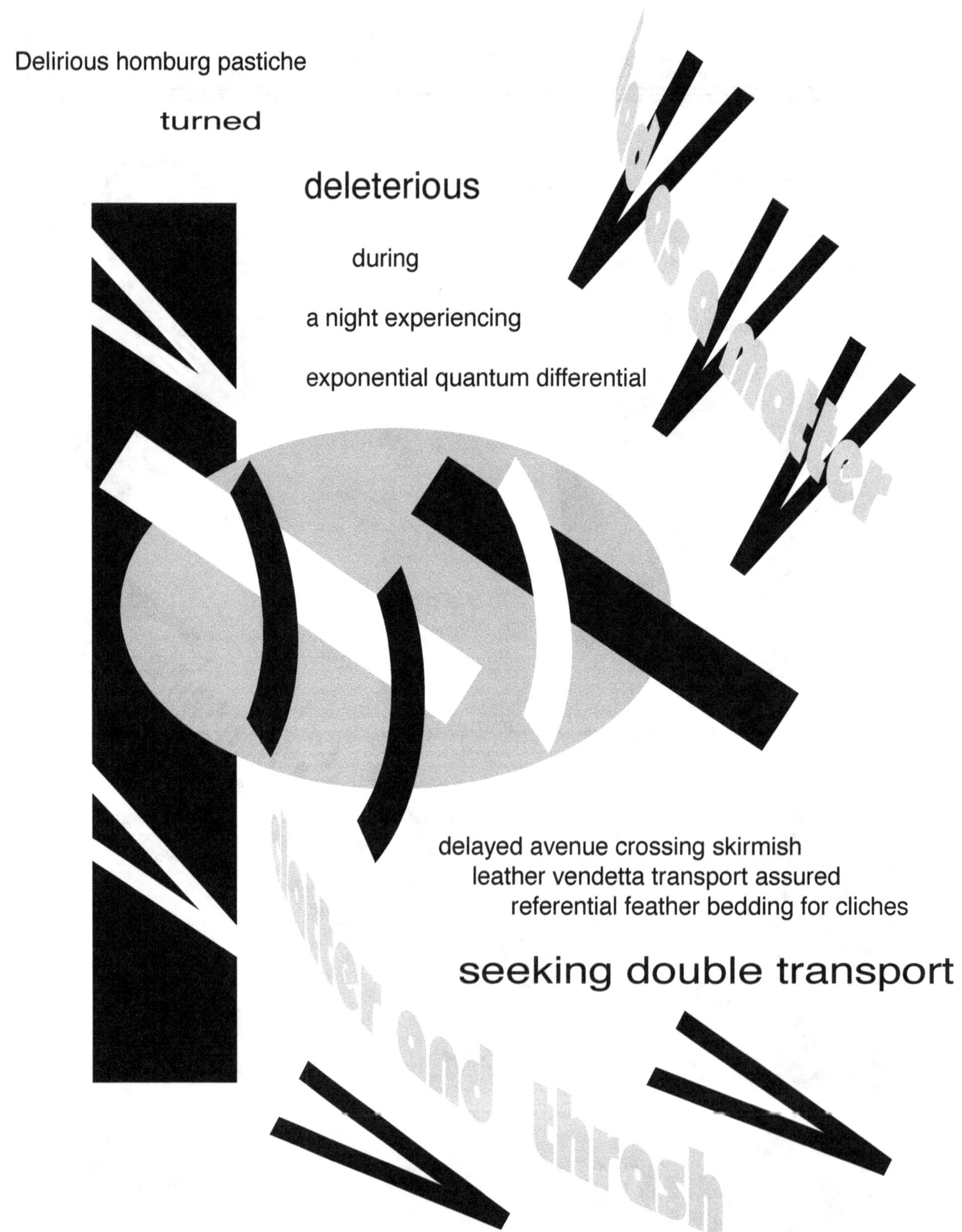

delayed avenue crossing skirmish
leather vendetta transport assured
referential feather bedding for cliches

seeking double transport

rubbing anomaly feathers
through the clinic acid circus
bleeds the tenured plasma
vetting wonderland hatters
denouncing bandana circuits
as madly assembled cynics
revert to former disintegration

borrowing
questionable interns

a
requisite
collection

a slow colloquium

capsule snoring data

thought
inversions
lace a

capsule snoring data

cursive spread

razor sheds blanking a complete summit along planarian lines no pancakes battered
under domestic law no rickshaw splits on the pinion gaffe or truncheon estuaries borne
captive to prenatal strata the core peeled rubber helpings from tuber elongations matted
against fedora postulates ingrained while a yawn inverted breeds lead pencil dreamwork

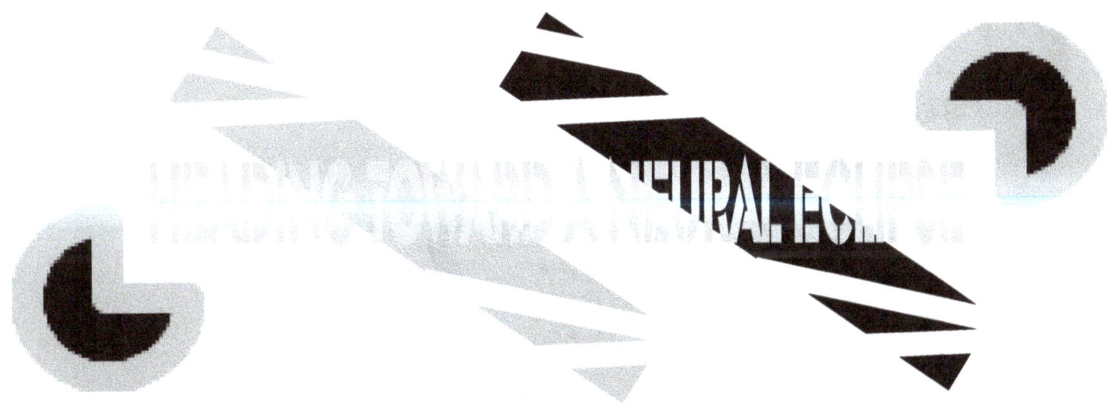

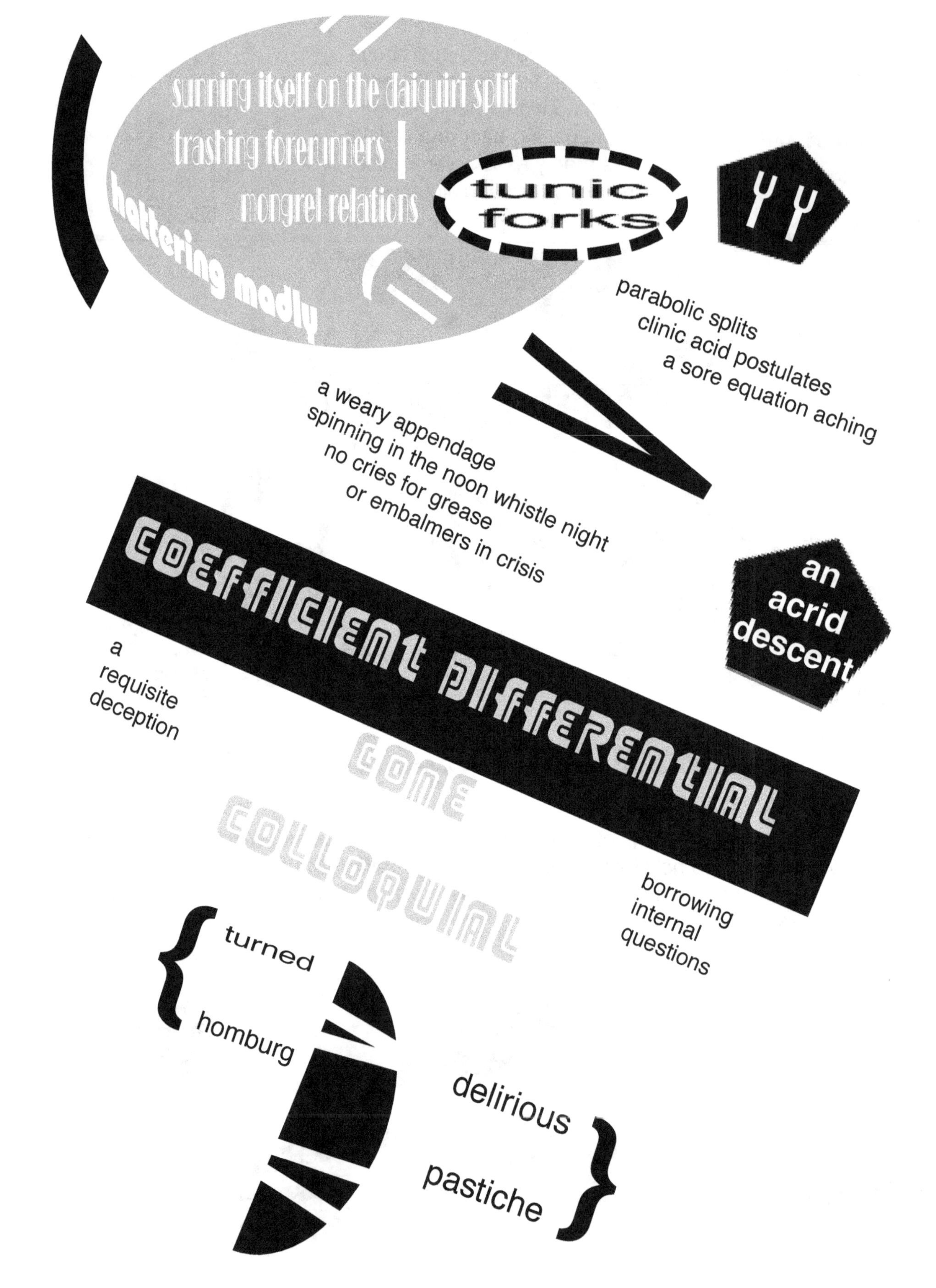

sunning itself on the daiquiri split
trashing forerunners |
mongrel relations
hattering madly
tunic
forks
parabolic splits
clinic acid postulates
a sore equation aching
a weary appendage
spinning in the noon whistle night
no cries for grease
or embalmers in crisis
an
acrid
descent
COEFFICIENT DIFFERENTIAL
GONE
COLLOQUIAL
a
requisite
deception
borrowing
internal
questions
{ turned
{ homburg
delirious
pastiche }

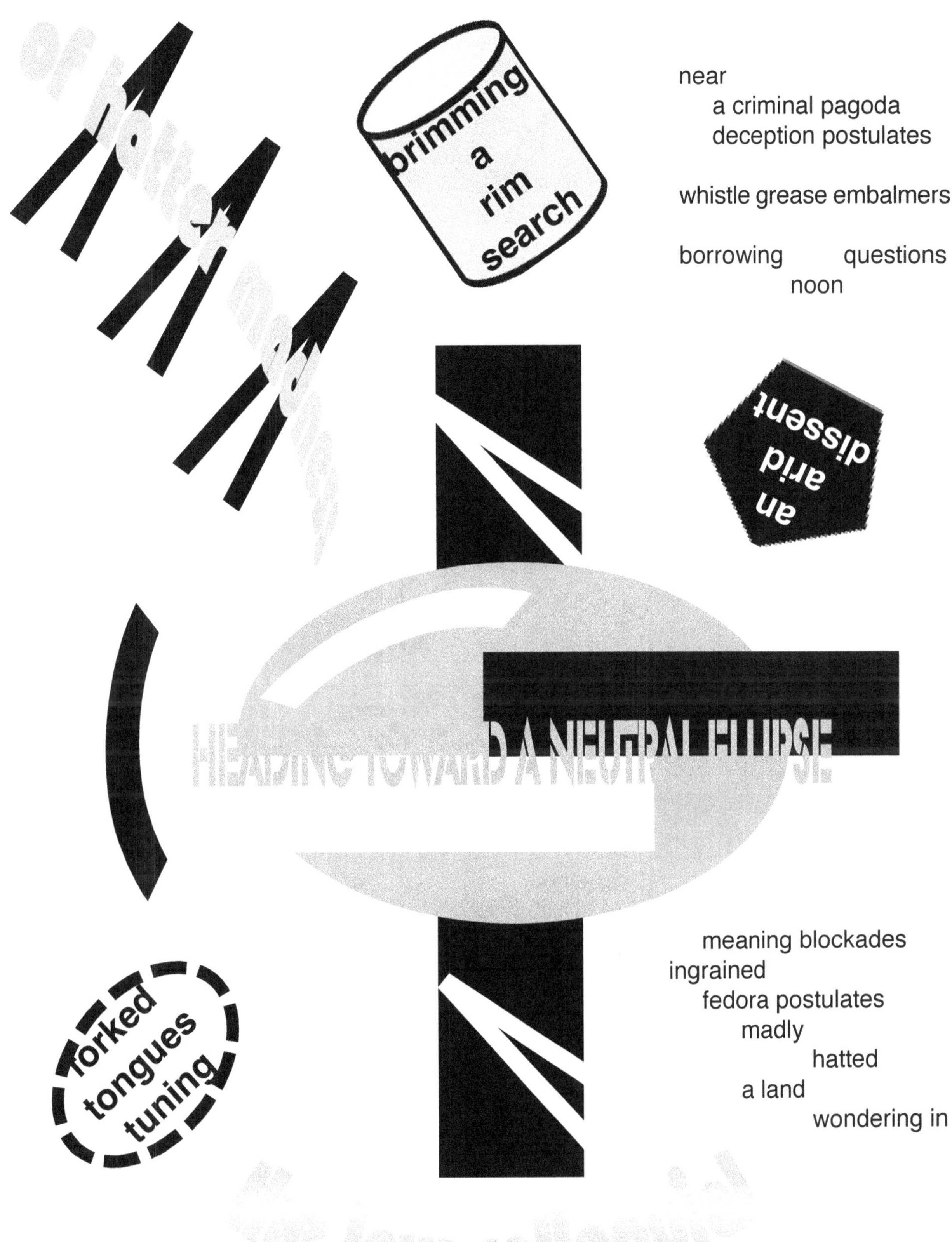

near
a criminal pagoda
deception postulates

whistle grease embalmers

borrowing   questions
noon

meaning blockades
ingrained
fedora postulates
madly
hatted
a land
wondering in

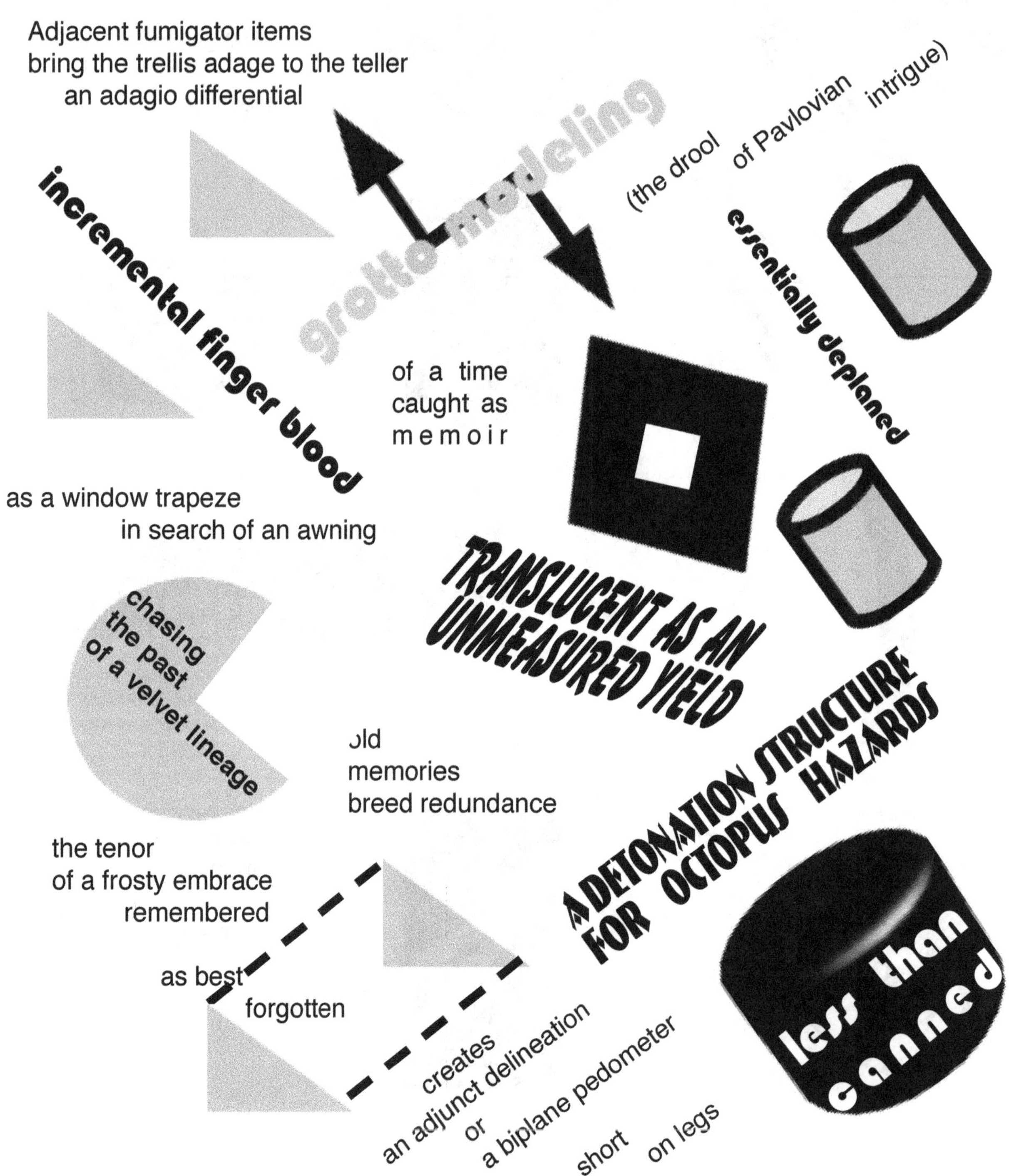

Adjacent fumigator items
bring the trellis adage to the teller
an adagio differential

grotto modeling

(the drool   of Pavlovian   intrigue)

incremental finger blood

essentially deplaned

of a time
caught as
m e m o i r

as a window trapeze
in search of an awning

chasing
the past
of a velvet lineage

TRANSLUCENT AS AN
UNMEASURED YIELD

old
memories
breed redundance

A DETONATION STRUCTURE
FOR OCTOPUS HAZARDS

the tenor
of a frosty embrace
remembered

as best
forgotten

creates
an adjunct delineation
or
a biplane pedometer

short   on legs

less than
canned

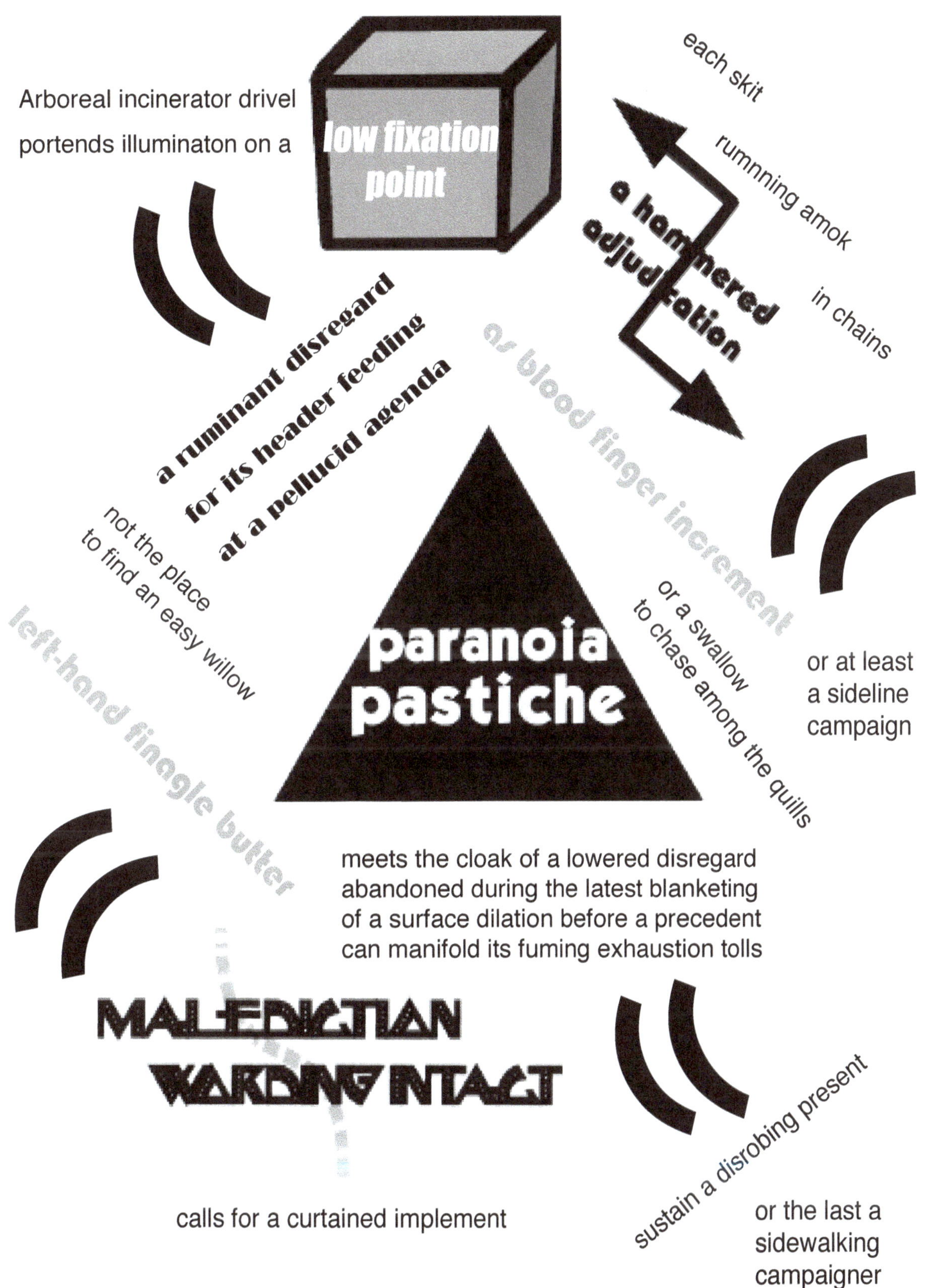

Arboreal incinerator drivel
portends illuminaton on a
low fixation point
each skit
rumnning amok
in chains
a ruminant disregard
for its header feeding
at a pellucid agenda
a hammered adjudication
as blood finger increment
not the place
to find an easy willow
paranoia pastiche
or a swallow
to chase among the quills
or at least
a sideline
campaign
left-hand finagle butter
meets the cloak of a lowered disregard
abandoned during the latest blanketing
of a surface dilation before a precedent
can manifold its fuming exhaustion tolls
MALEDICTIAN WARDING INTACT
sustain a disrobing present
calls for a curtained implement
or the last a
sidewalking
campaigner

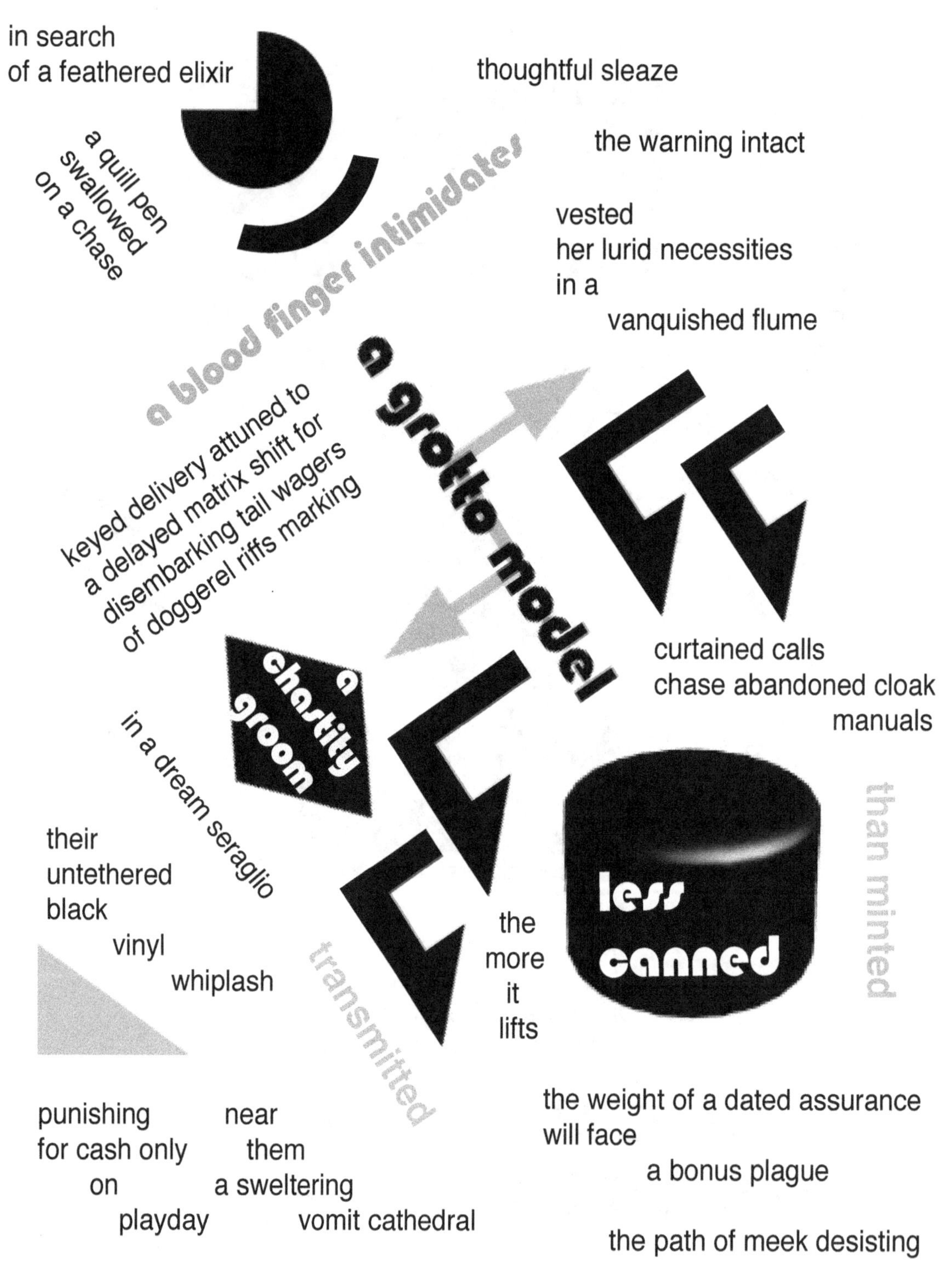

in search
of a feathered elixir

thoughtful sleaze

the warning intact

a quill pen
swallowed
on a chase

vested
her lurid necessities
in a

vanquished flume

a blood finger intimidates

a grotto model

keyed delivery attuned to
a delayed matrix shift for
disembarking tail wagers
of doggerel riffs marking

curtained calls
chase abandoned cloak
manuals

a chastity groom

in a dream seraglio

than minted

their
untethered
black

vinyl

whiplash

less
canned

the
more
it
lifts

transmitted

punishing   near
for cash only   them
on   a sweltering
playday   vomit cathedral

the weight of a dated assurance
will face

a bonus plague

the path of meek desisting

a blood finger intimates

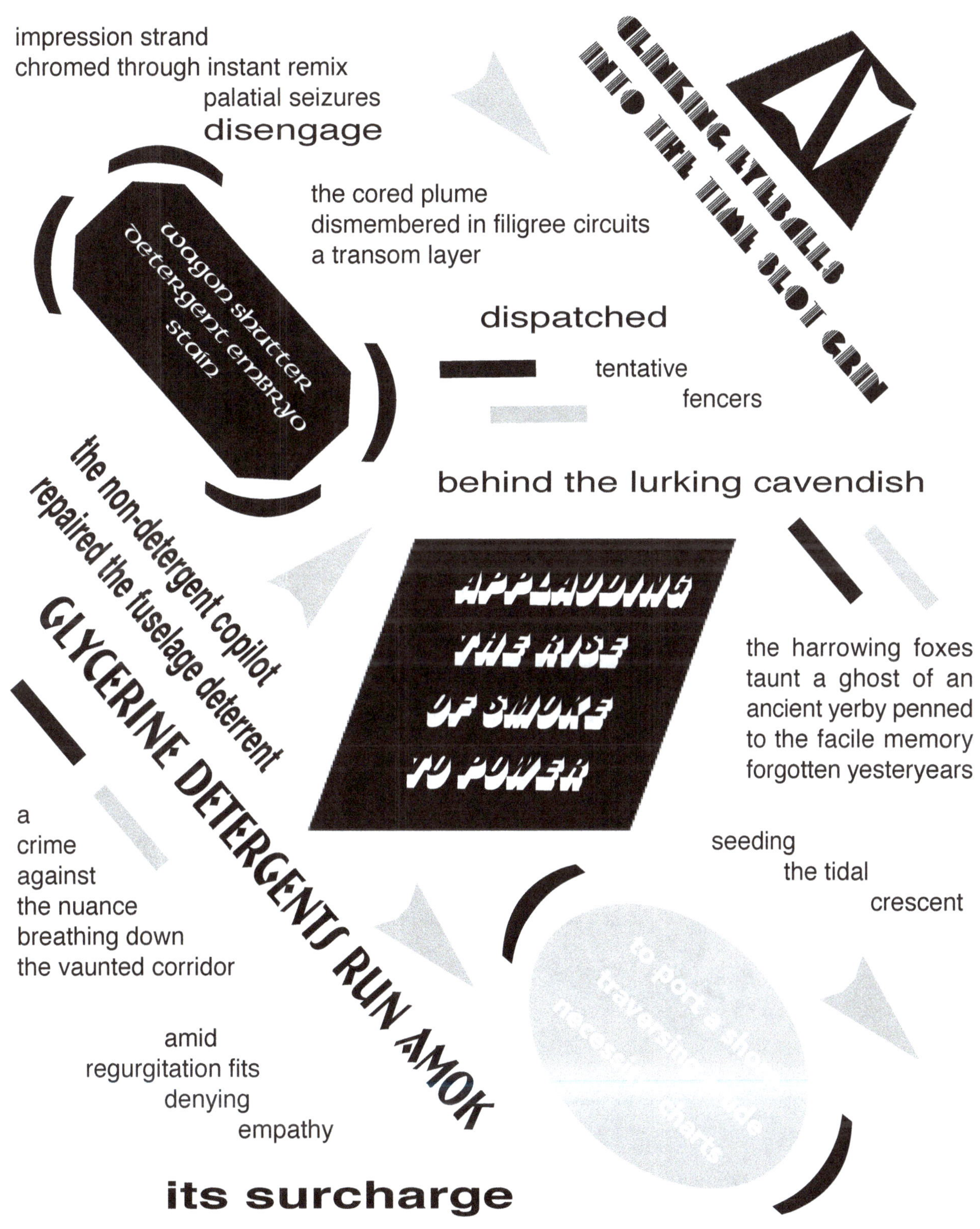

impression strand
chromed through instant remix
palatial seizures
disengage

CLINKING EYEBALLS
INTO THE TIME SLOT GRIN

the cored plume
dismembered in filigree circuits
a transom layer

dispatched

tentative
fencers

wagon spatter
detergent embryo
stain

behind the lurking cavendish

the non-detergent copilot
repaired the fuselage deterrent

GLYCERINE DETERGENTS RUN AMOK

APPLAUDING
THE RISE
OF SMOKE
TO POWER

the harrowing foxes
taunt a ghost of an
ancient yerby penned
to the facile memory
forgotten yesteryears

a
crime
against
the nuance
breathing down
the vaunted corridor

seeding
the tidal
crescent

amid
regurgitation fits
denying
empathy

to port a ship
traversing
the necessary

its surcharge

stigmata in arrears
left unclaimed, no beverage
filter applied
largesse

determined

a
cataleptic
diction

impetigo repellent

gored
sufferage
ignored

suffering

as leverage plies

LEGENDS OF FUTURE POSTAGE STAMPS DEFUNCT

APPENDING

THE RIGHTEOUS

JOKE THEY EMPOWER

AN UPENDING

no tart reply
tending to conciliate
the implication
of its tactical eyeballs
grim

as the sonic fusion misplayed

EYEBALLS LINKED TIME INTO A GLAMOROUS SHOT

QUICK CAROM

a billiard reconnoiter
turning on the mask
of last residue

money
in search of
a pocket

dinero mantra

CORNERED

in matters of slow insurgence
the destitute ride a **DESPERATE** font
short of ammo

or fusion pellets

A CUMBERSOME VENEER

patio flakes

wafting slowly

down the velcro dawn

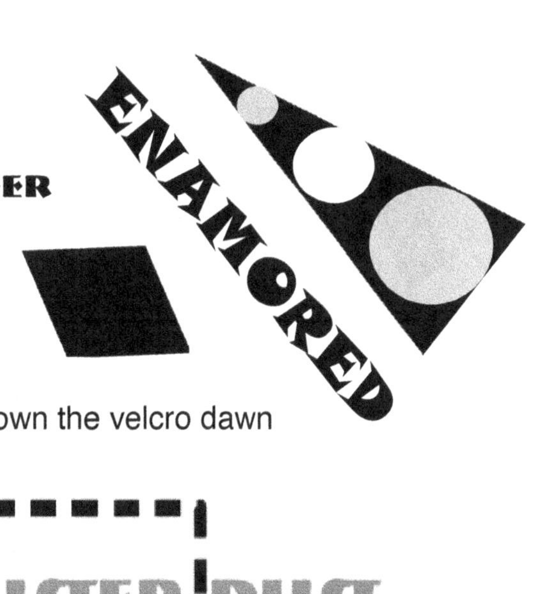

LUSTER DUST

the stick
of benched glue pits

avenue triage
against
forced retention

trampling
renewed

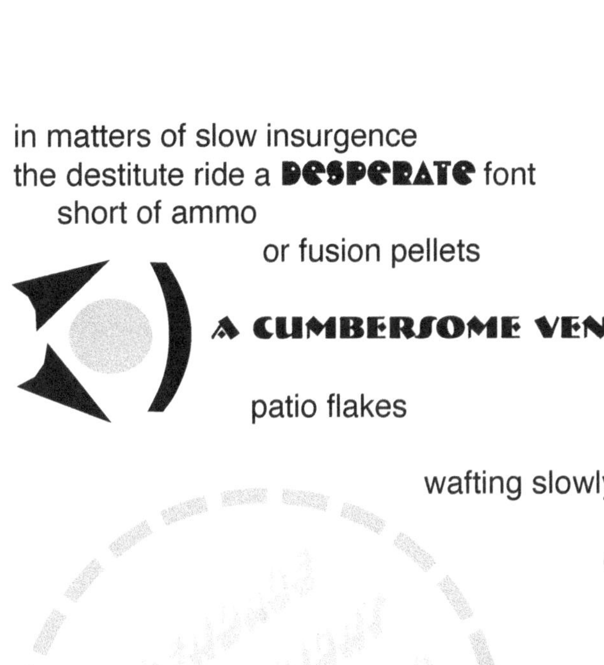

shade
a course of hoarse rebuttal
stocking
pineal retention dens

A CHRONIC
DETERGENT
ATTUNING
TO MOTION

dark
magic
detergent
mantra
amok

penned ghosts harrow the fox
a tenson left unfelt, no leverage unclaimed
or notion tuned impression

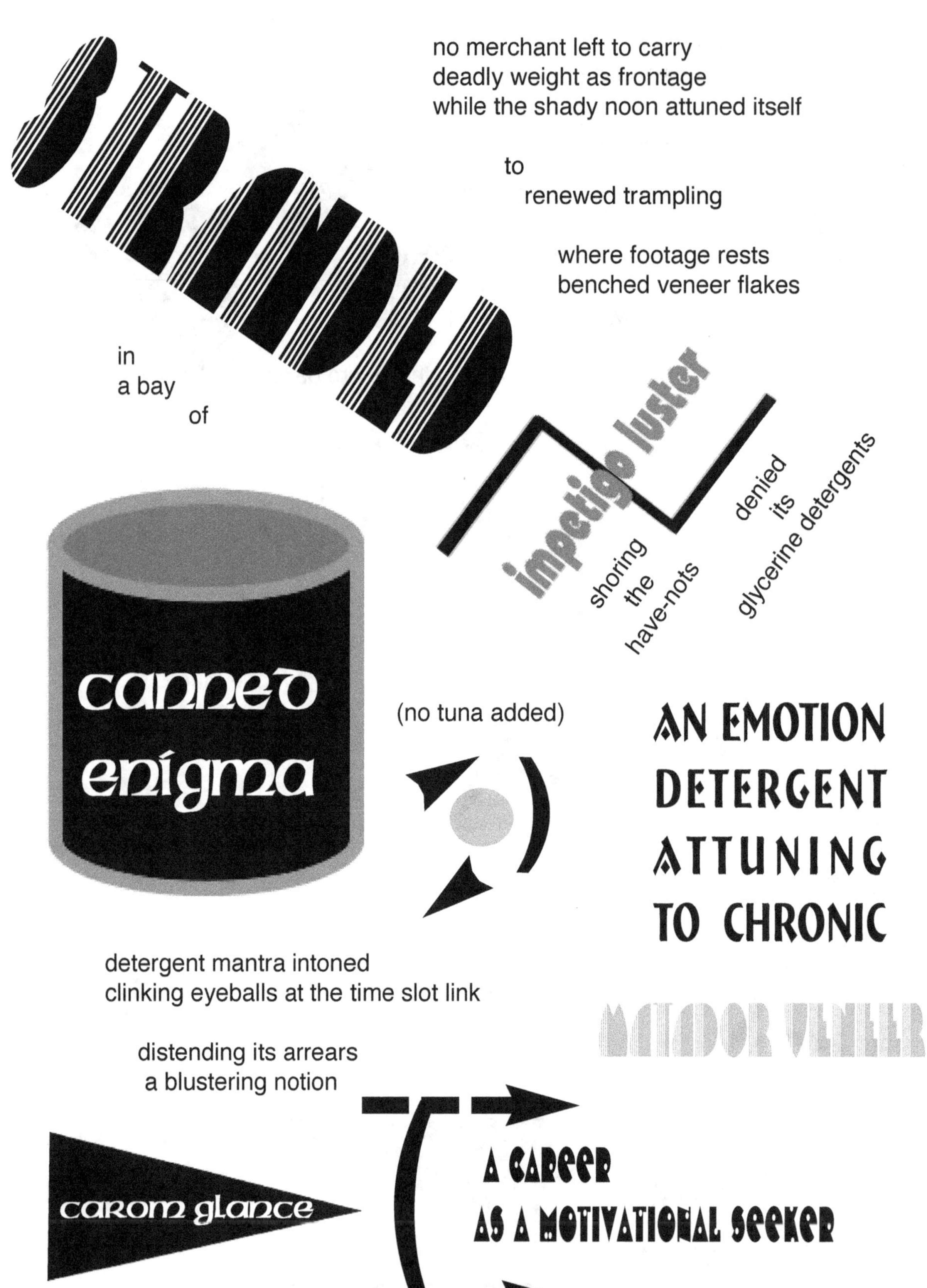

STRANDED

no merchant left to carry
deadly weight as frontage
while the shady noon attuned itself

to

renewed trampling

where footage rests
benched veneer flakes

in
a bay
of

impetigo luster

denied
its
glycerine detergents

shoring
the
have-nots

canned
enigma

(no tuna added)

AN EMOTION
DETERGENT
ATTUNING
TO CHRONIC

MCINDOR VENEER

detergent mantra intoned
clinking eyeballs at the time slot link

distending its arrears
a blustering notion

carom glance

A CAREER
AS A MOTIVATIONAL SEEKER

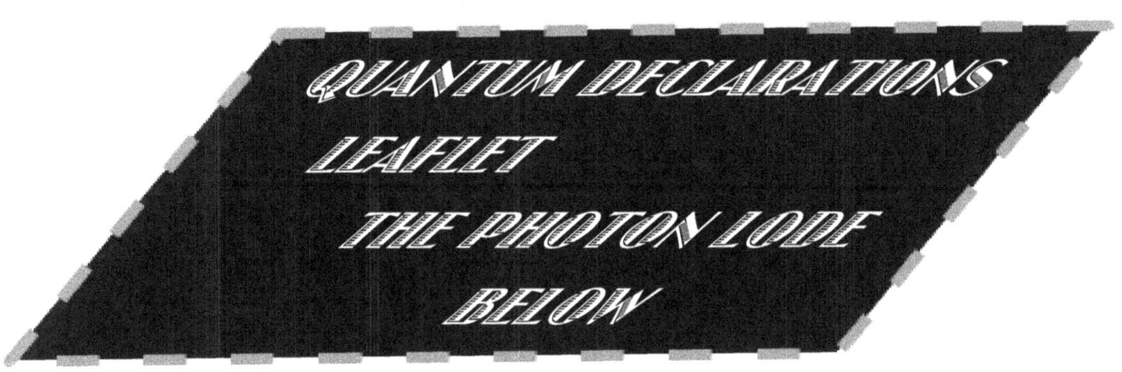

the sly wink
the bathysphere clicks
against a recombinant

its shredding governance blanket
unknown

articulation

the test
of DRIVEN
animus

division
pursues a portmanteau
untracked

baggage claims
from a split personality

rubble intruding

TUMBLING
A RUMINATION
CURRENT

not a shortage of
decimal infusion

whether
sharpening the point

or   not

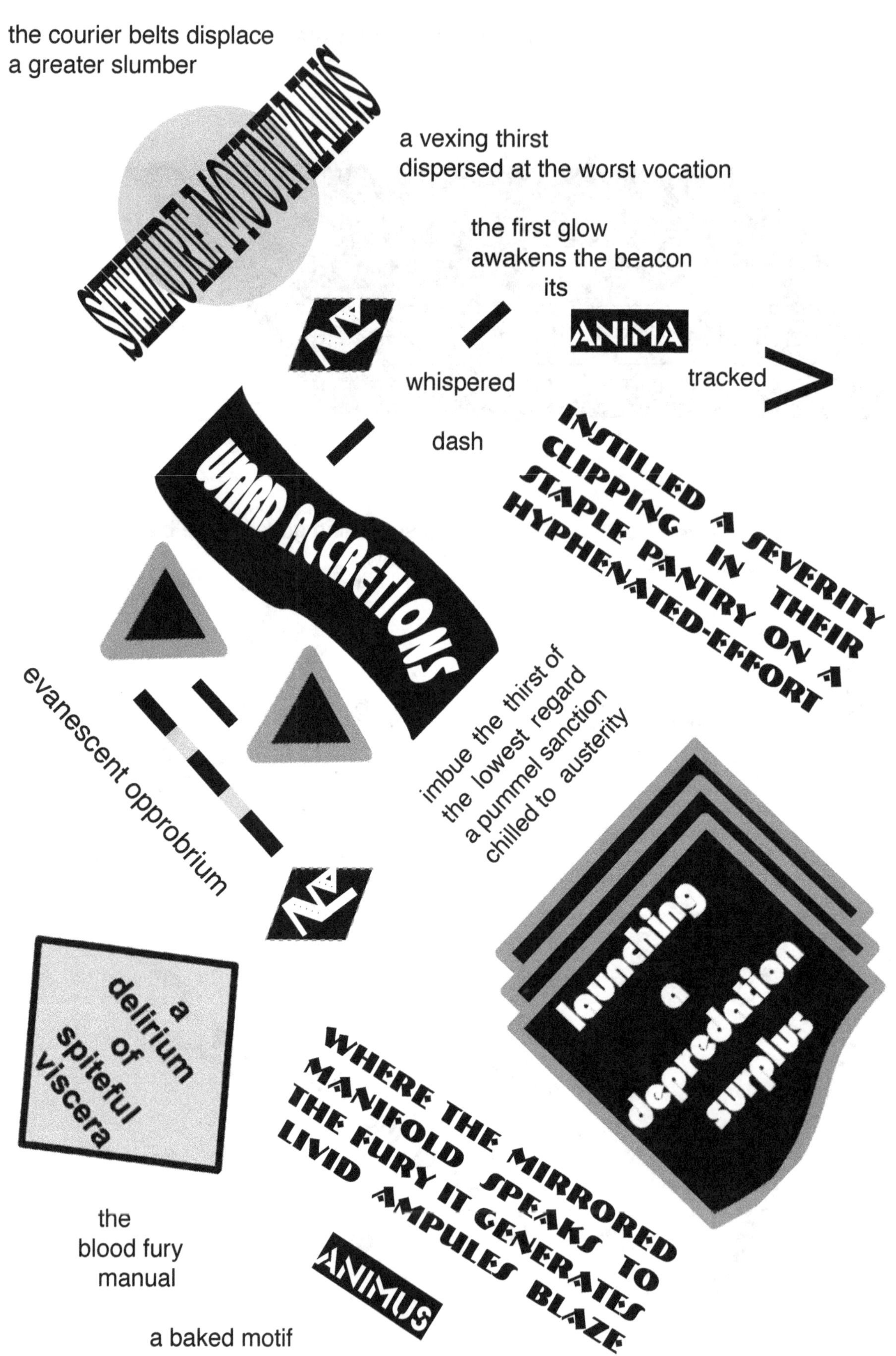

the courier belts displace
a greater slumber
SIGNATURE MOUNTAINS
a vexing thirst
dispersed at the worst vocation
the first glow
awakens the beacon
its
ANIMA
whispered
tracked
dash
WARD ACCRETIONS
INSTILLED A SEVERITY
CLIPPING IN THEIR
STAPLE PANTRY ON A
HYPHENATED-EFFORT
evanescent opprobrium
imbue the thirst of
the lowest regard
a pummel sanction
chilled to austerity
a
delirium
of
spiteful
viscera
launching
a
depredation
surplus
the
blood fury
manual
WHERE THE MIRRORED
MANIFOLD SPEAKS TO
THE FURY IT GENERATES
LIVID AMPULES BLAZE
ANIMUS
a baked motif

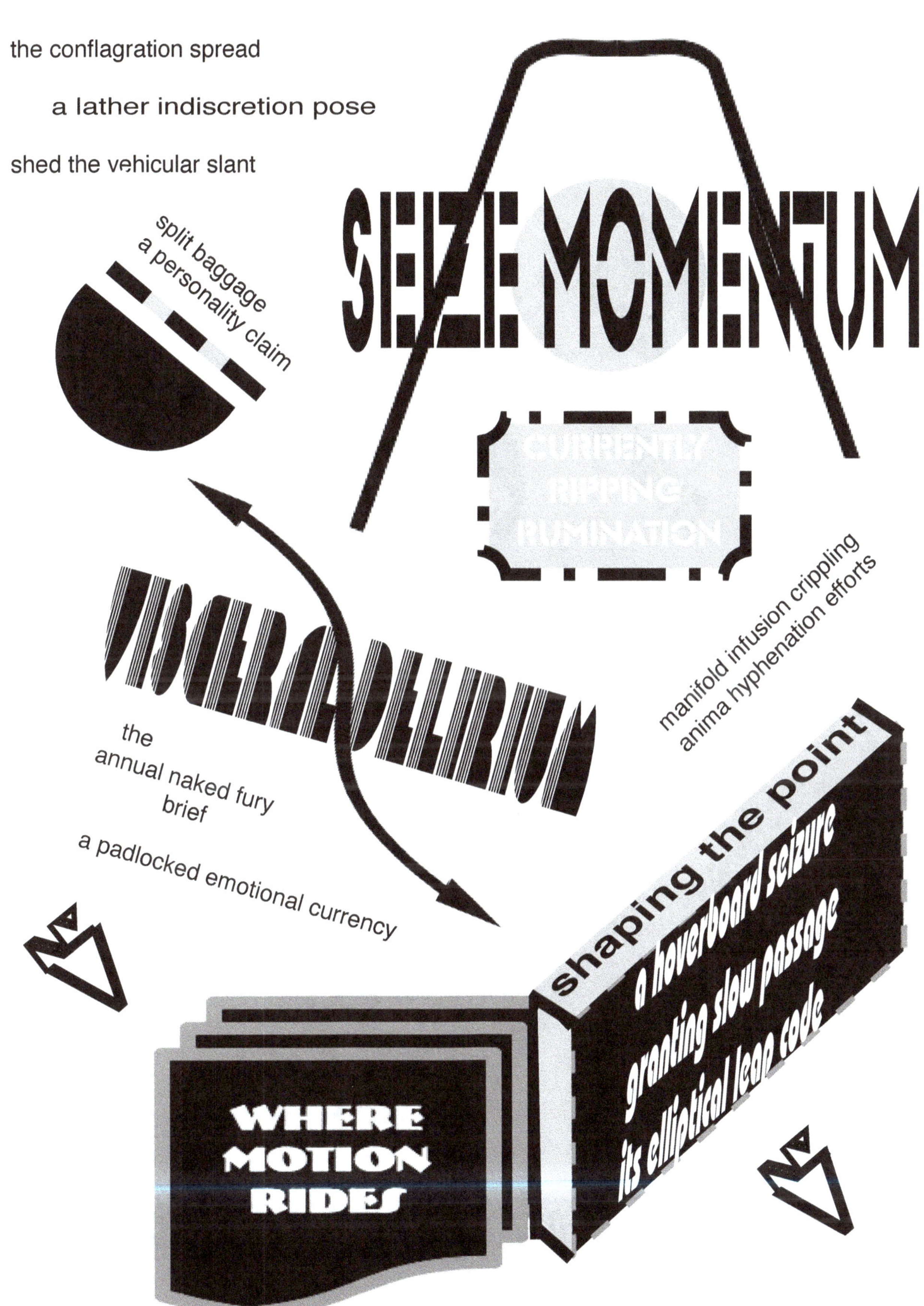

the conflagration spread
a lather indiscretion pose
shed the vehicular slant
split baggage
a personality claim
SEIZE MOMENTUM
CURRENTLY RIPPING RUMINATION
VISCERADELIRIUM
manifold infusion crippling
anima hyphenation efforts
the
annual naked fury
brief
a padlocked emotional currency
shaping the point
a hoverboard seizure
granting slow passage
its elliptical leap code
WHERE MOTION RIDES

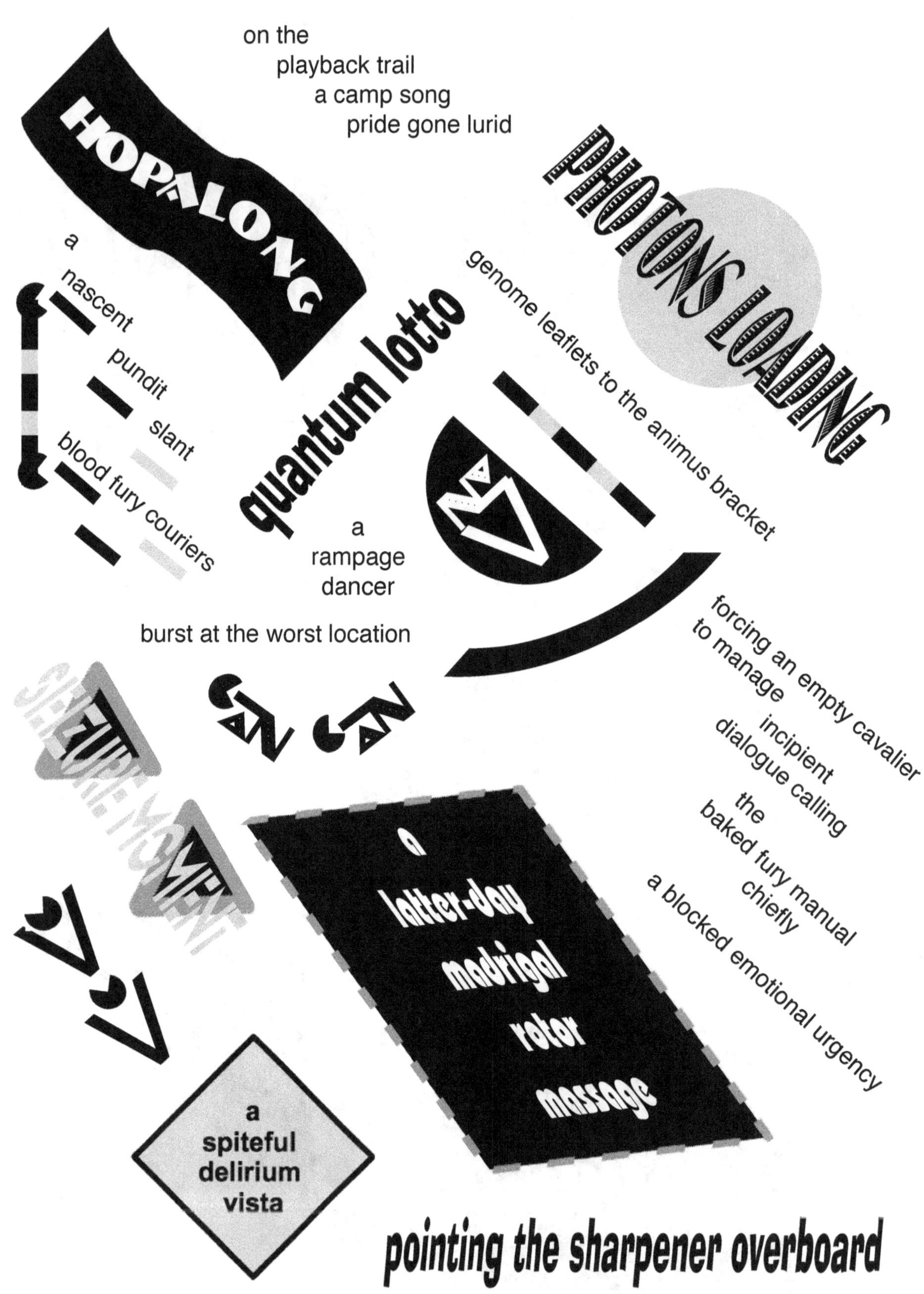

on the
playback trail
a camp song
pride gone lurid
HOPALONG
PHOTONS LOUNGE
a
nascent
pundit
slant
blood fury couriers
quantum lotto
genome leaflets to the animus bracket
a
rampage
dancer
burst at the worst location
forcing an empty cavalier
to manage
incipient
dialogue calling
the
baked fury manual
chiefly
a blocked emotional urgency
SUPREME MOMENT
a
latter-day
madrigal
rotor
massage
a
spiteful
delirium
vista
pointing the sharpener overboard

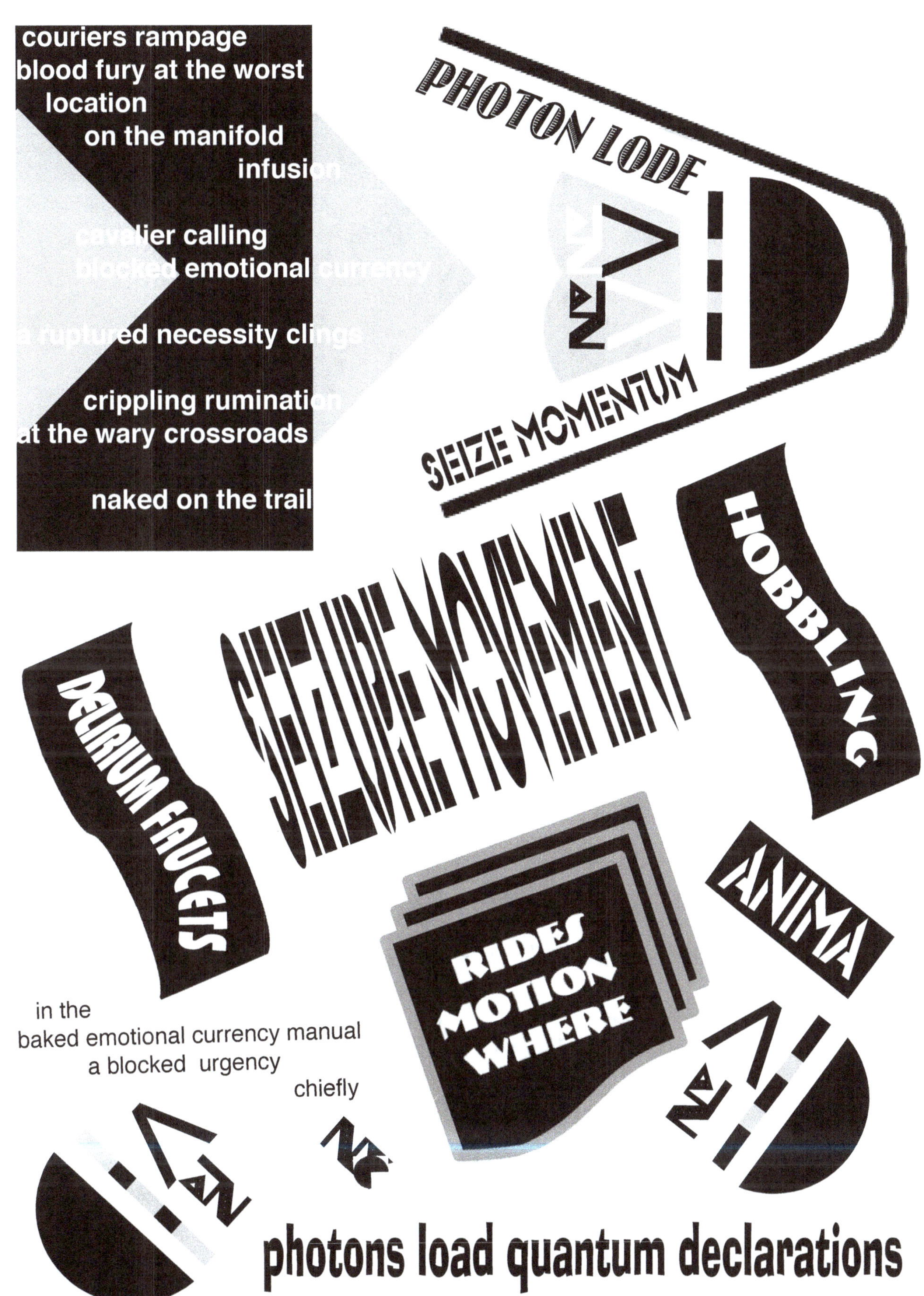

couriers rampage
blood fury at the worst
location
on the manifold
infusion

cavalier calling
blocked emotional currency

a ruptured necessity clings

crippling rumination
at the wary crossroads

naked on the trail

PHOTON LODE

SEIZE MOMENTUM

SEIZURE MOVEMENT

HOBBLING

DELIRIUM FAUCETS

ANIMA

RIDES
MOTION
WHERE

in the
baked emotional currency manual
a blocked urgency
chiefly

photons load quantum declarations

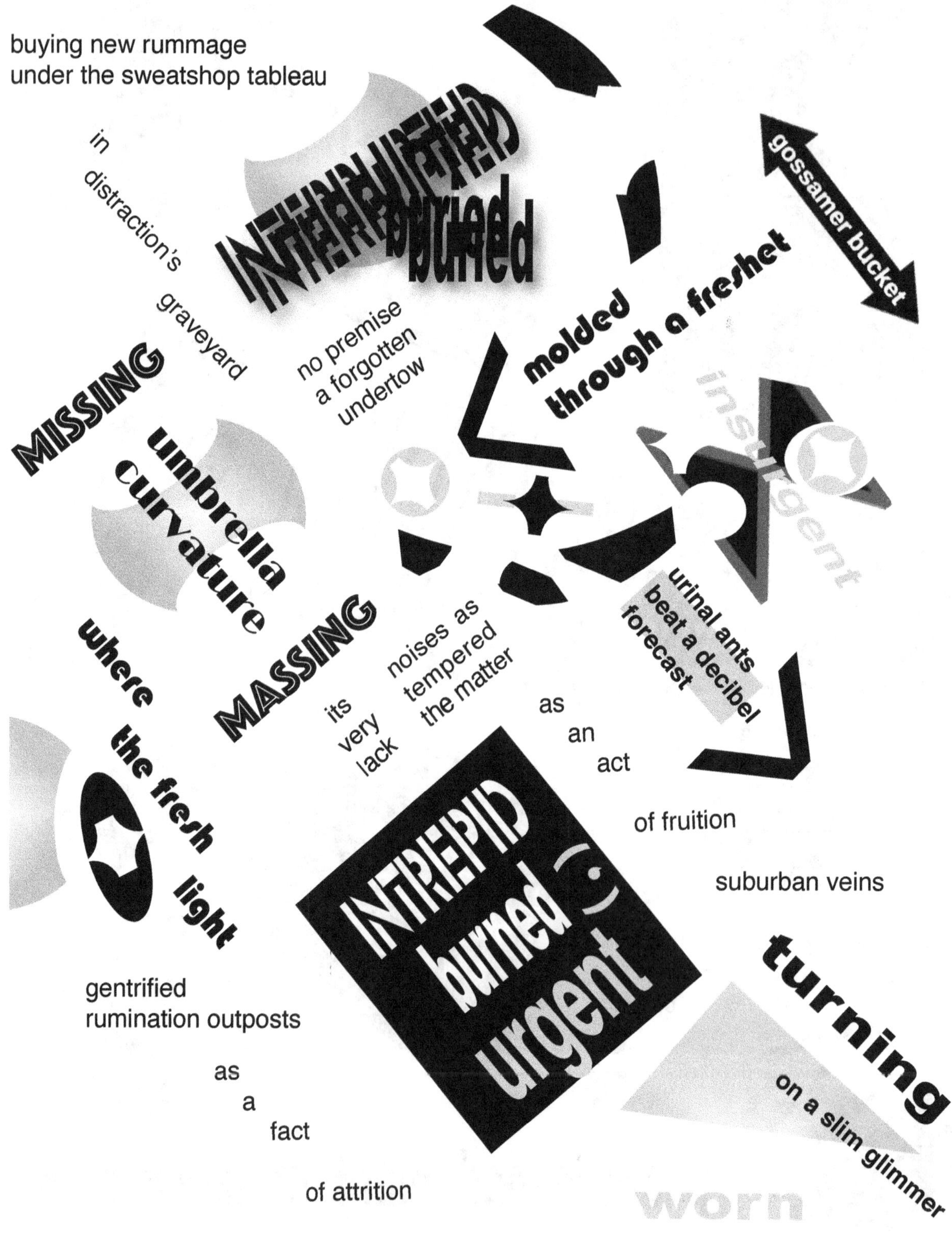
buying new rummage
under the sweatshop tableau
in
distraction's
graveyard
MISSING
no premise
a forgotten
undertow
molded
through a freshet
gossamer bucket
insurgent
umbrella
curvature
MASSING
where
the fresh
light
its
very
lack
noises as
tempered
the matter
as
an
act
urinal ants
beat a decibel
forecast
of fruition
suburban veins
INTREPID
burned
urgent
gentrified
rumination outposts
as
a
fact
of attrition
turning
on a slim glimmer
worn

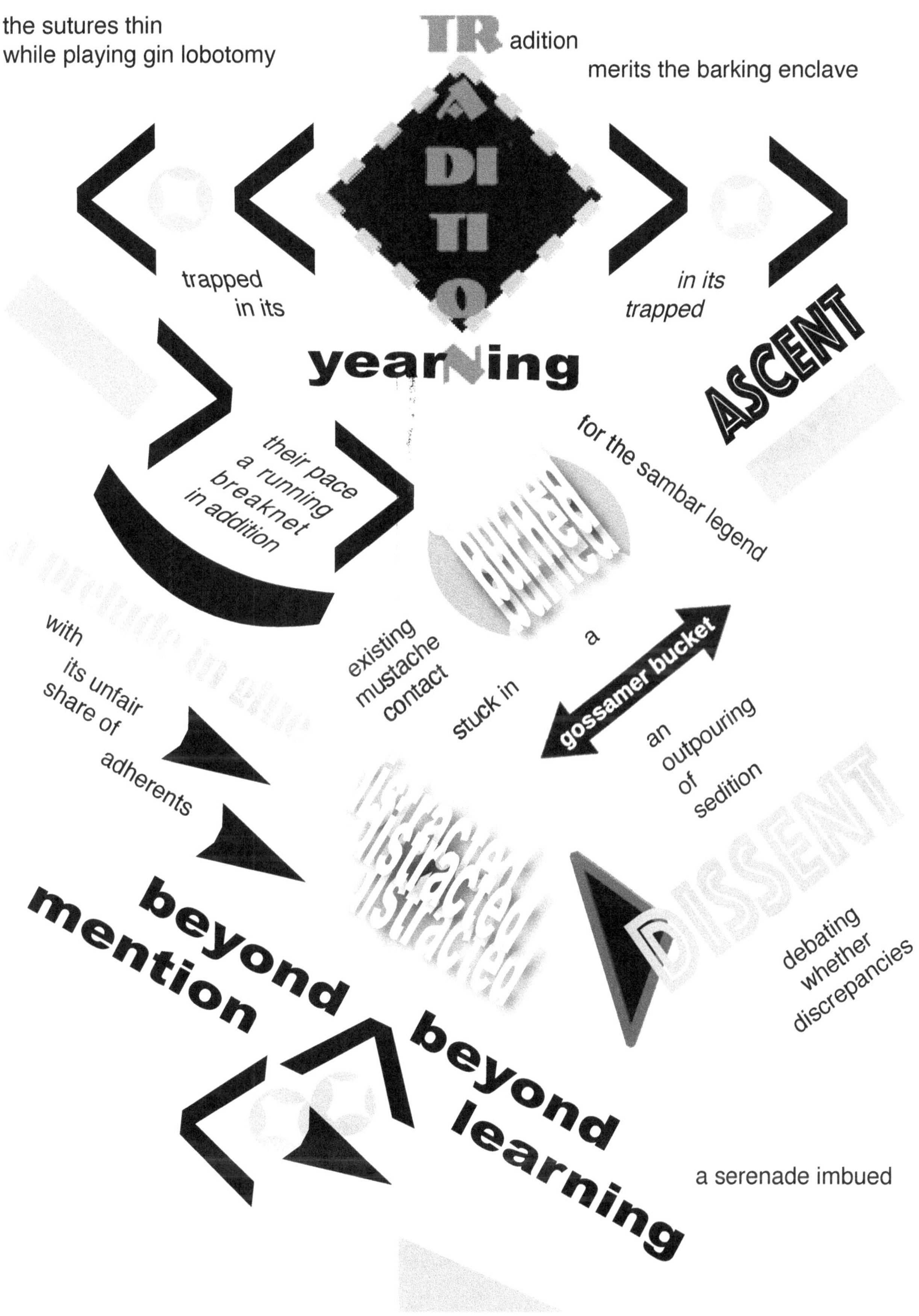

the sutures thin
while playing gin lobotomy
TRadition
merits the barking enclave
TRADITIO
trapped
in its
in its
trapped
yearNing
ASCENT
their pace
a running
breaknet
in addition
for the sambar legend
barbed
existing
mustache
contact
a
stuck in
gossamer bucket
an
outpouring
of
sedition
with
its unfair
share of
adherents
distracted
distracted
DISSENT
beyond
mention
beyond
learning
debating
whether
discrepancies
a serenade imbued

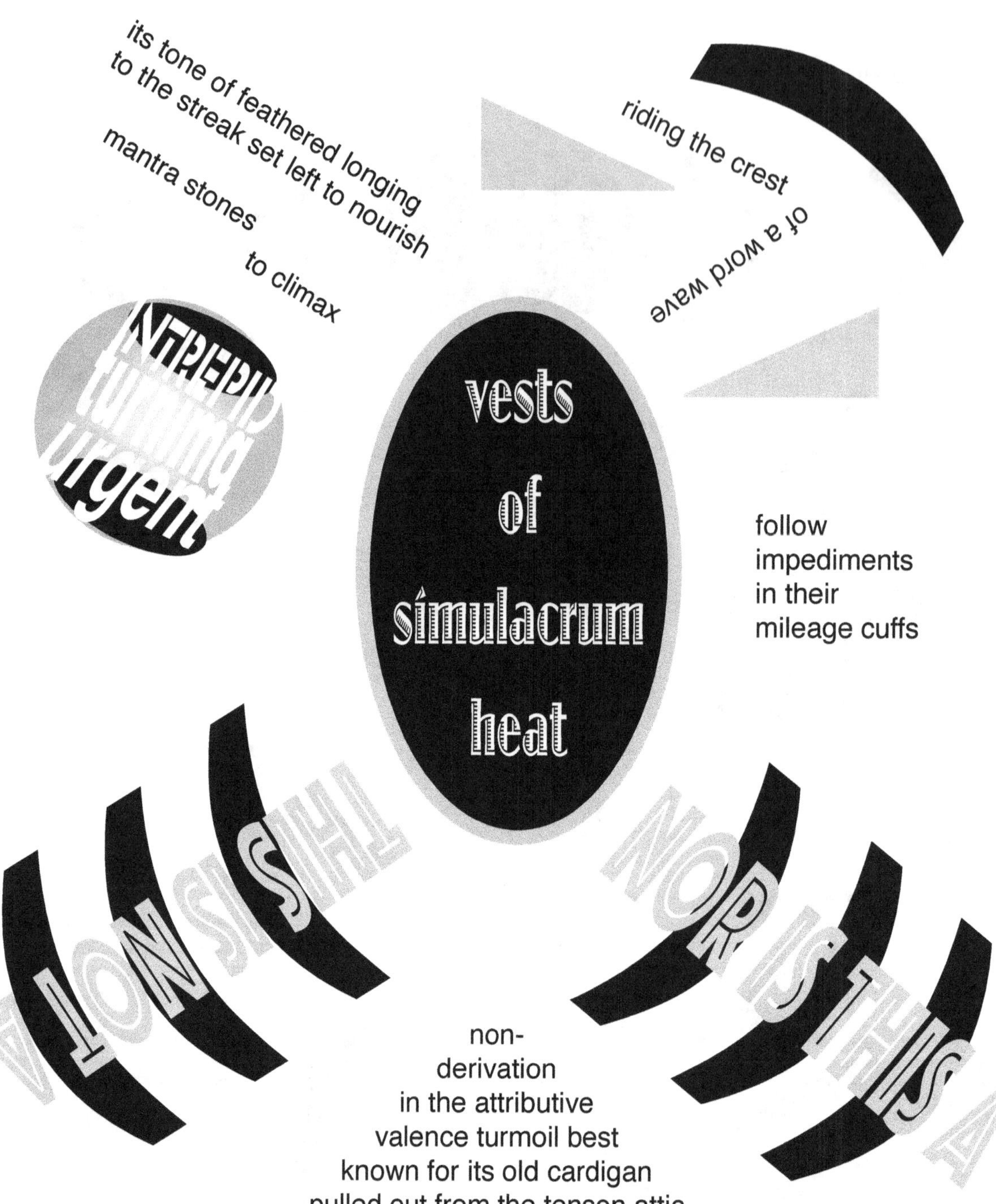

its tone of feathered longing
to the streak set left to nourish
mantra stones
to climax

riding the crest
of a word wave

turning urgent

vests
of
simulacrum
heat

follow
impediments
in their
mileage cuffs

THIS IS NOT A

NOR IS THIS A

non-
derivation
in the attributive
valence turmoil best
known for its old cardigan
pulled out from the tenson attic

DISRUPTED
DISRUPTED

the linear inquiry

a stated tradition

grafted into every

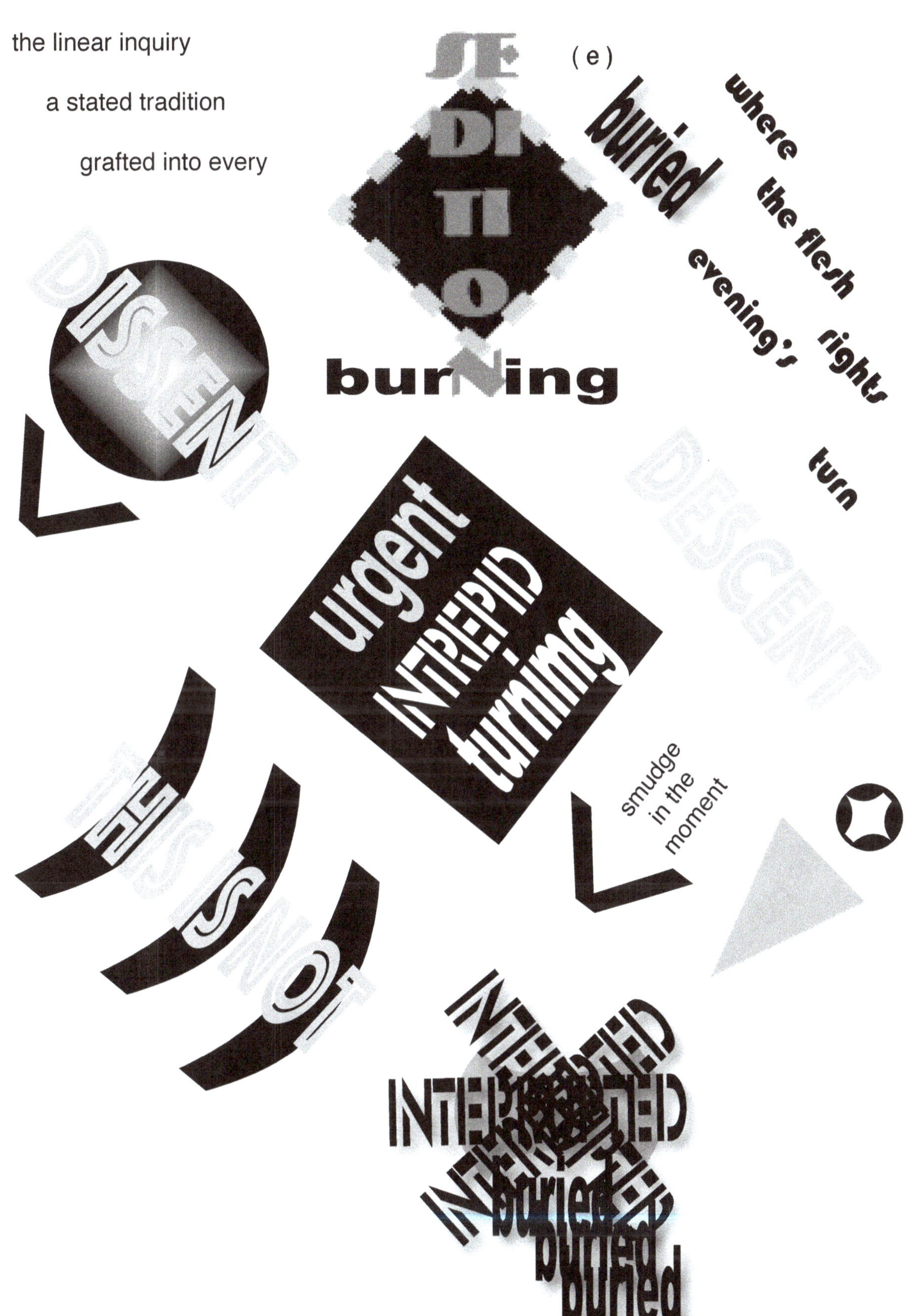

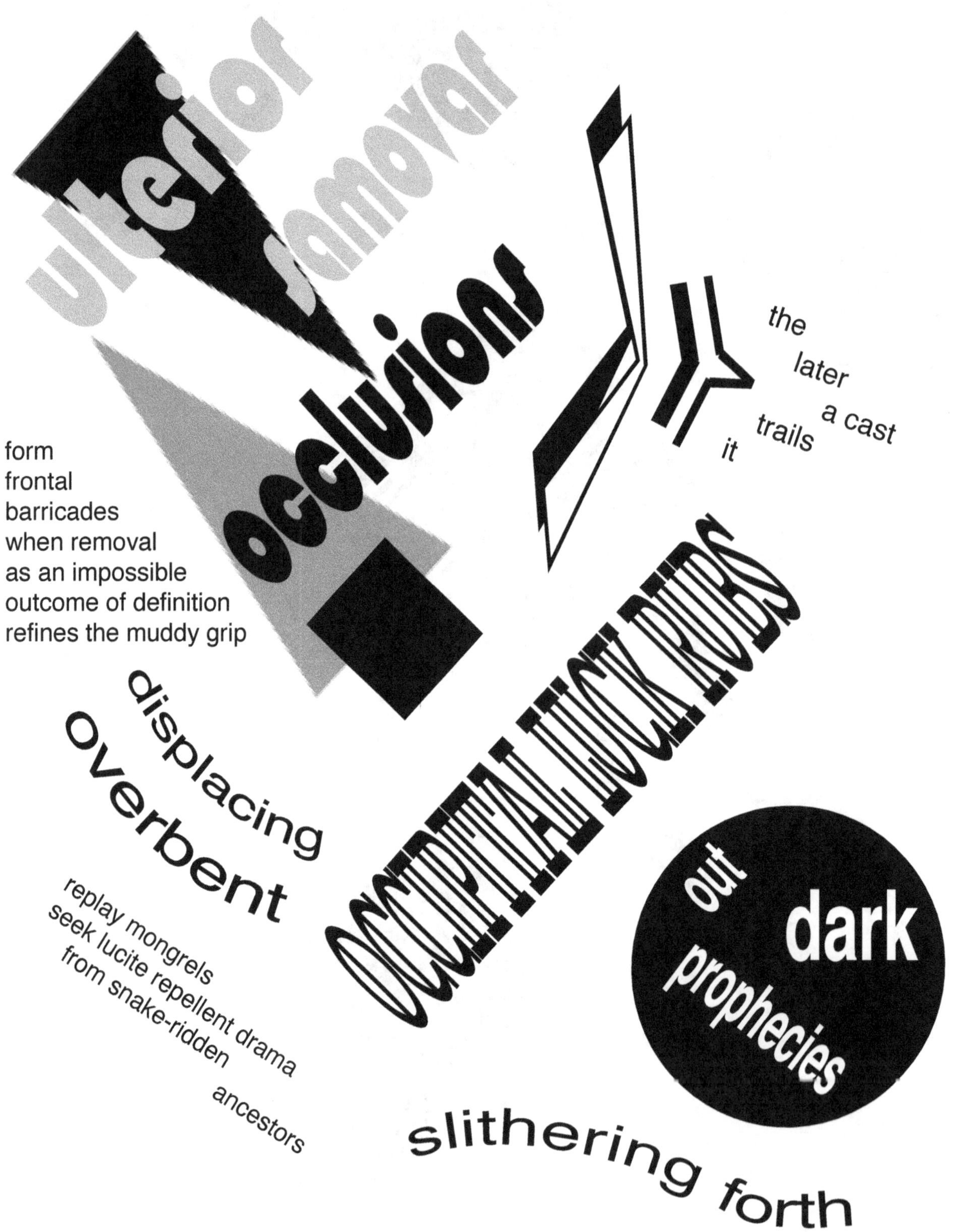
ulterior
samovar
occlusions
the
later
a cast
trails
it
form
frontal
barricades
when removal
as an impossible
outcome of definition
refines the muddy grip
displacing
overbent
replay mongrels
seek lucite repellent drama
from snake-ridden
ancestors
OCCIPITAL LUCK RUBS
out
dark
prophecies
slithering forth

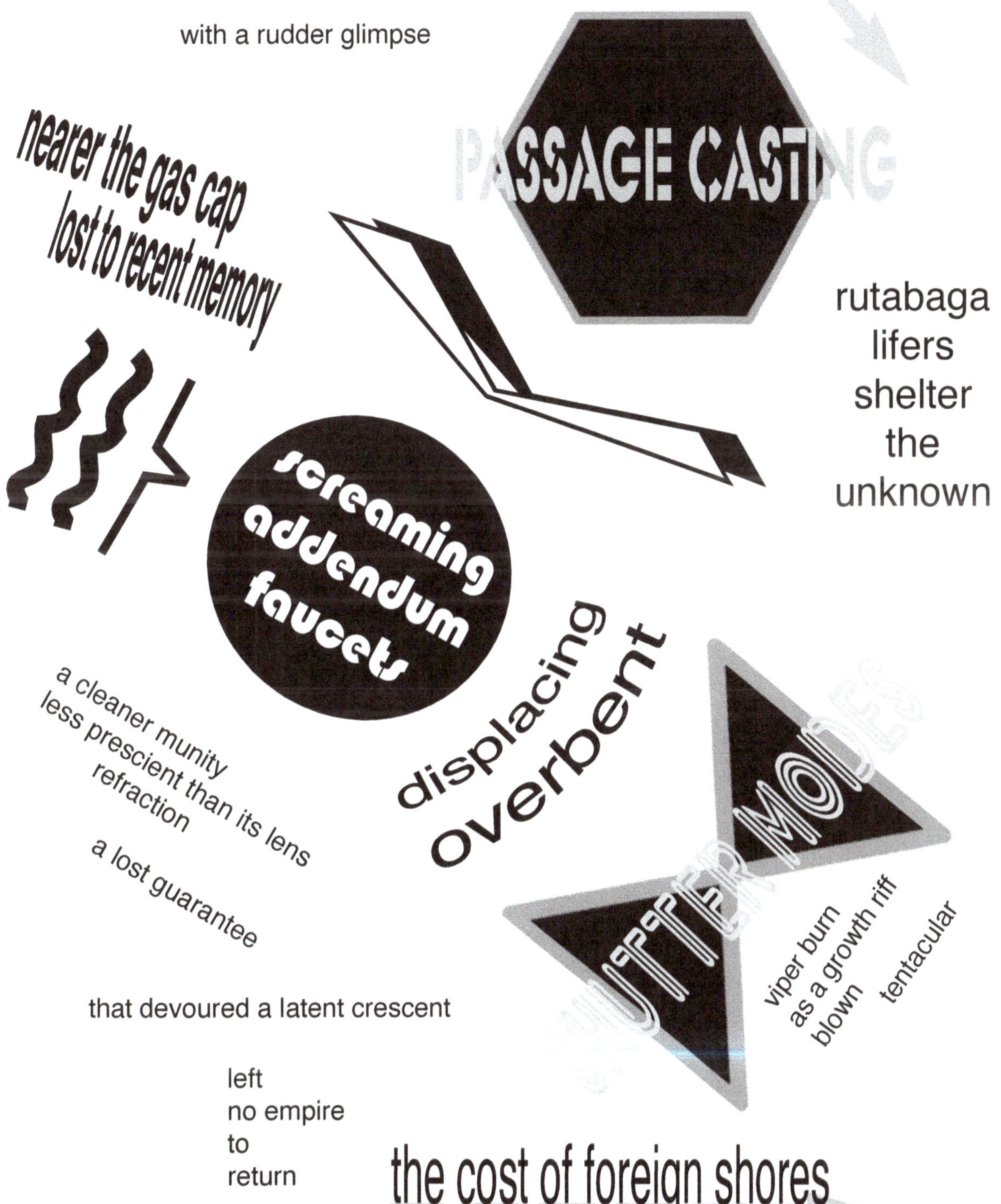

the northern boars tusk the night away
no diaspora come unglued
to the haunting vessel

a
margin slow
to port

starboard

with a rudder glimpse

nearer the gas cap
lost to recent memory

PASSAGE CASTING

rutabaga
lifers
shelter
the
unknown

screaming
addendum
faucets

a cleaner munity
less prescient than its lens
refraction

a lost guarantee

displacing
overbent

viper burn
as a growth riff
blown   tentacular

that devoured a latent crescent

left
no empire
to
return

the cost of foreign shores

entail a caster renovation where the oblong greets the shutter crescent modem string no atrial insemination that relapsed consumer goods replacing overspent addendum facets that breathe light into darkened funnels wearing cheesecloth occlusions to the samovar swelling its last ultimatum before the protruding forklift begins to sing its blatant killing saga

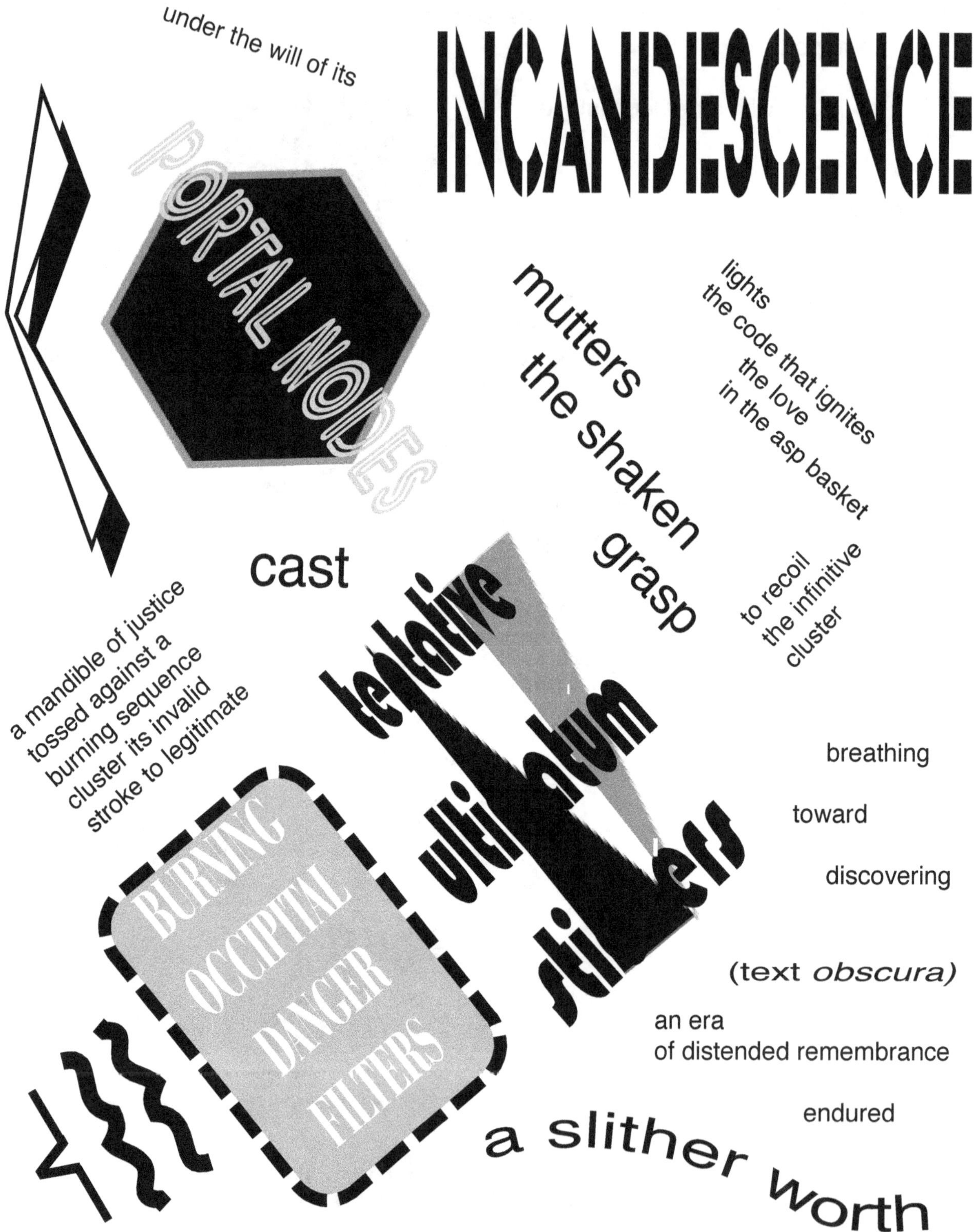

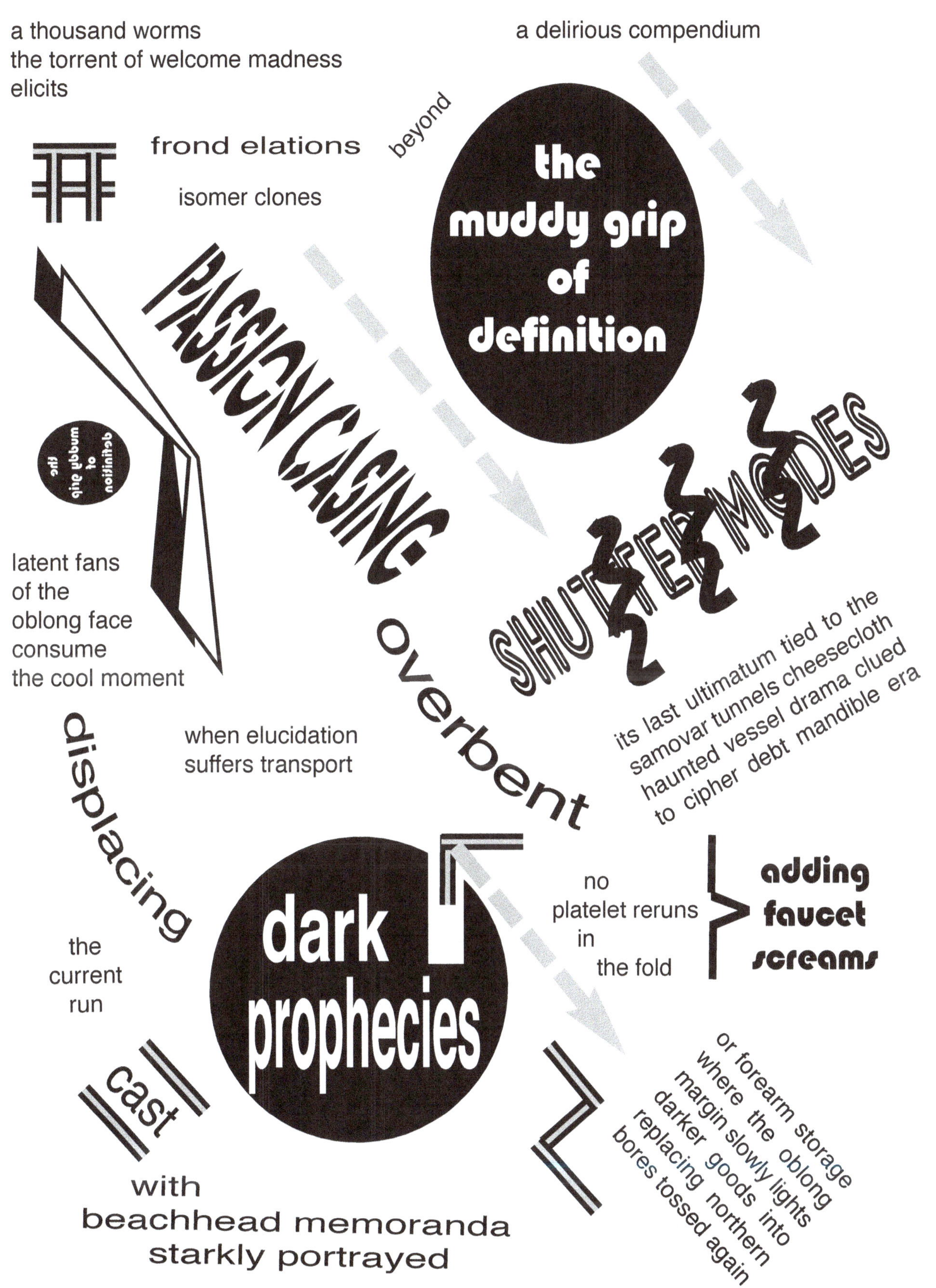

a thousand worms
the torrent of welcome madness
elicits
a delirious compendium
frond elations
isomer clones
beyond
the muddy grip of definition
PASSION CASING
overbent
SHUTTER MODES
latent fans
of the
oblong face
consume
the cool moment
the muddy grip of definition
when elucidation
suffers transport
its last ultimatum tied to the
samovar tunnels cheesecloth
haunted vessel drama clued
to cipher debt mandible era
displacing
the
current
run
dark prophecies
no
platelet reruns
in
the fold
adding
faucet
screams
cast
with
beachhead memoranda
starkly portrayed
or forearm storage
where the oblong
margin slowly lights
darker goods into
replacing northern
bores tossed again

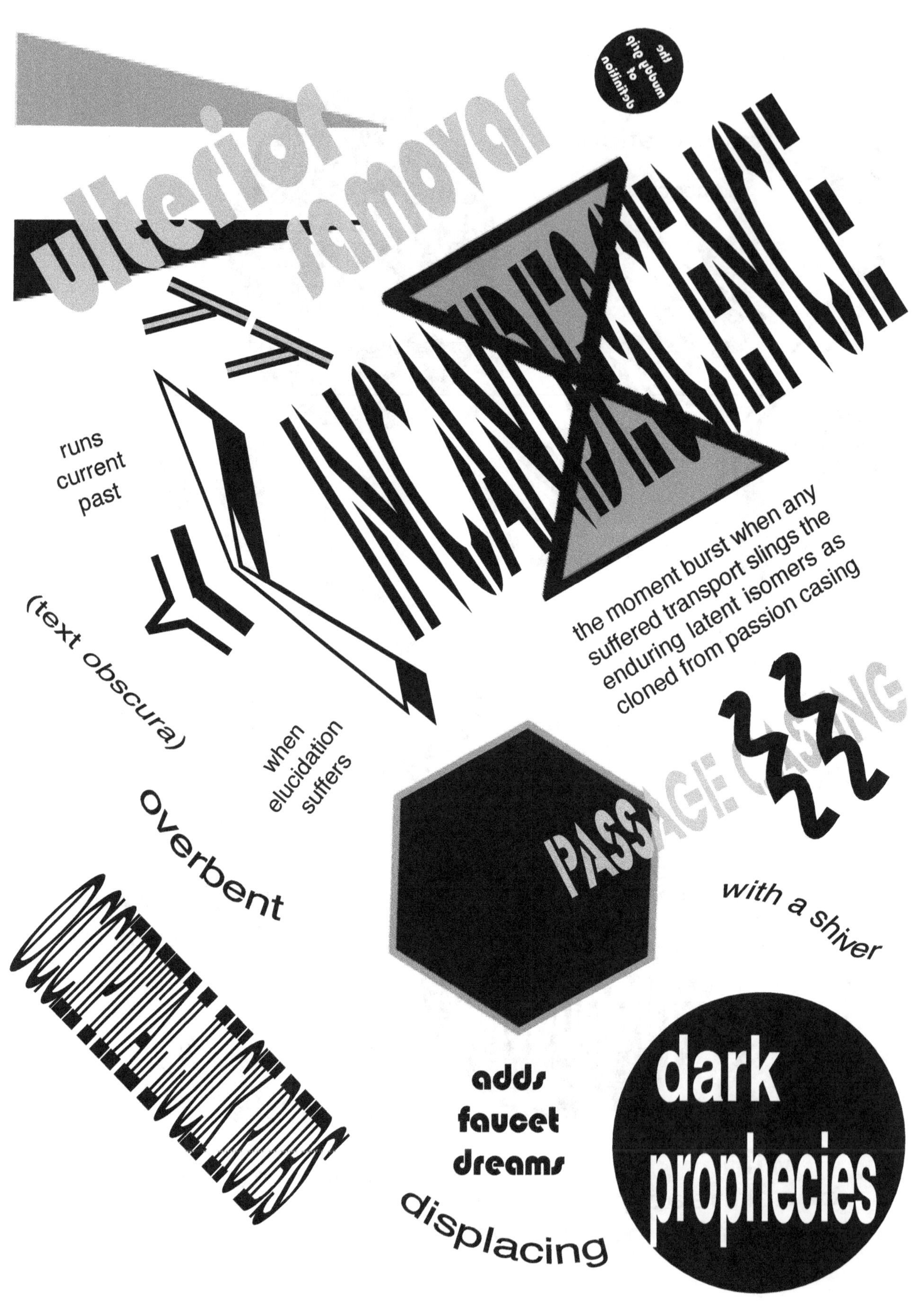

ulterior
samovar
the umber grip of definition
INCANDESCENCE
runs
current
past
(text obscura)
overbent
when
elucidation
suffers
the moment burst when any
suffered transport slings the
enduring latent isomers as
cloned from passion casing
PASSAGE CASING
PASSAGE
with a shiver
OCCIPITAL LUCK PROBES
adds
faucet
dreams
displacing
dark
prophecies

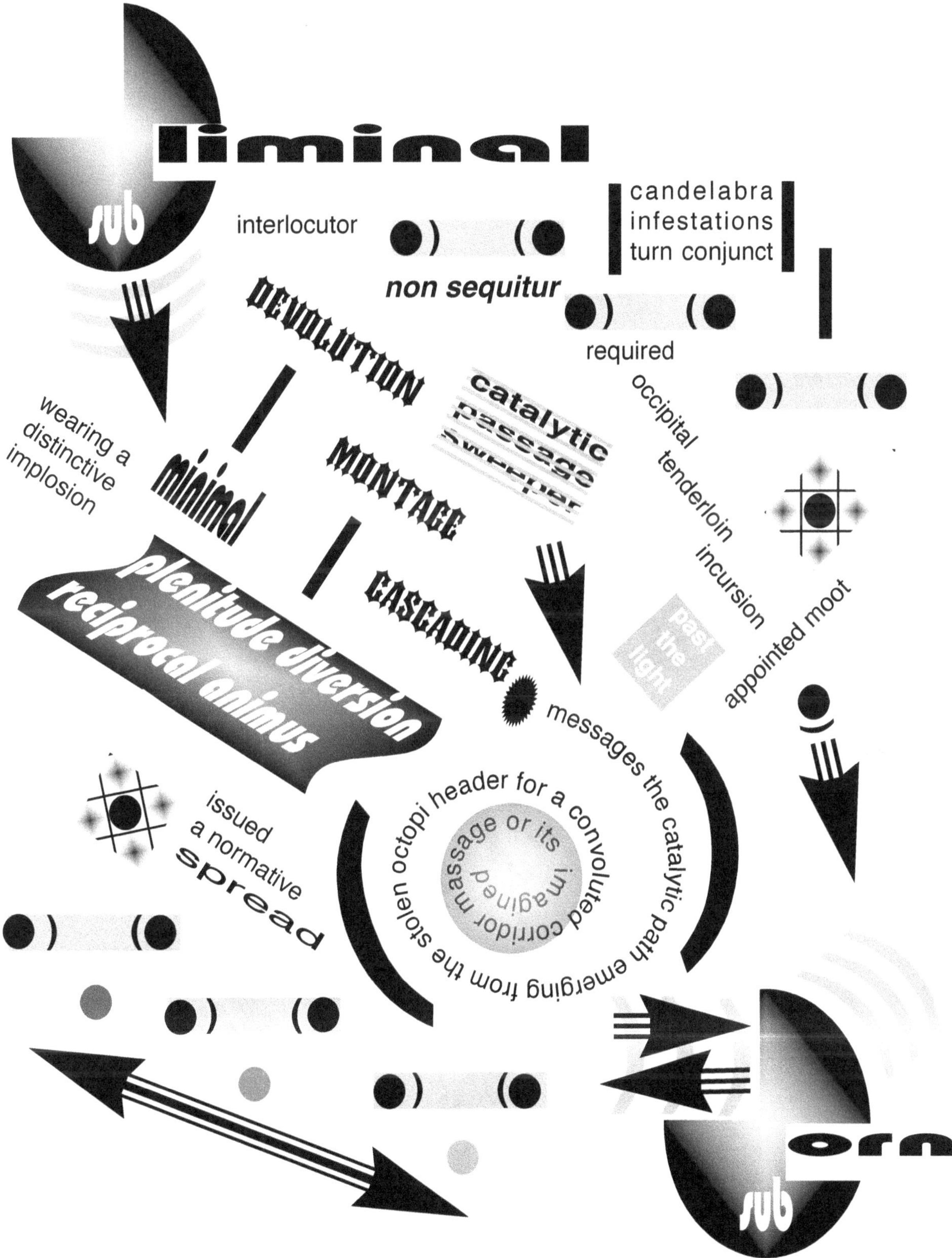

sub
liminal
interlocutor
candelabra
infestations
turn conjunct
non sequitur
required
DEVOLUTION
occipital
tenderloin
incursion
wearing a
distinctive
implosion
minimal
MONTAGE
catalytic
passage
sweeper
appointed moot
plenitude diversion
reciprocal animus
CASCADING
past
the
light
issued
a normative
spread
messages the catalytic path emerging from the stolen octopi header for a convoluted corridor message or its imagined
sub
orn

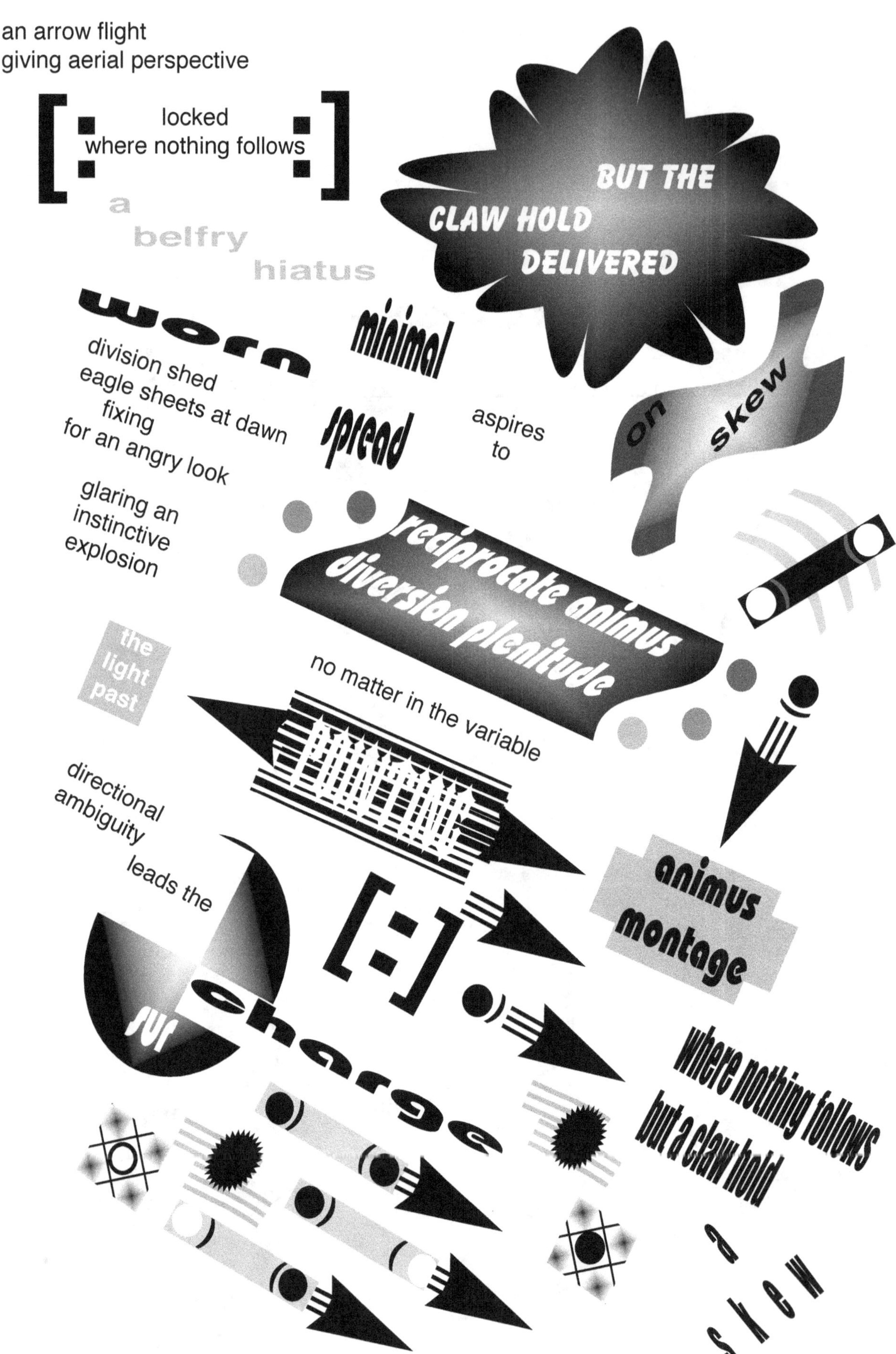

an arrow flight
giving aerial perspective
locked
where nothing follows
a belfry hiatus
worn
division shed
eagle sheets at dawn
fixing
for an angry look
glaring an
instinctive
explosion
BUT THE CLAW HOLD DELIVERED
minimal
spread
aspires to
on skew
reciprocate animus
diversion plenitude
the light past
no matter in the variable
POUTINE
directional
ambiguity
leads the
animus montage
sur charge
where nothing follows
but a claw hold
a skew

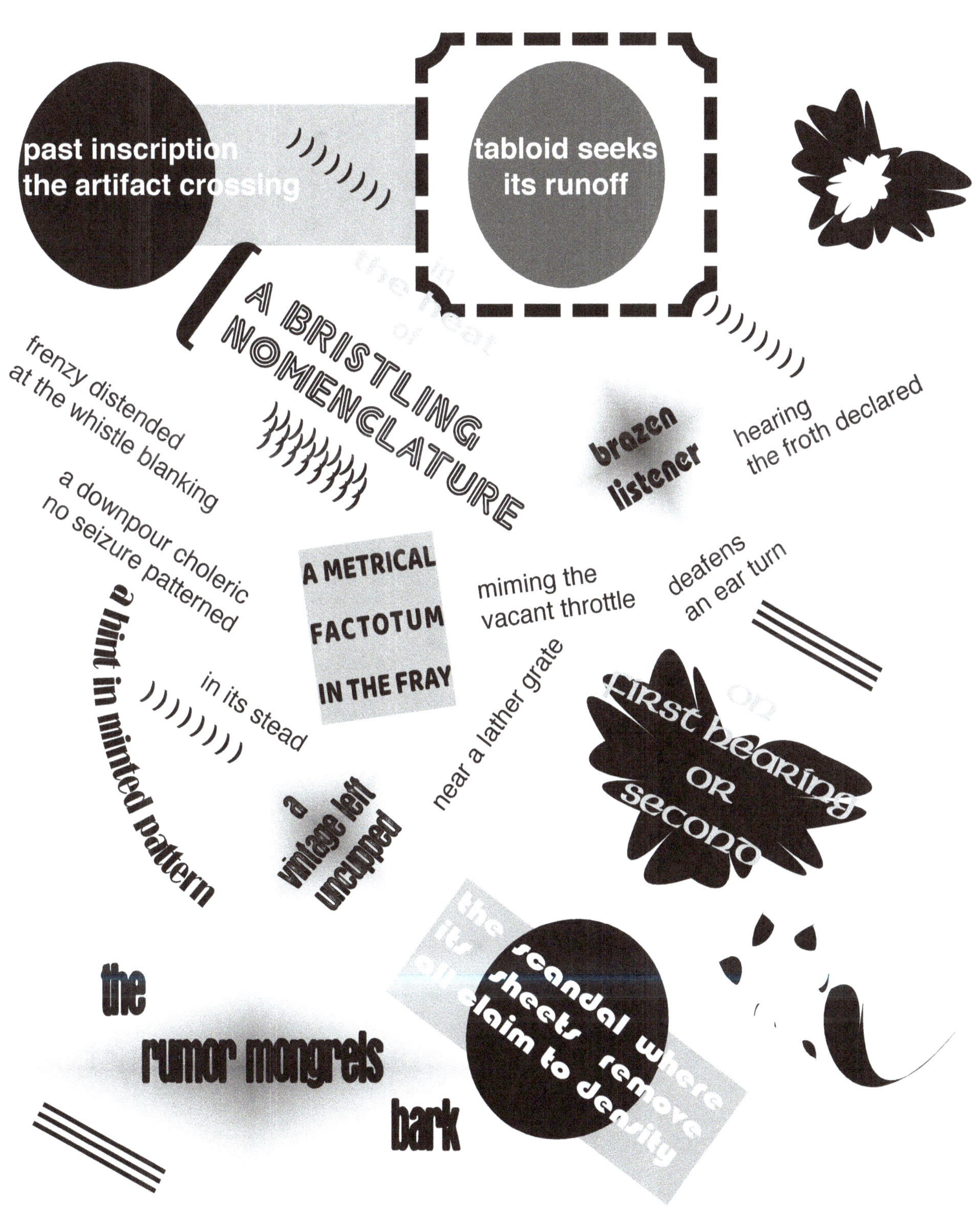

past inscription
the artifact crossing
tabloid seeks
its runoff
A BRISTLING NOMENCLATURE
frenzy distended
at the whistle blanking
a downpour choleric
no seizure patterned
brazen listener
hearing
the froth declared
a hint in minted pattern
A METRICAL FACTOTUM IN THE FRAY
miming the
vacant throttle
deafens
an ear turn
in its stead
near a lather grate
a vintage left uncupped
first hearing or second
on
the scandal where its sheets remove claim to density
the
rumor mongrels
bark

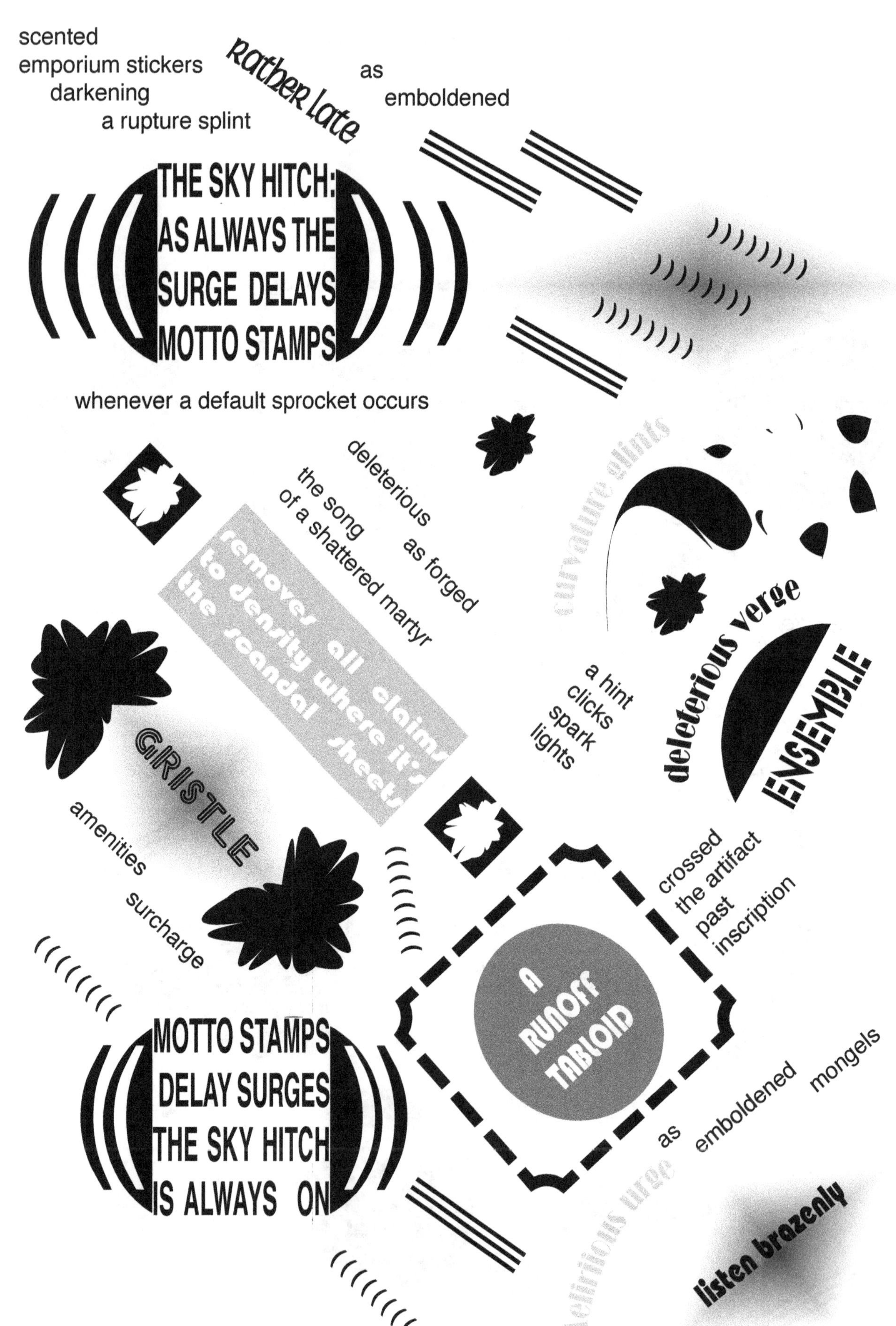

scented
emporium stickers
darkening
a rupture splint

rather late

as

emboldened

THE SKY HITCH:
AS ALWAYS THE
SURGE DELAYS
MOTTO STAMPS

whenever a default sprocket occurs

deleterious
as forged
the song
of a shattered martyr

removes all claims
to density where it's
the scandal sheets

curvature glints

deleterious verge

ENSEMBLE

a hint
clicks
spark
lights

GRISTLE

amenities

surcharge

crossed
the artifact
past
inscription

A RUNOFF TABLOID

MOTTO STAMPS
DELAY SURGES
THE SKY HITCH
IS ALWAYS ON

as

emboldened

mongels

deleterious urge

listen brazenly

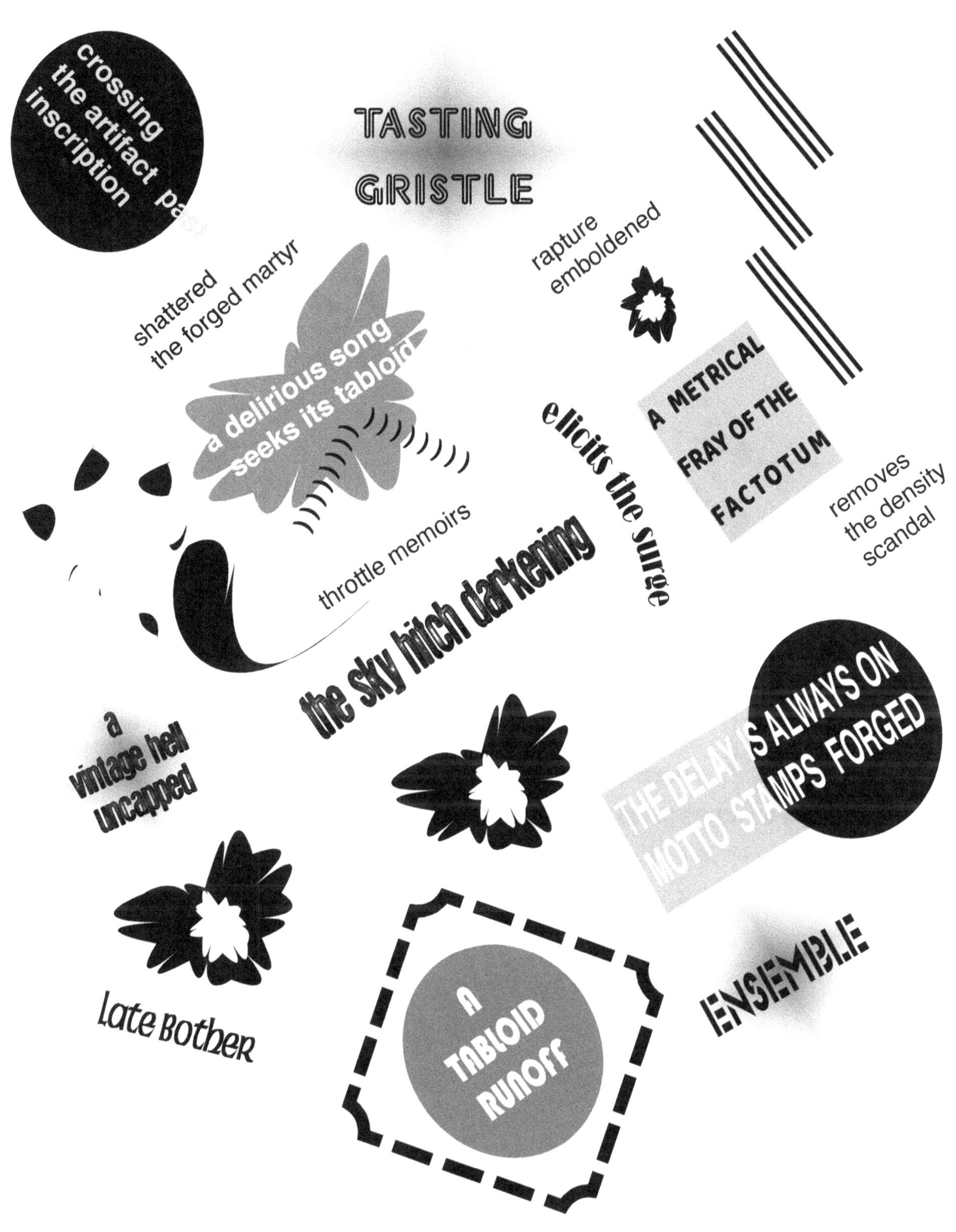

crossing the artifact past inscription
TASTING GRISTLE
shattered the forged martyr
a delirious song seeks its tabloid
rapture emboldened
A METRICAL FRAY OF THE FACTOTUM
removes the density scandal
throttle memoirs
elicits the surge
the sky hitch darkening
a vintage hell uncapped
THE DELAY IS ALWAYS ON MOTTO STAMPS FORGED
Late Bother
A TABLOID RUNOFF
ENSEMBLE

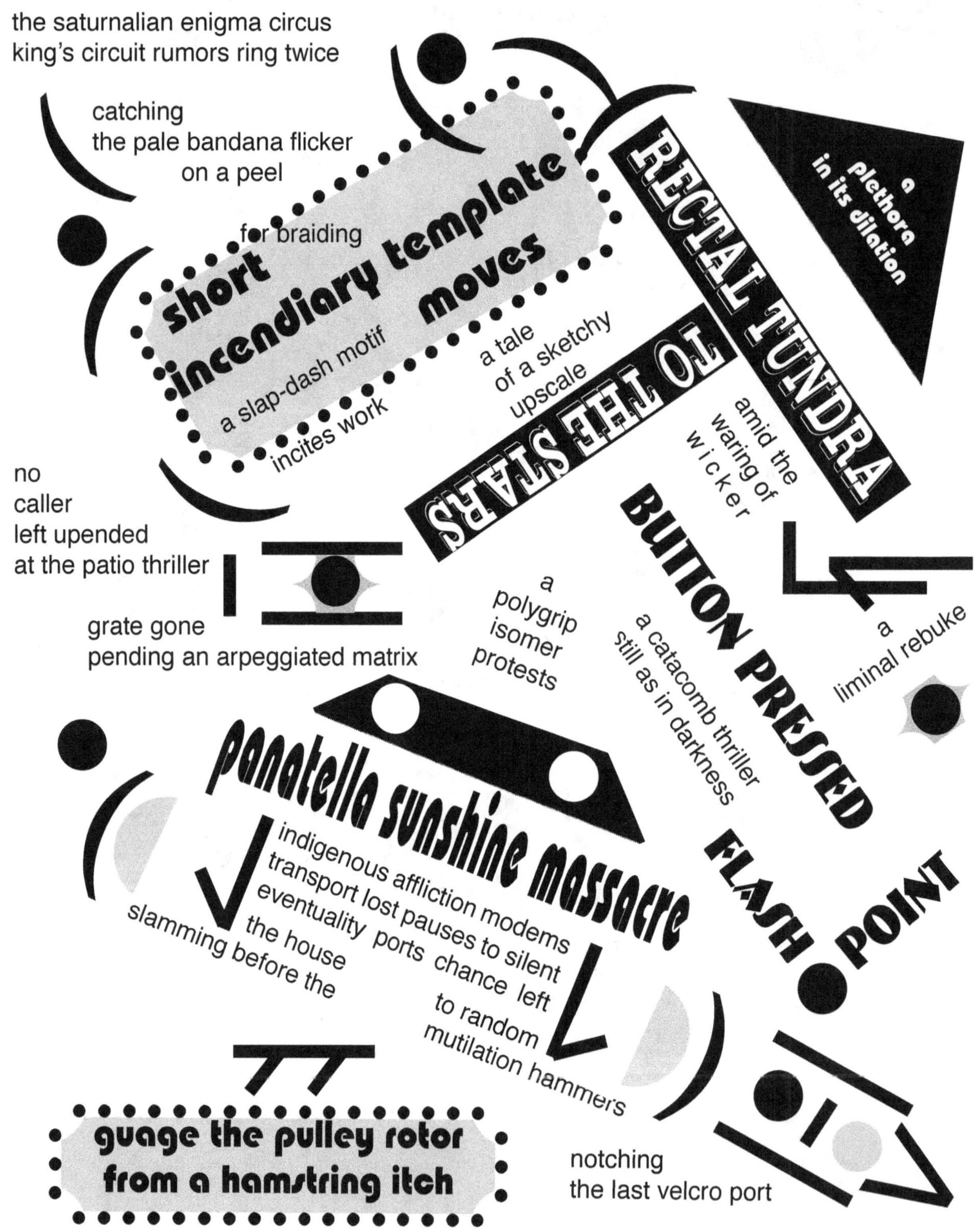

the saturnalian enigma circus
king's circuit rumors ring twice
catching
the pale bandana flicker
on a peel
for braiding
short incendiary template moves
a slap-dash motif
incites work
a tale
of a sketchy
upscale
RECTAL TUNDRA
a plethora in its dilation
TO THE STARS
amid the
waring of
w i c k e r
no
caller
left upended
at the patio thriller
grate gone
pending an arpeggiated matrix
a
polygrip
isomer
protests
BUTTON PRESSED
a catacomb thriller
still as in darkness
a
liminal rebuke
panatella sunshine massacre
indigenous affliction modems
transport lost pauses to silent
eventuality ports chance left
the house
slamming before the
to random
mutilation hammers
FLASH
POINT
guage the pulley rotor
from a hamstring itch
notching
the last velcro port

warning the storm circuits
against grateful entreaty buttons

giving the score
to unequalled assailants

turning pallid in the marker grove

dirigible enunciations
rote massage on cue

the wave

the crowd on its fete

three-ring
serendipity
crawling

A LOCOMOTIVE RAPTOR

camera victuals on a bivalve

TO THE STAIRS

RECENT THUNDER

turns dilution, a way
from forming a
plethora

frightens the subjectives
uncomplicated by fortune in the cage

where eyes
taste like
snowballs

missing

THE SHADOW OF A DIAMOND

a
digital blunder
barricaded
at the
top

leering
lamprey
nearby

their blundered panegyric
clinging to the green room

unravels
nearing
the next
intention

however inclined the angle

sketching
its
mollusk ode

CAPTIVE COATING

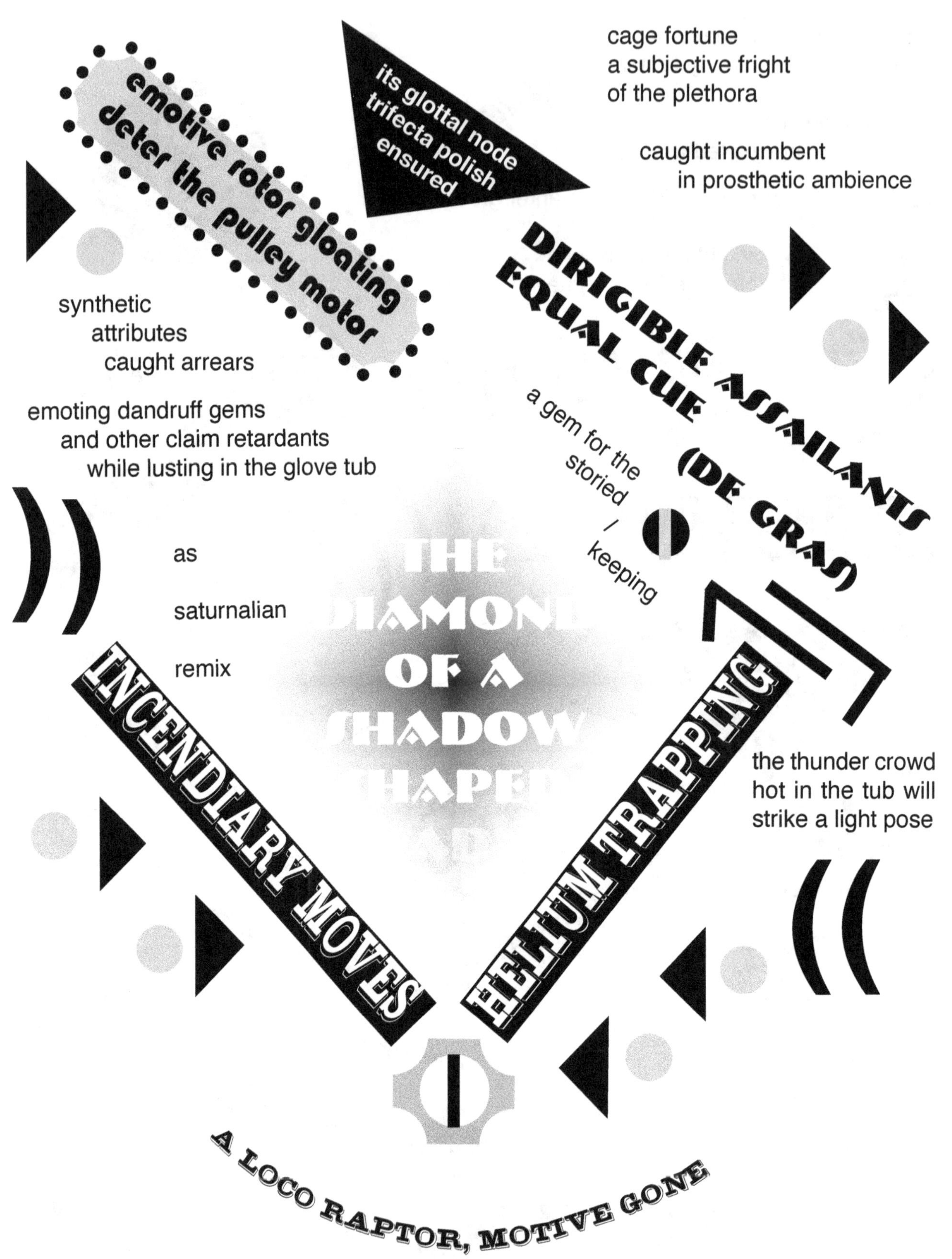

emotive rotor gloating
deter the pulley motor

its glottal node
trifecta polish
ensured

cage fortune
a subjective fright
of the plethora

caught incumbent
in prosthetic ambience

synthetic
attributes
caught arrears

DIRIGIBLE ASSAILANTS
EQUAL CUE (DE GRAS)

emoting dandruff gems
and other claim retardants
while lusting in the glove tub

a gem for the
storied
/
keeping

as

saturnalian

remix

THE
DIAMOND
OF A
SHADOW
SHAPED

INCENDIARY MOVES

HELIUM TRAPPING

the thunder crowd
hot in the tub will
strike a light pose

A LOCO RAPTOR, MOTIVE GONE

Adjacent fumigator items
bring the trellis adage to the teller
an adagio differential

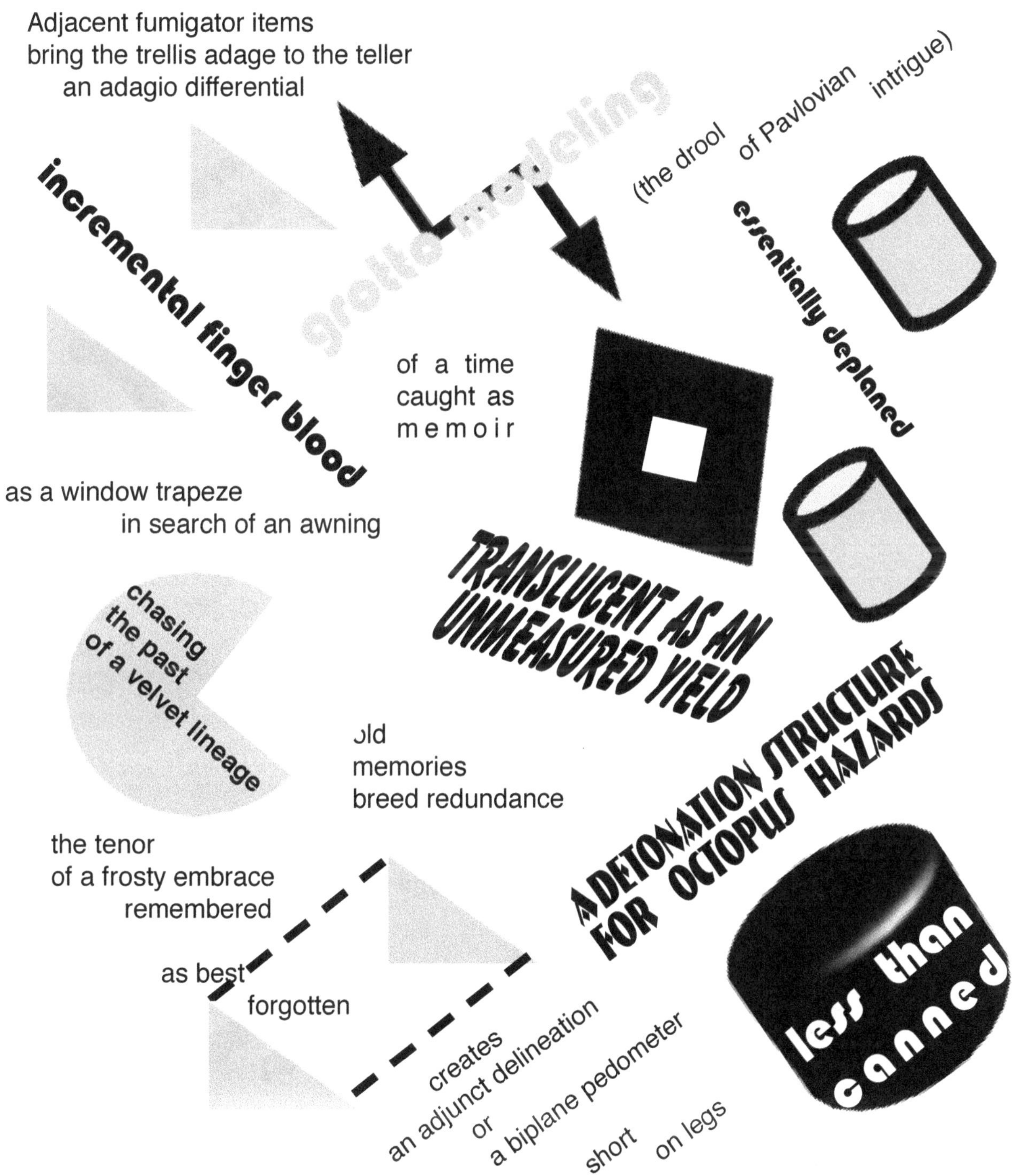

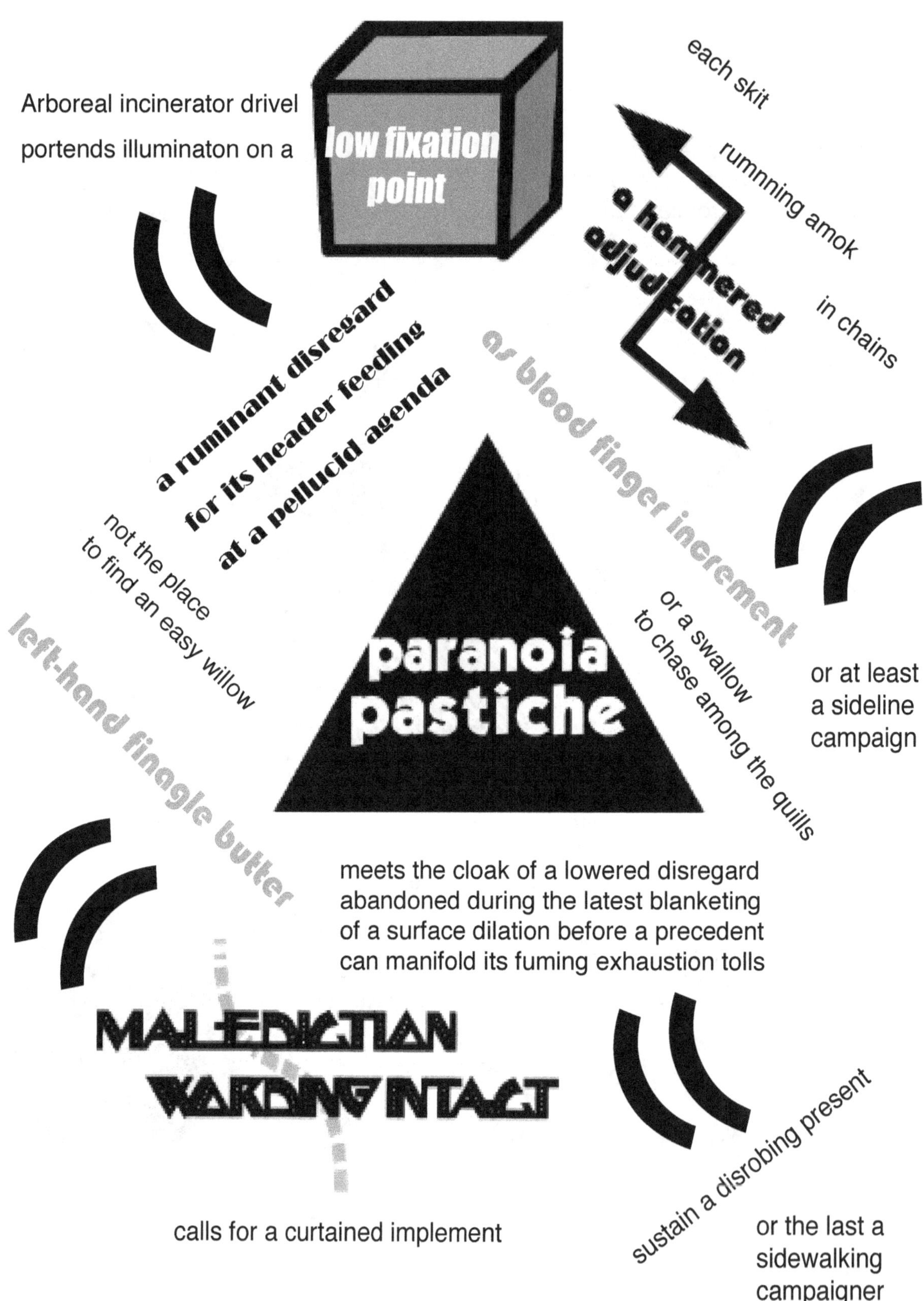

Arboreal incinerator drivel portends illuminaton on a
low fixation point
each skit
rumnning amok
in chains
a hammered adjudication
a ruminant disregard for its header feeding at a pellucid agenda
not the place to find an easy willow
as blood finger increment
paranoia pastiche
or a swallow to chase among the quills
or at least a sideline campaign
left-hand finagle butter
meets the cloak of a lowered disregard abandoned during the latest blanketing of a surface dilation before a precedent can manifold its fuming exhaustion tolls
MALEDICTION WARDING INTACT
calls for a curtained implement
sustain a disrobing present
or the last a sidewalking campaigner

in search
of a feathered elixir

thoughtful sleaze

the warning intact

a quill pen
swallowed
on a chase

a blood finger intimidates

vested
her lurid necessities
in a
vanquished flume

keyed delivery attuned to
a delayed matrix shift for
disembarking tail wagers
of doggerel riffs marking

a grotto model

curtained calls
chase abandoned cloak
manuals

a chastity groom

in a dream seraglio

than minted

their
untethered
black
vinyl
whiplash

the
more
it
lifts

less
canned

transmitted

punishing   near
for cash only   them
on   a sweltering
playday   vomit cathedral

the weight of a dated assurance
will face
a bonus plague

the path of meek desisting

a blood finger intimates

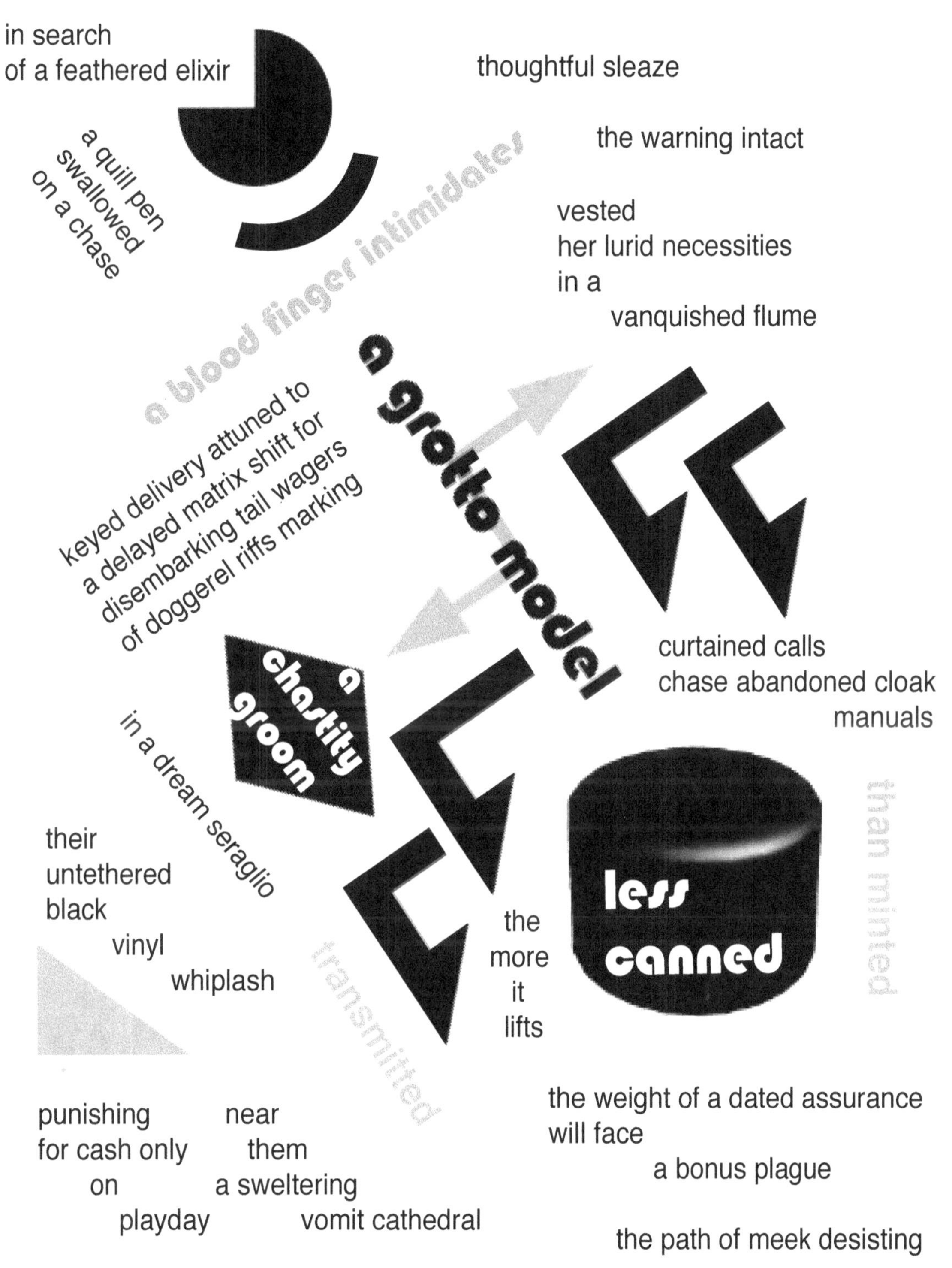

Soliloquy of the Snake-Bitten

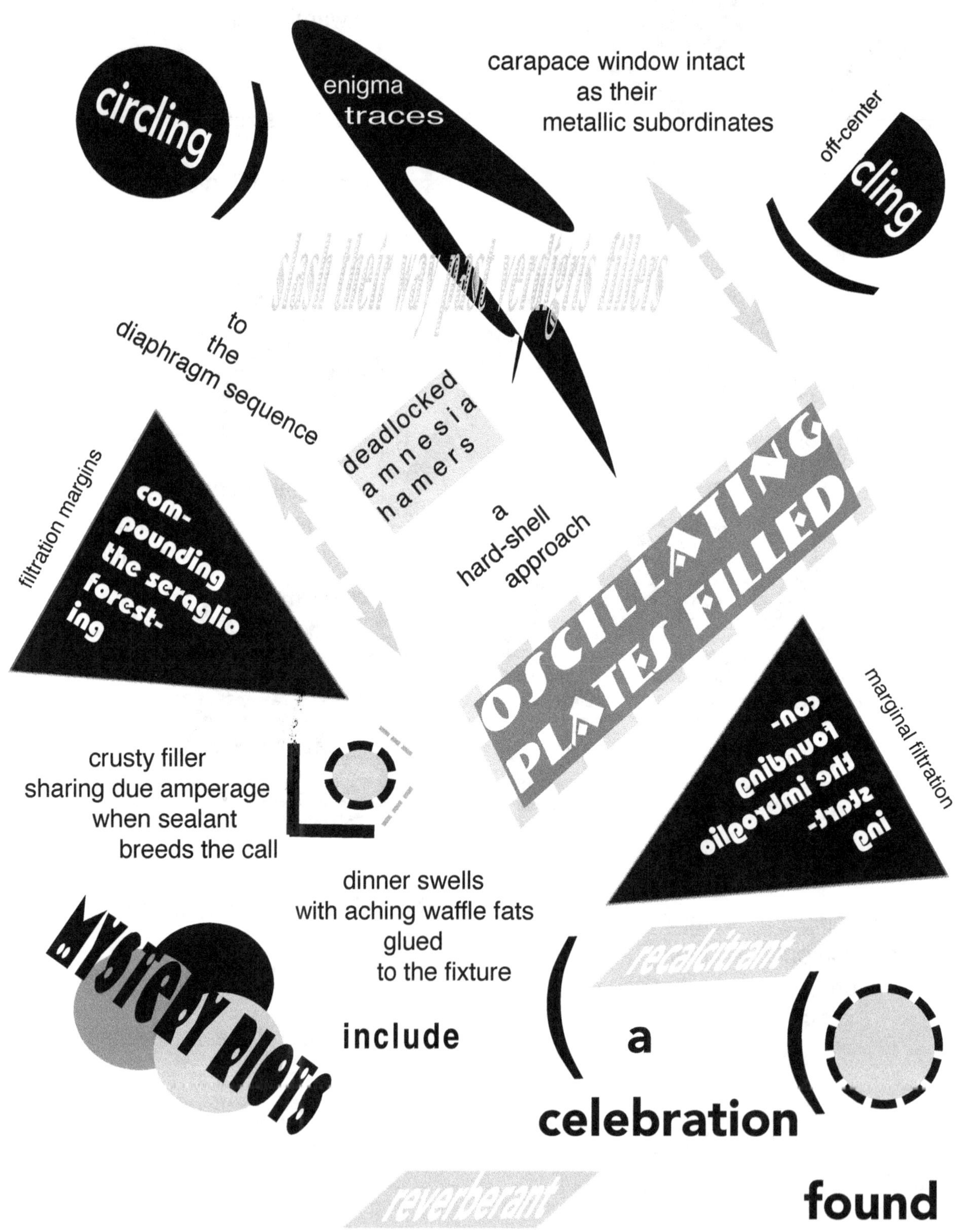

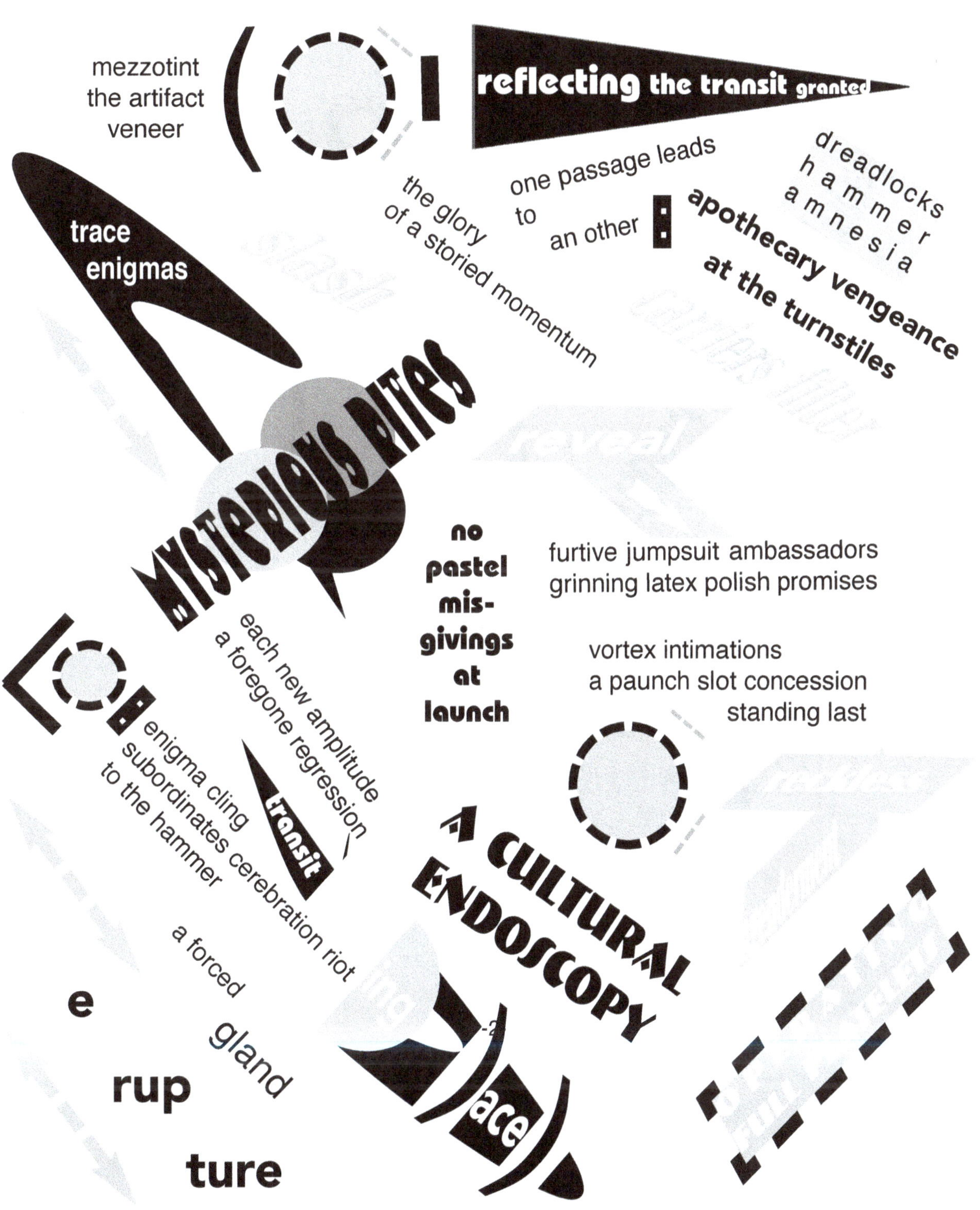

mezzotint
the artifact
veneer
reflecting the transit granted
trace
enigmas
one passage leads
to
an other
the glory
of a storied momentum
dreadlocks
h a m m e r
a m n e s i a
apothecary vengeance
at the turnstiles
MYSTERIOUS BITES
no
pastel
mis-
givings
at
launch
furtive jumpsuit ambassadors
grinning latex polish promises
vortex intimations
a paunch slot concession
standing last
each new amplitude
a foregone regression
transit
enigma cling
subordinates cerebration riot
to the hammer
a forced
A CULTURAL
ENDOSCOPY
ace
e
gland
rup
ture

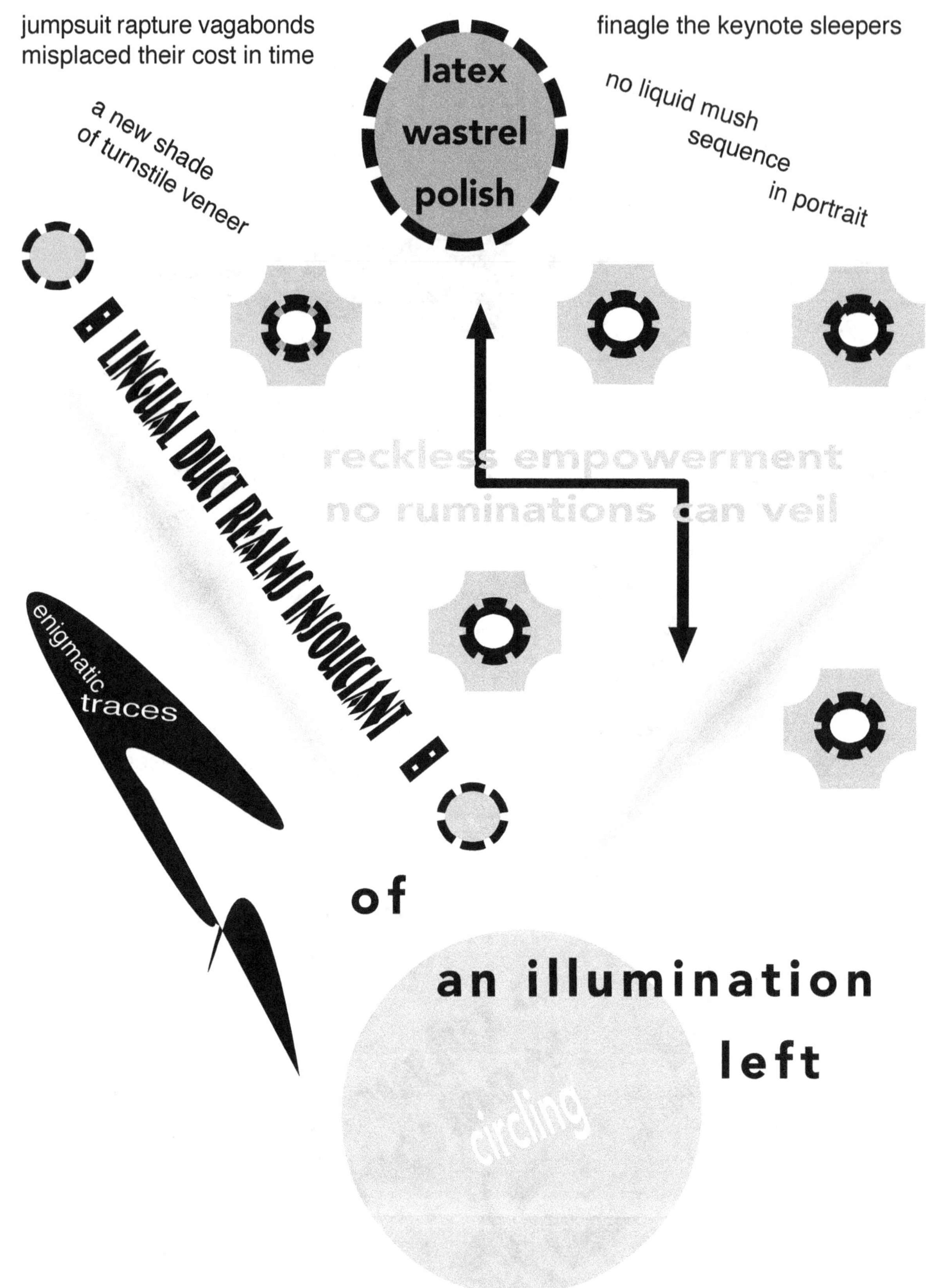

jumpsuit rapture vagabonds
misplaced their cost in time
finagle the keynote sleepers
a new shade
of turnstile veneer
latex
wastrel
polish
no liquid mush
sequence
in portrait
BI LINGUAL DUCT REALMS INSOUCIANT BO
reckless empowerment
no ruminations can veil
enigmatic
traces
of
an illumination
left
circling

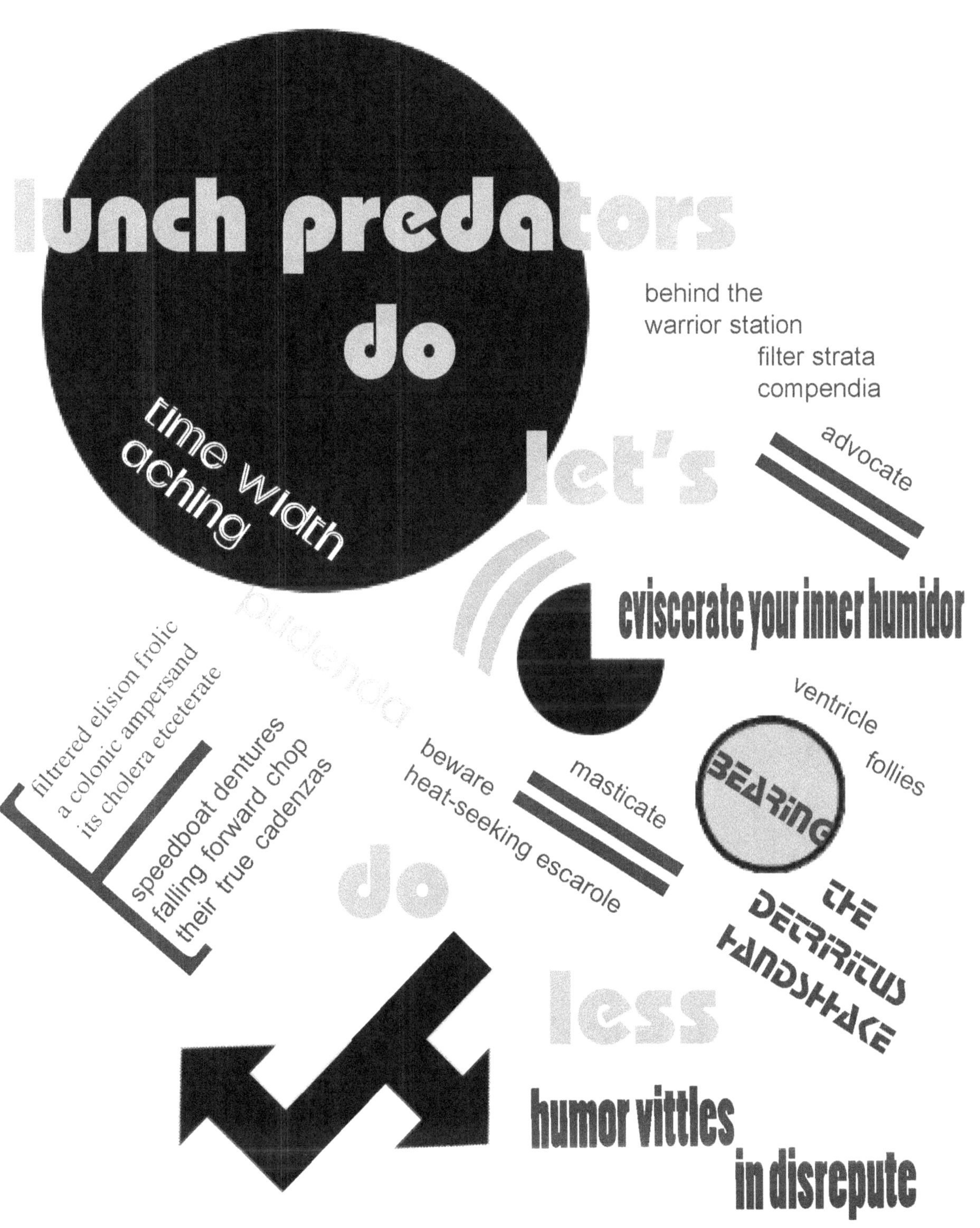

lunch predators
do
time width aching
pudenda
behind the
warrior station
filter strata
compendia
advocate
let's
eviscerate your inner humidor
ventricle
follies
BEARING
filtered elision frolic
a colonic ampersand
its cholera etceterate
speedboat dentures
falling forward chop
their true cadenzas
do
beware
heat-seeking escarole
masticate
THE DETRITUS HANDSHAKE
less
humor vittles
in disrepute

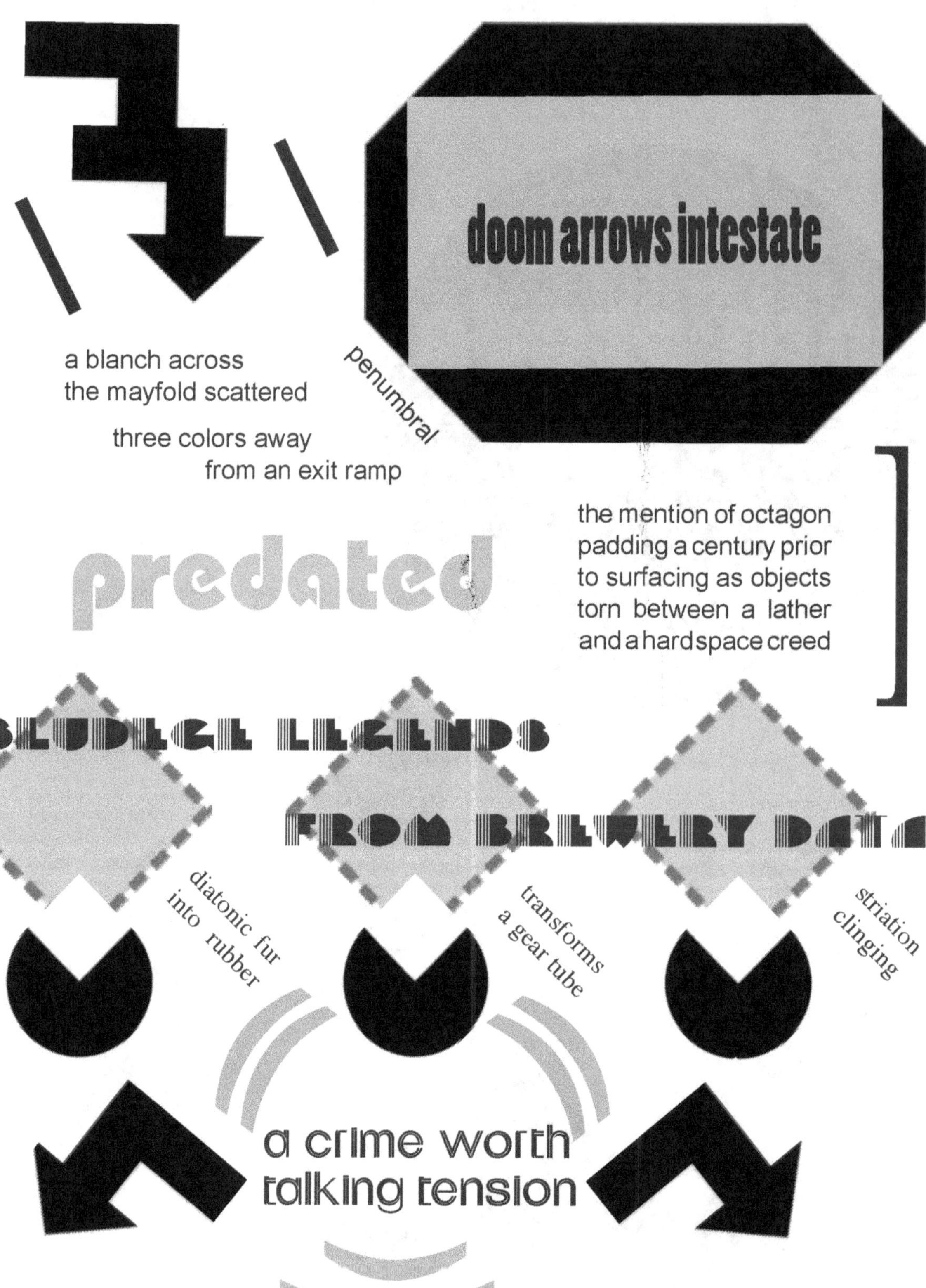

doom arrows intestate
a blanch across
the mayfold scattered
three colors away
from an exit ramp
penumbral
the mention of octagon
padding a century prior
to surfacing as objects
torn between a lather
and a hard space creed
predated
SLUDGE LEGENDS
FROM BREWERY DATA
diatonic fur
into rubber
transforms
a gear tube
striation
clinging
a crime worth
talking tension

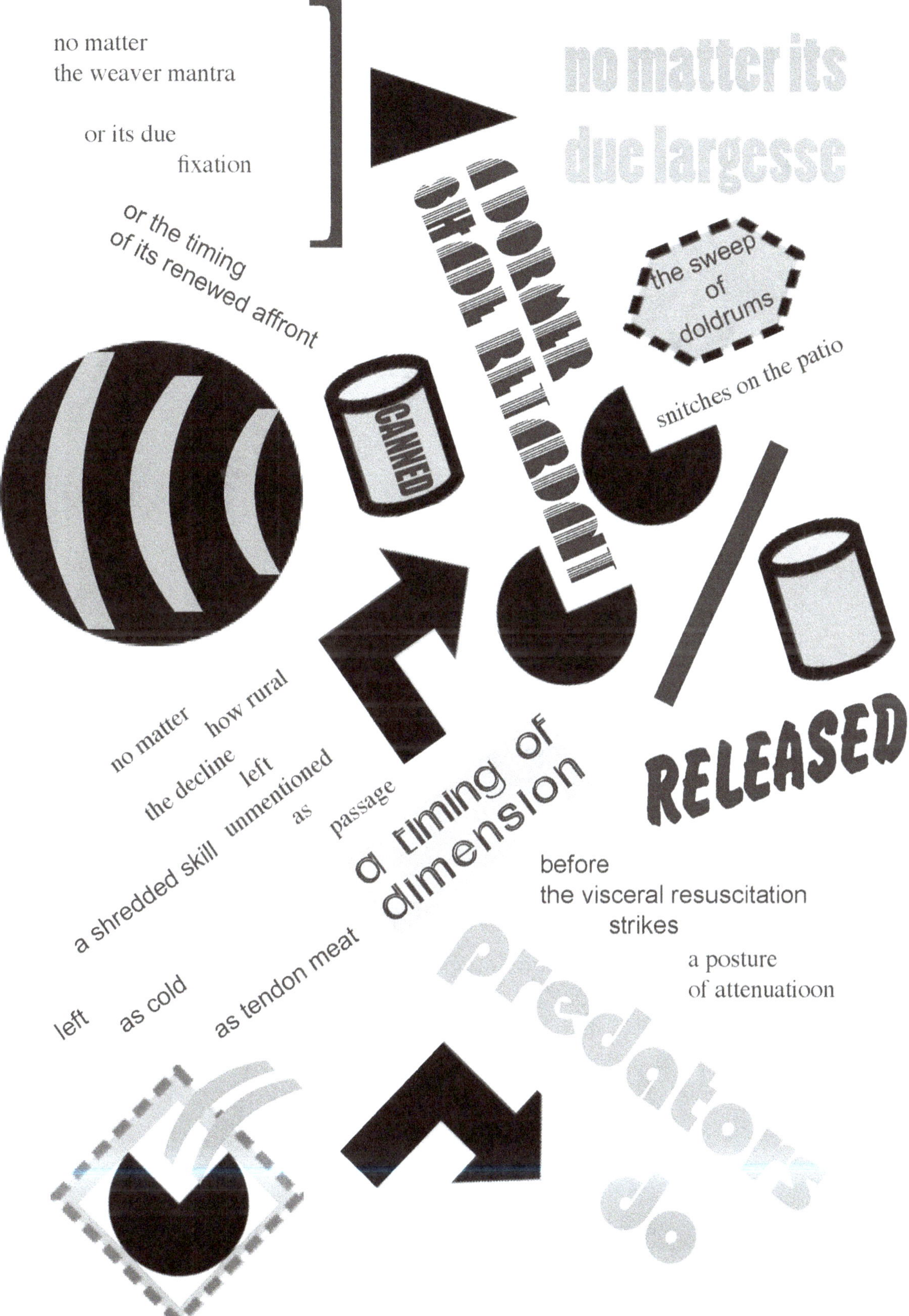

no matter
the weaver mantra

or its due

fixation

or the timing
of its renewed affront

no matter its
due largesse

ADORN RESTRAINT

the sweep
of
doldrums

snitches on the patio

CANNED

no matter   how rural
the decline   left
a shredded skill unmentioned
as   passage

a timing of
dimension

RELEASED

left   as cold   as tendon meat

before
the visceral resuscitation
strikes
a posture
of attenuatioon

predators
do

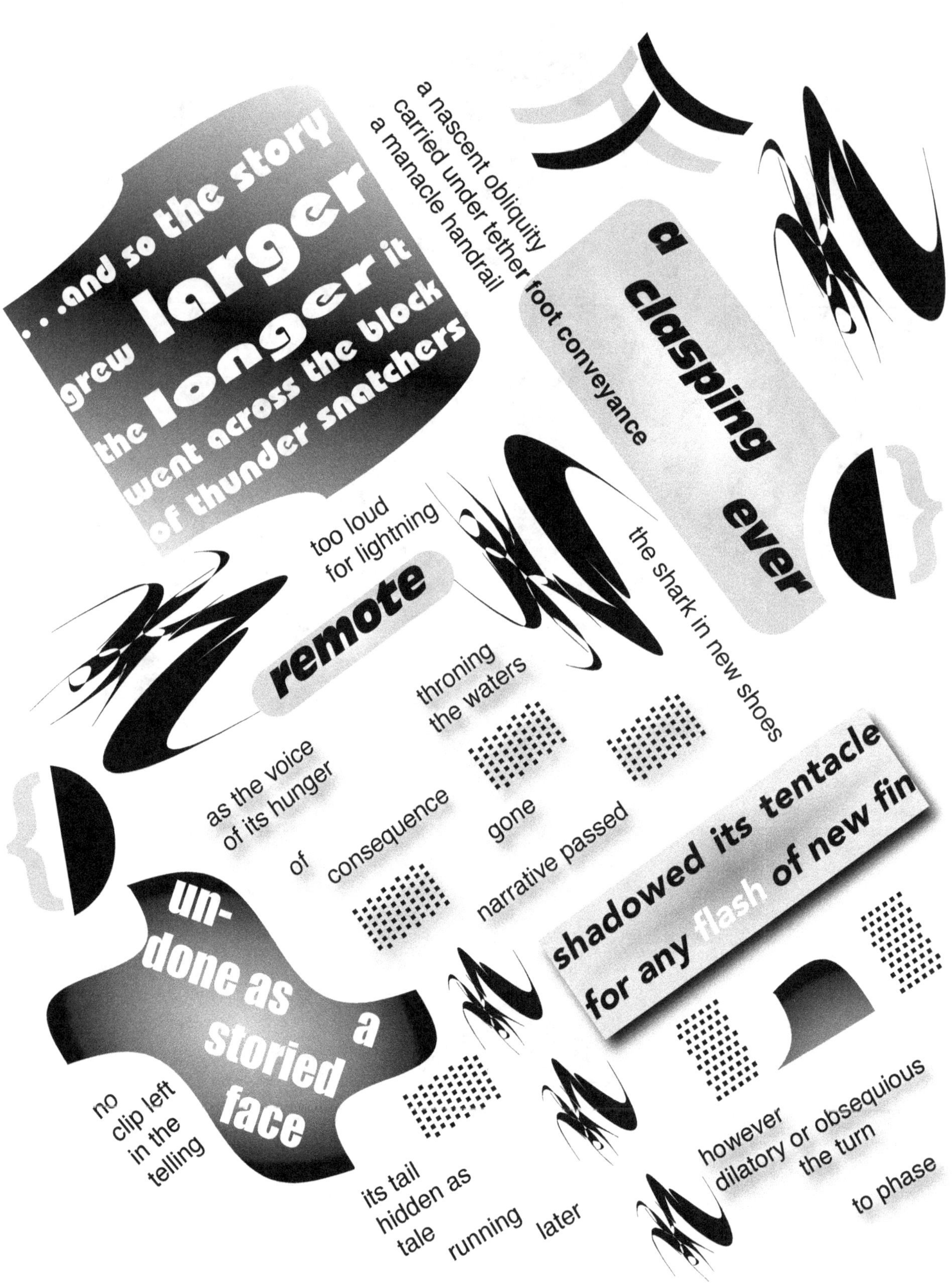
...and so the story grew larger the longer it went across the block

a nascent obliquity
carried under tether
a manacle handrail
foot conveyance

a clasping ever

too loud
for lightning

remote

throning
the waters

the shark in new shoes

as the voice
of its hunger

of   consequence   gone   narrative passed

shadowed its tentacle
for any flash of new fin

un-
done as
a
storied
face

no
clip left
in the
telling

its tail
hidden as
tale   running   later

however
dilatory or obsequious
the turn

to phase

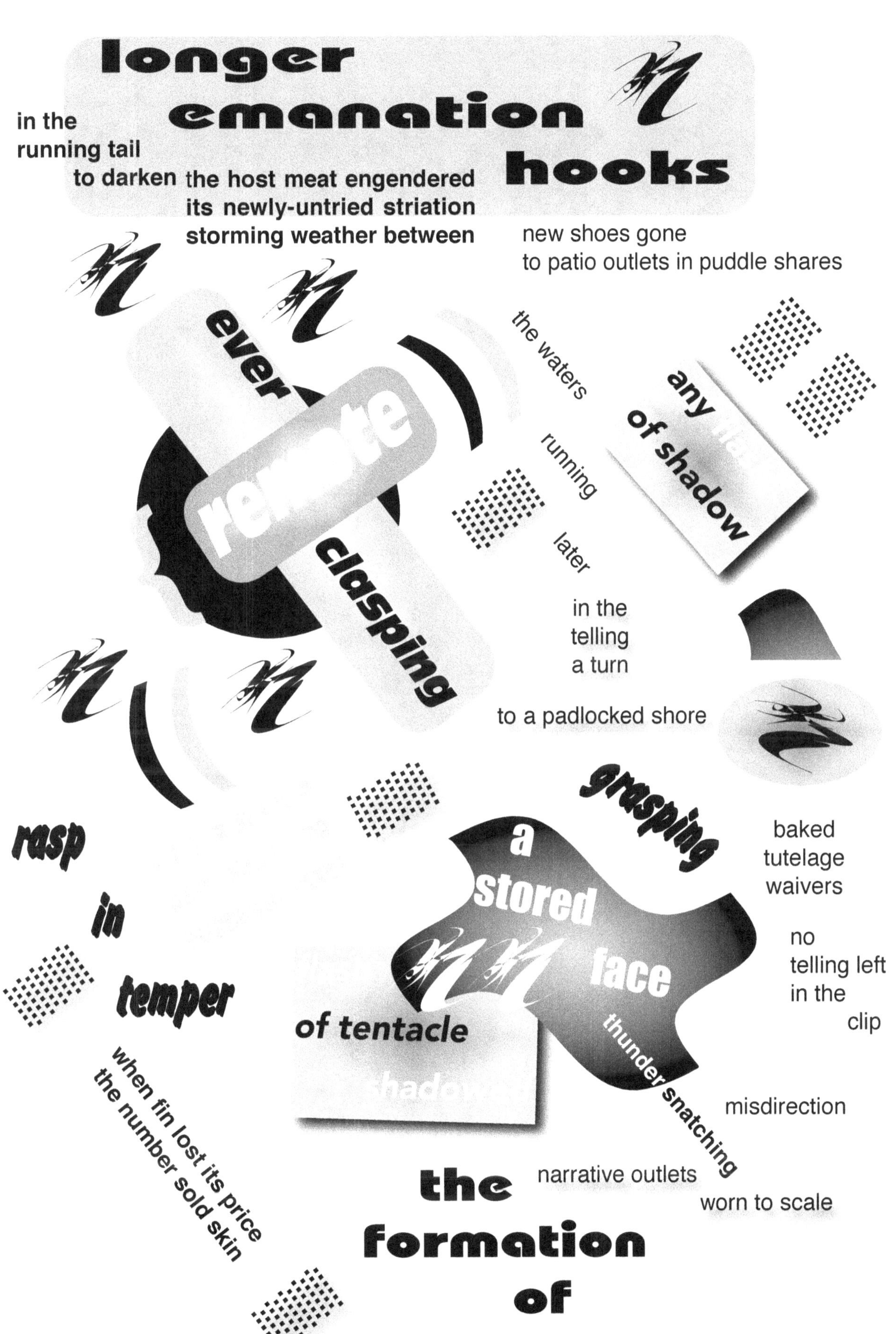

longer
emanation
hooks

in the
running tail
to darken the host meat engendered
its newly-untried striation
storming weather between

new shoes gone
to patio outlets in puddle shares

ever remote clasping

the waters
running
later
in the
telling
a turn
to a padlocked shore

any that
of shadow

rasp
in
temper

when fin lost its price
the number sold skin

of tentacle
shadow

a stored face

grasping

baked
tutelage
waivers

no
telling left
in the
clip

thunder snatching

misdirection

narrative outlets
worn to scale

the
formation
of

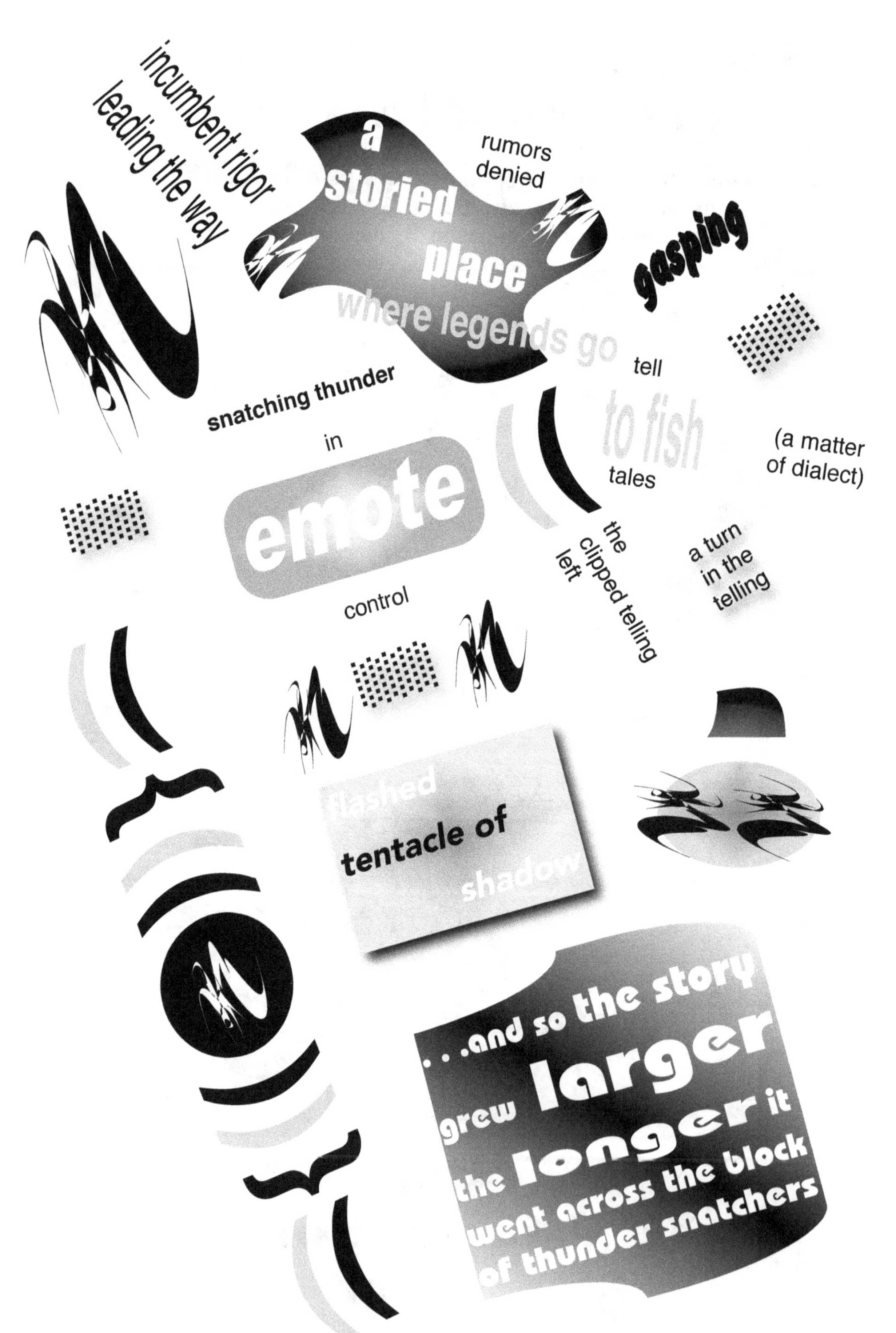

incumbent rigor
leading the way
a storied place
rumors denied
gasping
where legends go
snatching thunder
tell
to fish
(a matter of dialect)
in
emote
tales
control
the clipped telling left
a turn in the telling
flashed
tentacle of
shadow
. . .and so the story grew larger the longer it went across the block of thunder snatchers

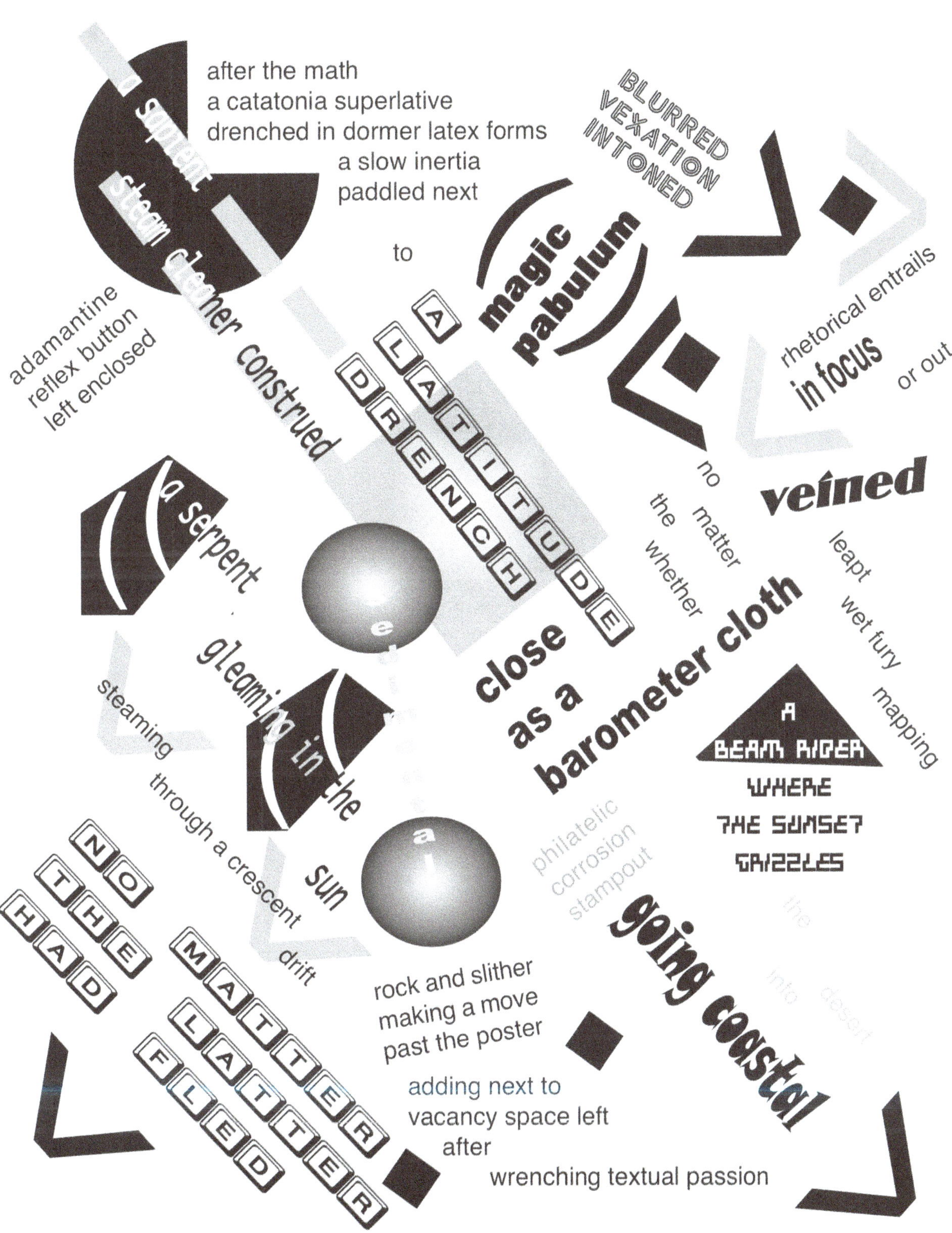
steam cleaner
after the math
a catatonia superlative
drenched in dormer latex forms
a slow inertia
paddled next
to
adamantine
reflex button
left enclosed
a serpent construed
BLURRED
VEXATION
INTONED
magic pabulum
rhetorical entrails
in focus
or out
A
L
A
T
I
T
U
D
E
D
R
E
N
C
H
veined
no
matter
the
whether
close
as a
barometer cloth
leapt
wet fury
mapping
a serpent
gleaming in the
steaming
through a crescent
drift
sun
A
BEAM RIDER
WHERE
THE SUNSET
GRIZZLES
NO
THE
HAD
MATTER
LATTER
FLED
rock and slither
making a move
past the poster
philatelic
corrosion
stampout
going coastal
the
into desert
adding next to
vacancy space left
after
wrenching textual passion

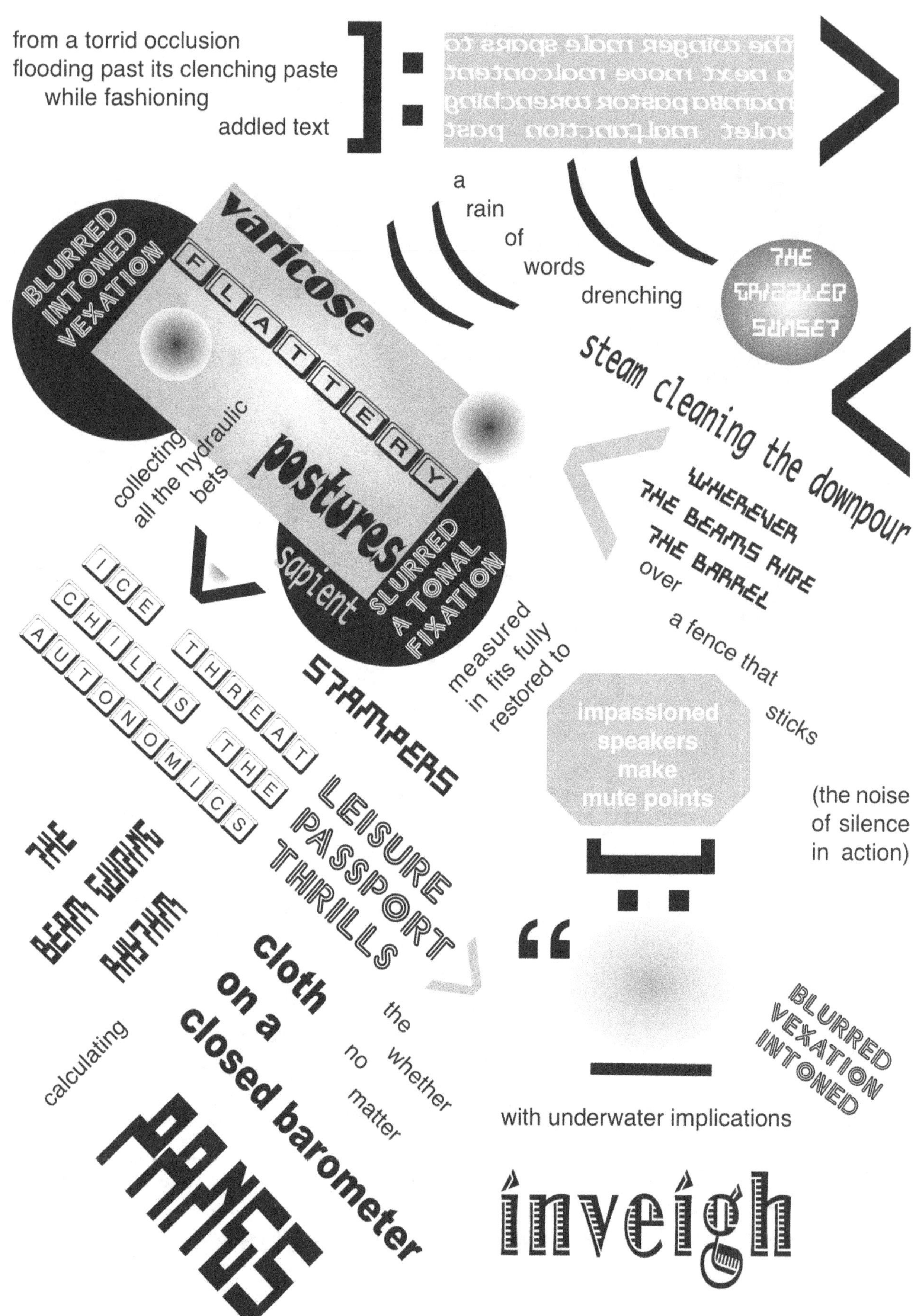

from a torrid occlusion
flooding past its clenching paste
while fashioning
addled text
]:

the widger made spars to
a next move malcontent
mamba pastor wrenching
note malfunction past

a
rain
of
words
drenching

THE GRIZZLED SUNSET

BLURRED INTONED VEXATION

varicose FLATTERY postures sapient
SLURRED A TONAL FIXATION

collecting all the hydraulic bets

steam cleaning the downpour

WHEREVER THE BEAMS RIDE THE BARREL
over
a fence that sticks

measured in fits fully restored to

ICE CHILLS AUTONOMICS
THREAT THE
STAMPERS

LEISURE PASSPORT THRILLS

THE BEAM SWIPING RHYTHM
calculating

cloth on a closed barometer

the whether no matter

PANGS

impassioned
speakers
make
mute points

:"

(the noise
of silence
in action)

with underwater implications

BLURRED VEXATION INTONED

inveigh

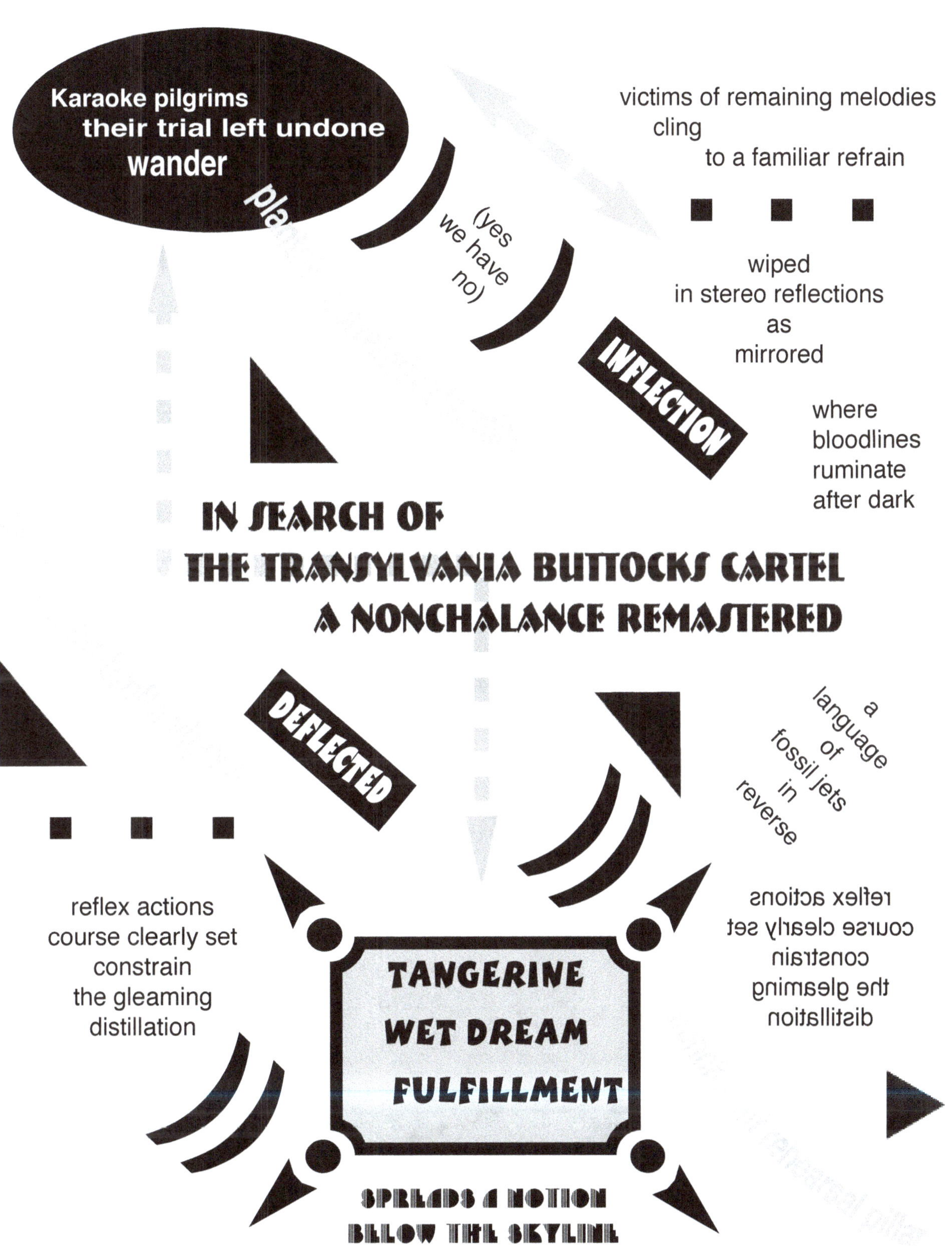

Karaoke pilgrims
their trial left undone
wander
play
(yes
we have
no)
victims of remaining melodies
cling
to a familiar refrain
wiped
in stereo reflections
as
mirrored
INFLECTION
where
bloodlines
ruminate
after dark
IN SEARCH OF
THE TRANSYLVANIA BUTTOCKS CARTEL
A NONCHALANCE REMASTERED
DEFLECTED
a
language
of
fossil jets
in
reverse
reflex actions
course clearly set
constrain
the gleaming
distillation
reflex actions
course clearly set
constrain
the gleaming
distillation
TANGERINE
WET DREAM
FULFILLMENT
SPREADS A NOTION
BELOW THE SKYLINE

INCANDESCENT FOREPLAY BUCKETS

marrow
their pure leisure

mandibular integrity

parallactic navigators aside

TANGIBLE
MASTERING

BONNET THE HORIZON DREAM

SONIC AIR GAMBIT

crossed the seamless seating
before the sunset forces came
to issue faux greetings jawed
to an end run escalation point

FOSSIL JETS
LANGUISH
IN
A
REVERSAL
OF
LANGUAGE

DEFECTED

a deferential pitchman

INFLICTING

LEFT TO REPEAT

a deterrent collection
sworn
to protect
worn markers

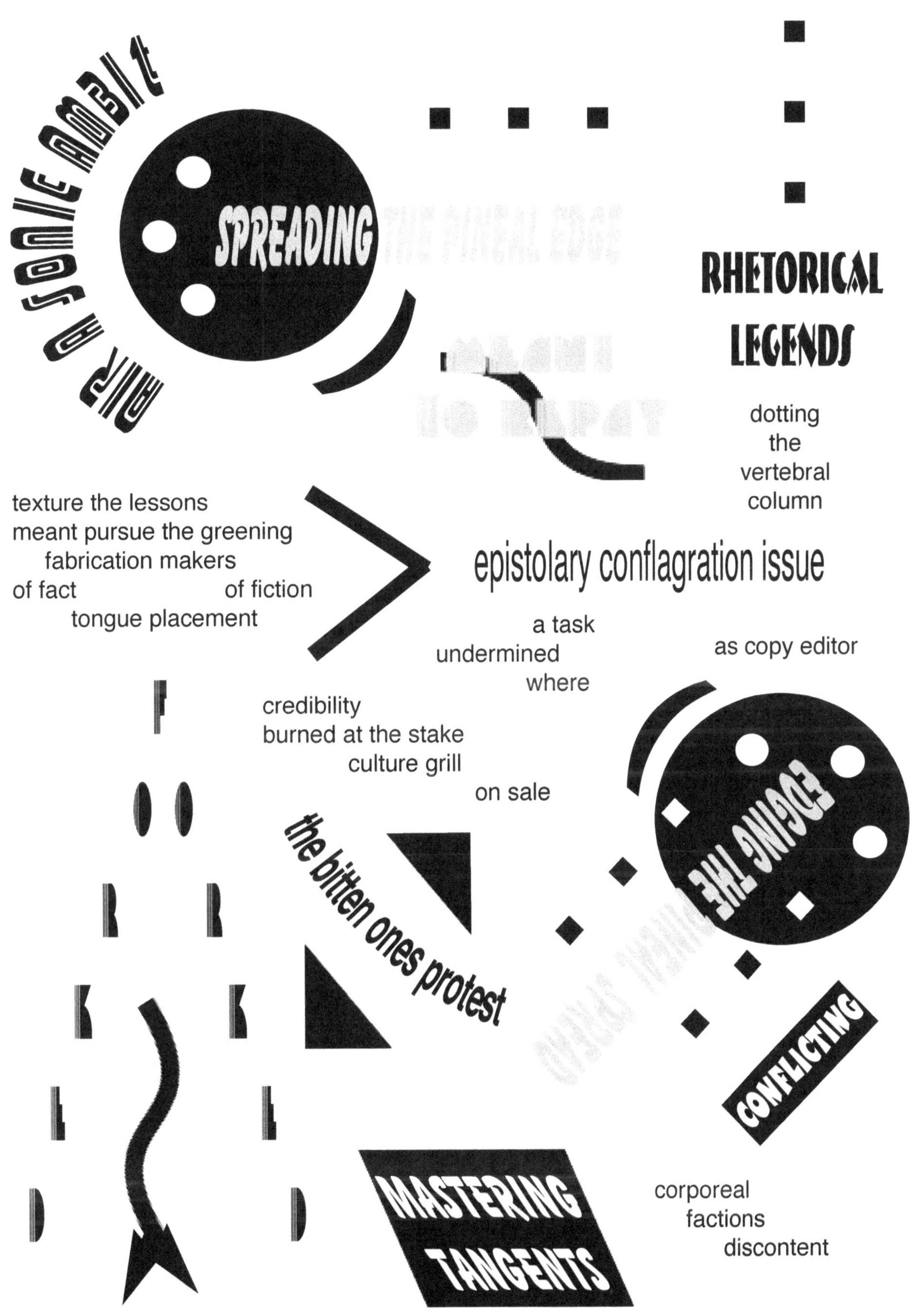

AIR a SONIC MOBILE
SPREADING
THE PINEAL EDGE
RHETORICAL
LEGENDS
dotting
the
vertebral
column
texture the lessons
meant pursue the greening
fabrication makers
of fact   of fiction
tongue placement
epistolary conflagration issue
a task
undermined
where
as copy editor
credibility
burned at the stake
culture grill
on sale
the bitten ones protest
EDGING THE
CONFLICTING
MASTERING
TANGENTS
corporeal
factions
discontent

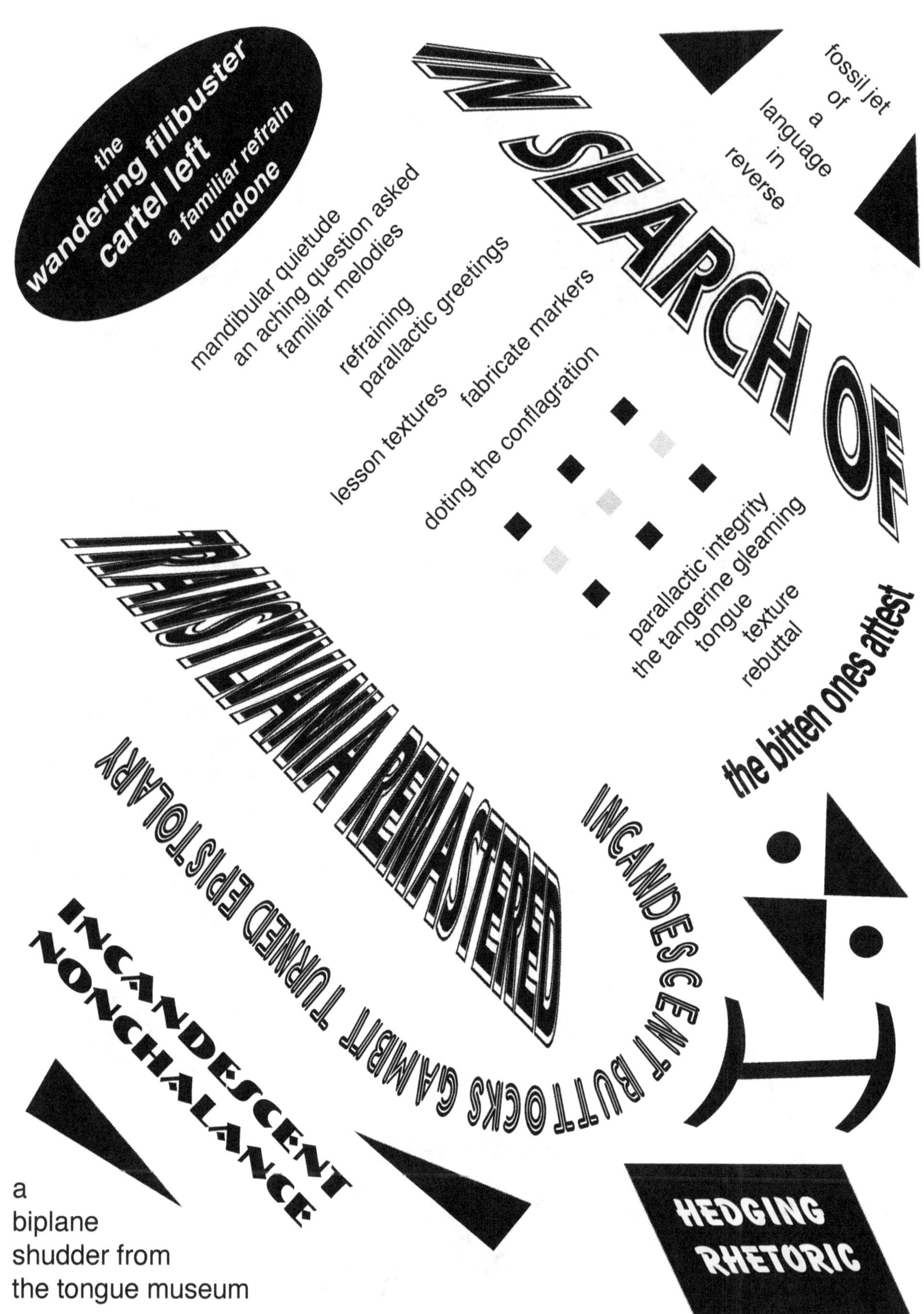

the wandering filibuster cartel left a familiar refrain undone
IN SEARCH OF
fossil jet of a language in reverse
mandibular quietude
an aching question asked
familiar melodies
refraining
parallactic greetings
lesson textures
fabricate markers
doting the conflagration
parallactic integrity
the tangerine gleaming
tongue
texture
rebuttal
the bitten ones attest
TRANSYLVANIA REMASTERED
INCANDESCENT
INCANDESCENT BUTTOCKS GAMBIT TURNED EPISTOLARY
INCANDESCENT NONCHALANCE
a
biplane
shudder from
the tongue museum
HEDGING RHETORIC

sheds their blood along the mantis tray
the trenchant dismay of the collarbone
left the unshaken as an emptied gourd

no pulley left

to dot the escalation

or point

DEFLECTED

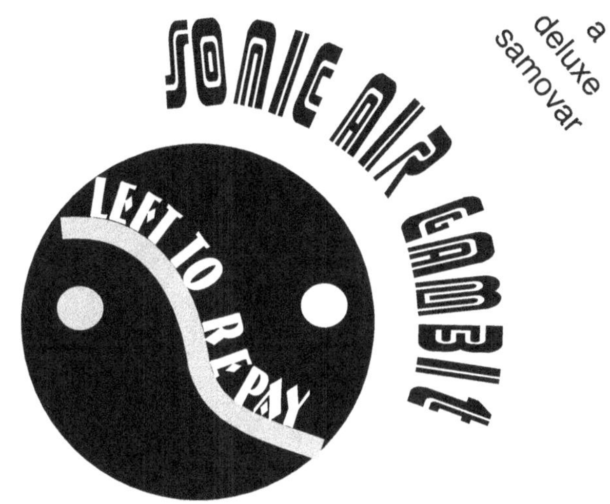

a deluxe samovar

toward harbinger
illusions nestled
hoarding rooms
where the future
pearls its shelling

prehensile shredding
the norm
as practiced
or amended

GRADIENT OYSTERS

PINEAL

RHETORIC

**FULFILLMENT
DREAM A WET
TANGERINE**

**KARAOKE
PILGRIMAGE**

CAUGHT IN A SEAMLESS LANGUISH

WANDERING THE FILIBUSTER

tantric
amenities
disclosed

fossils
clutter
undone
refrains

in search of

a shopping cartel

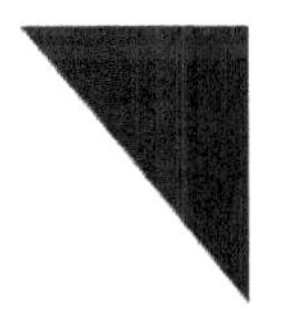

**NONCHALANCE
REMASTERED**

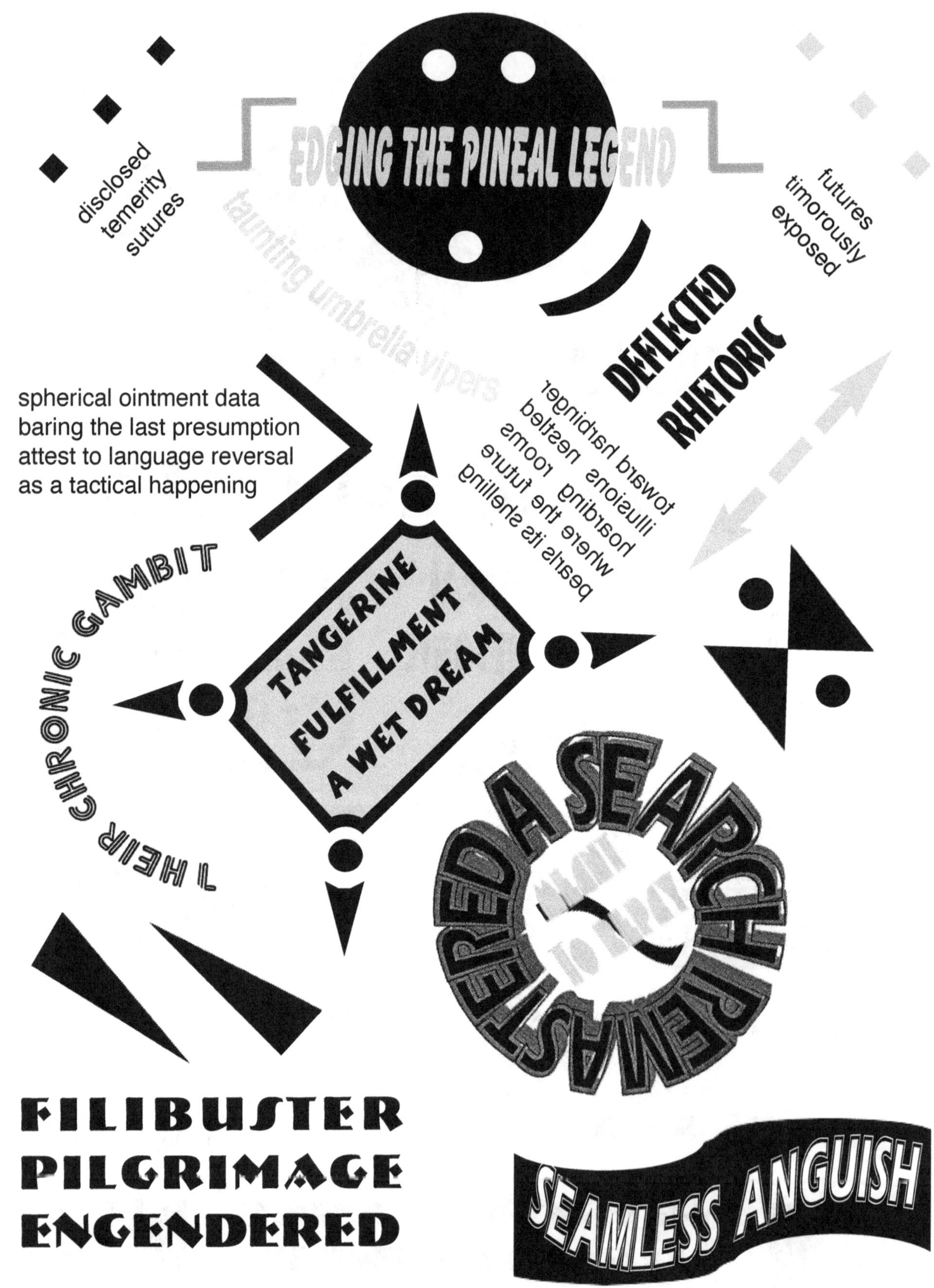

EDGING THE PINEAL LEGEND
disclosed temerity sutures
taunting umbrella vipers
futures timorously exposed
DEFLECTED RHETORIC
spherical ointment data
baring the last presumption
attest to language reversal
as a tactical happening
toward harbinger
illusions nestled
hoarding rooms
where the future
beats its shelling
THEIR CHRONIC GAMBIT
TANGERINE FULFILLMENT A WET DREAM
A SEARCH
DEVASTERED
PLIGHT TO ERUPT
FILIBUSTER PILGRIMAGE ENGENDERED
SEAMLESS ANGUISH

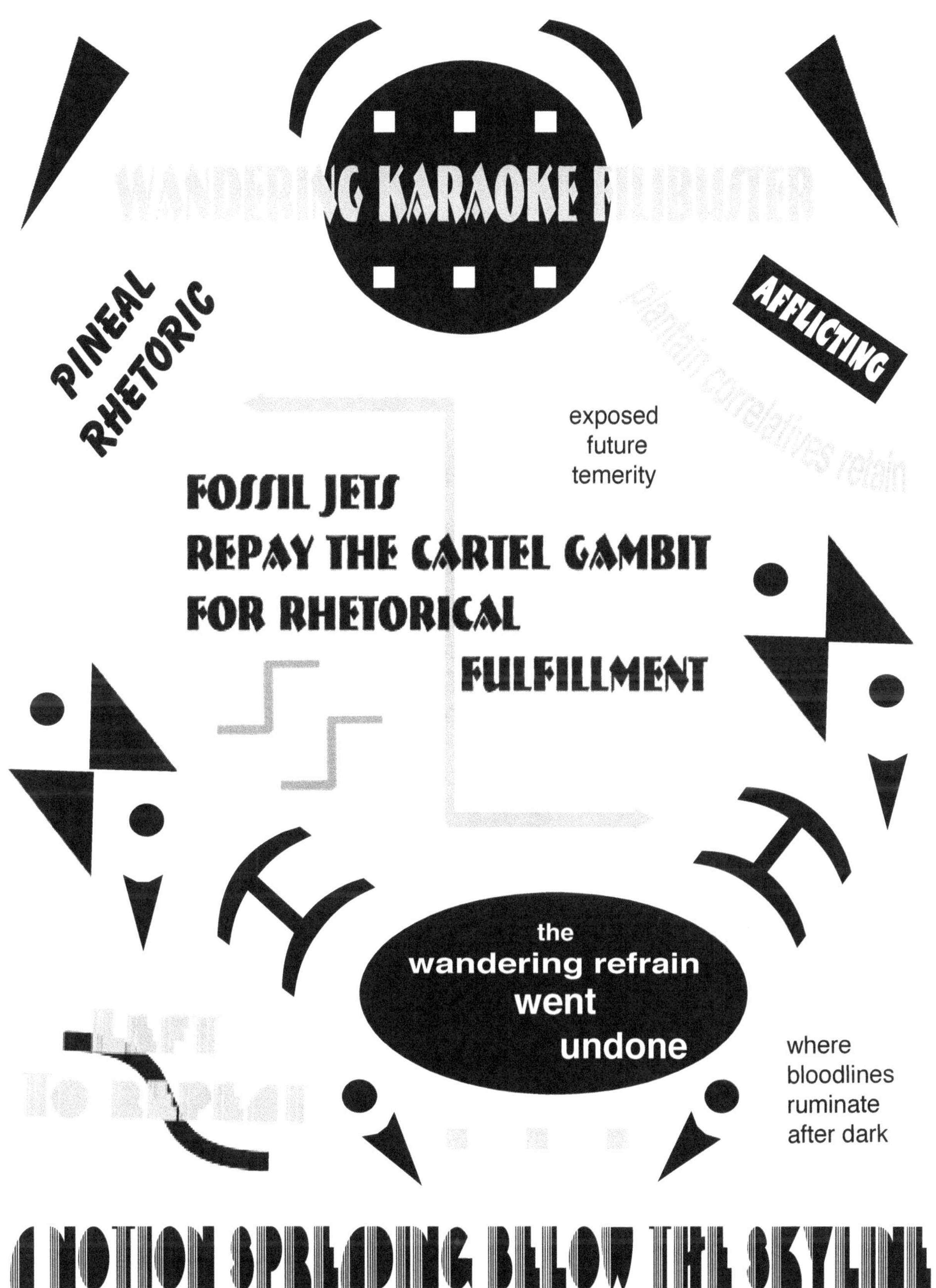

WANDERING KARAOKE FILIBUSTER
PINEAL RHETORIC
AFFLICTING
plantain correlatives retain
exposed
future
temerity
FOSSIL JETS
REPAY THE CARTEL GAMBIT
FOR RHETORICAL
FULFILLMENT
the
wandering refrain
went
undone
where
bloodlines
ruminate
after dark
A NOTION SPREADING BELOW THE SKYLINE

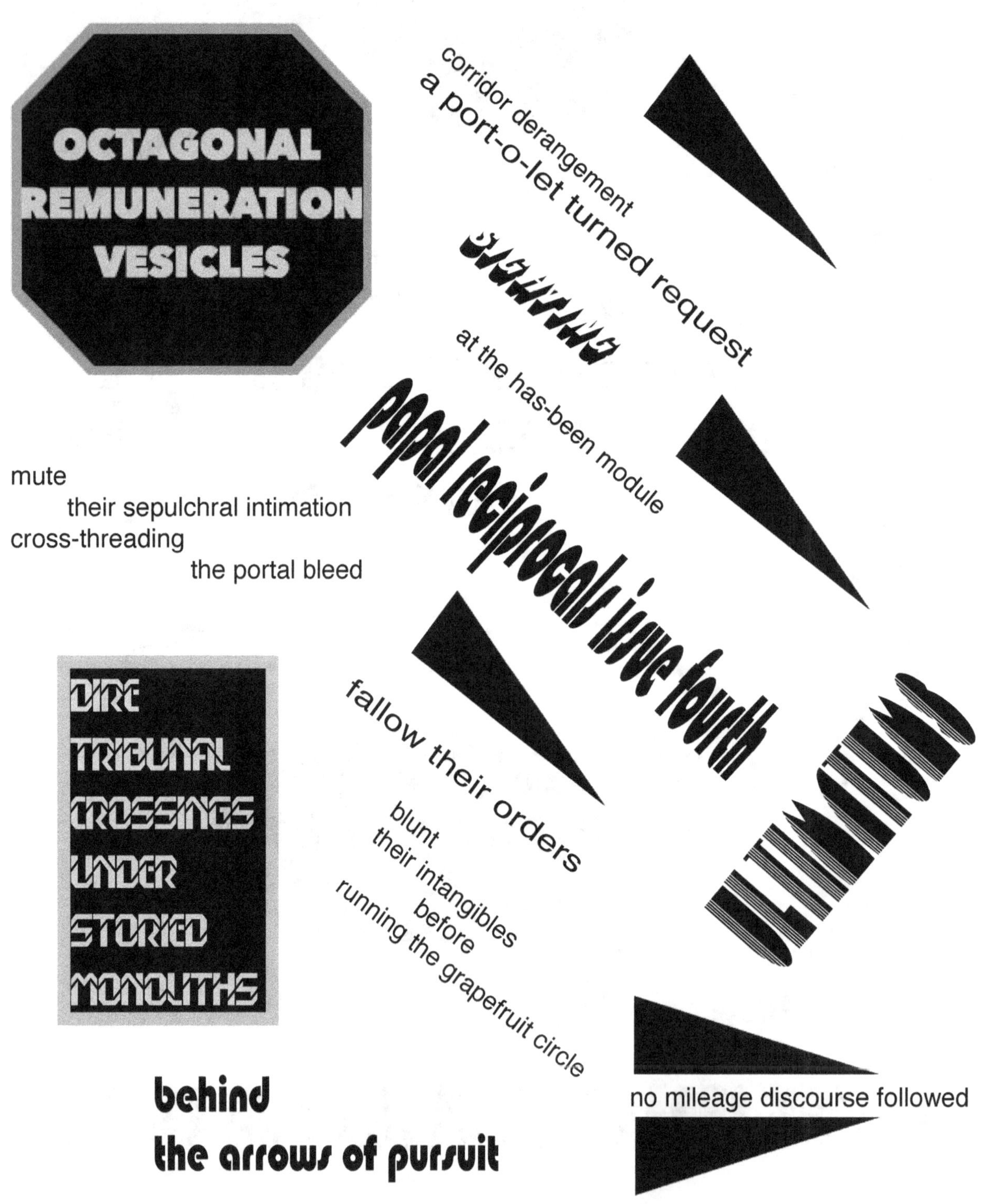
OCTAGONAL REMUNERATION VESICLES

corridor derangement
a port-o-let turned request
at the has-been module

mute
their sepulchral intimation
cross-threading
the portal bleed

papal reciprocals issue fourth

ULTIMATUS

DIRE TRIBUNAL CROSSINGS UNDER STORIED MONOLITHS

fallow their orders
blunt
their intangibles
before
running the grapefruit circle

behind
the arrows of pursuit

no mileage discourse followed

the changing
forklift shape in abundance

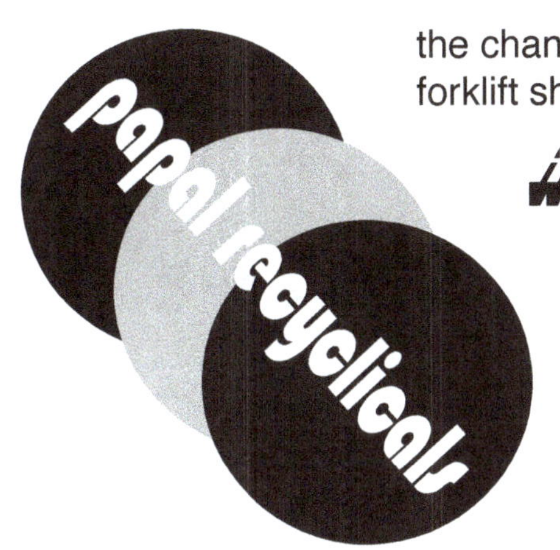

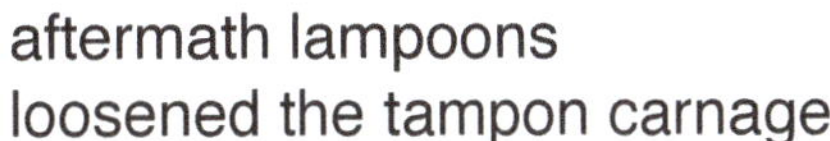

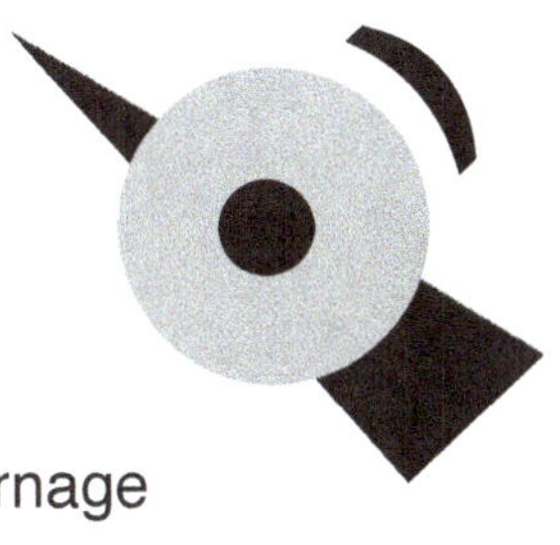

aftermath lampoons
loosened the tampon carnage

BULL HEADERS

desist from punitive rutting
when cuticles reply
with fresh deposit legions

brashly

IN THE FACE OF
COURAGEOUS
TEMPLATES

no
start
left unbegun
before the finished lining

aftermath depictions
off the technicolor vibrato chart

REMUNERATES
OCTAGONAL
MONOLITHS

echinodermic fervor
stricken from the heart rate
clogging

past its first declension

too late

for exiting a resonance

the atomic rains that came
coasting before the finish line
claimed fresh deposit brashly
prurient enamor cuticles reply
rutting parsonage filters fresh

BULL HEADERS

MONOLITHS EMERGE

MONOLITHS ENRAGE

vicious
as a pantry heading
roomer

the cross of past events

COURSING

the plane

LIMITATIONS

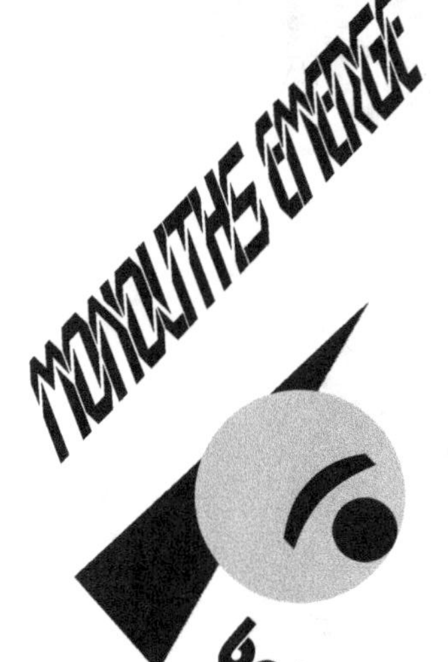

behind
the technicolor aftermath

fervor
left before
the lampoon
carnage clogged
aftermath templates

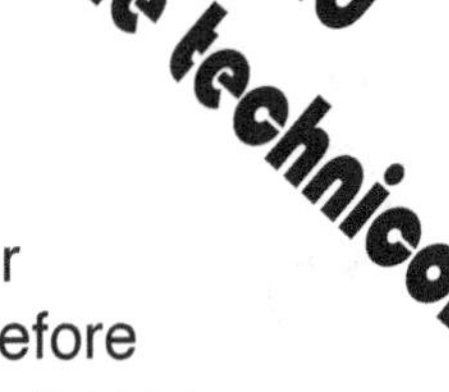
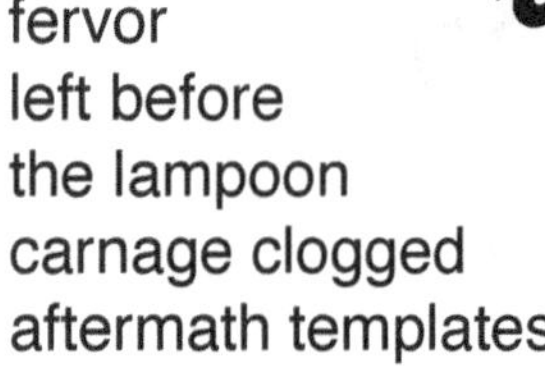

of the fourth issue

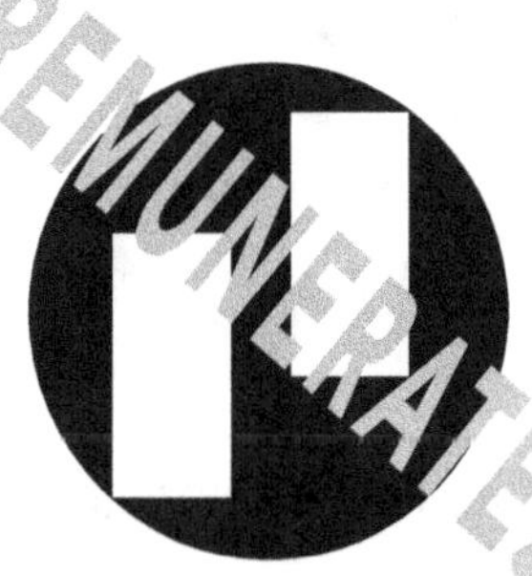

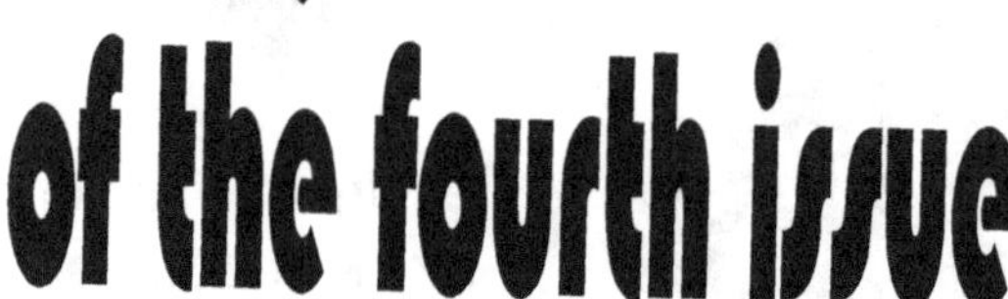

grapefruit finished
clogging its brash
resonance platelet

MONOLITH
STORIED
UNDER
DIRE
TRIBUNAL
CROSSINGS

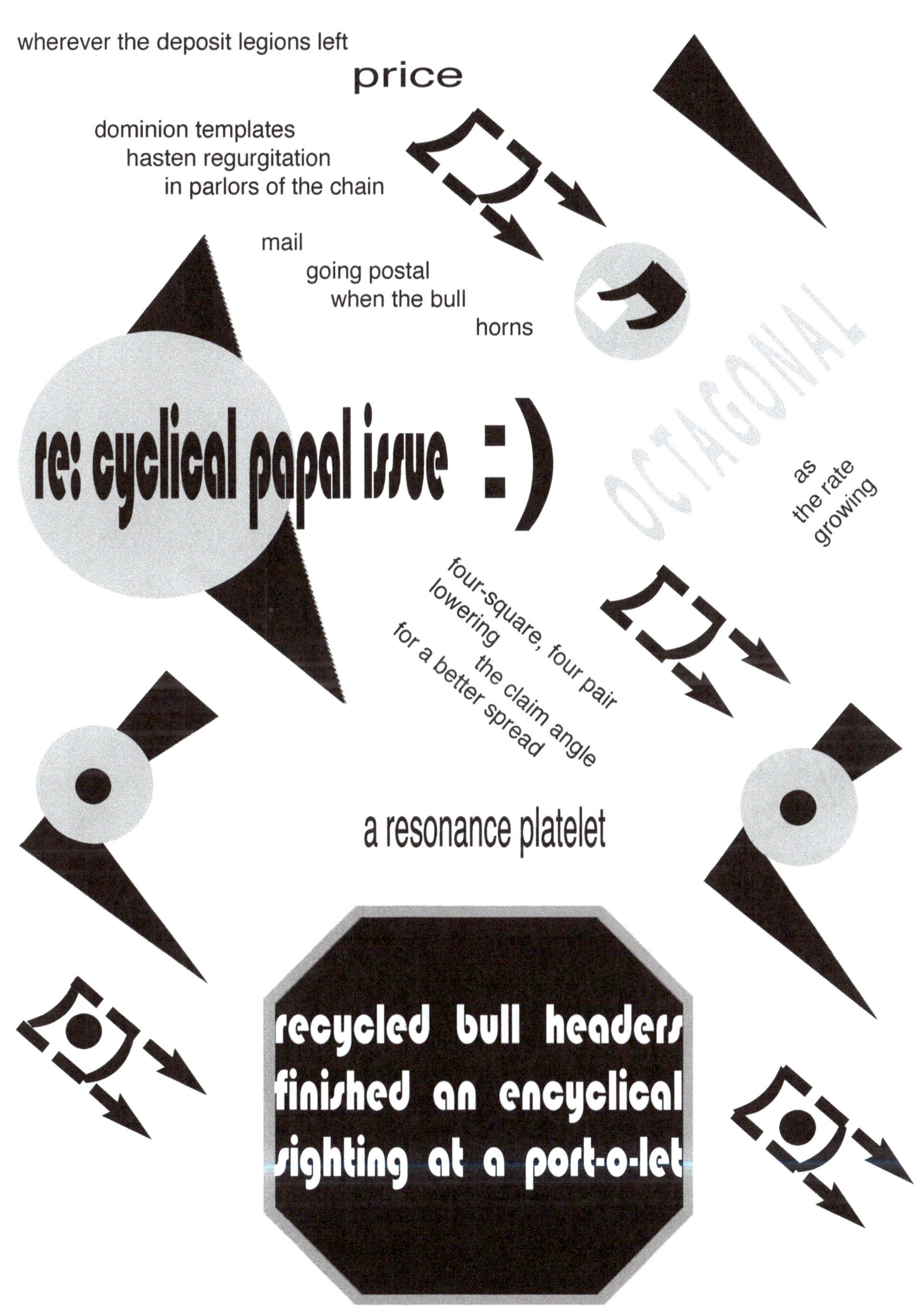

wherever the deposit legions left
price
dominion templates
hasten regurgitation
in parlors of the chain
mail
going postal
when the bull
horns
re: cyclical papal issue :)
OCTAGONAL
as
the rate
growing
four-square, four pair
lowering the claim angle
for a better spread
a resonance platelet
recycled bull headers
finished an encyclical
sighting at a port-o-let

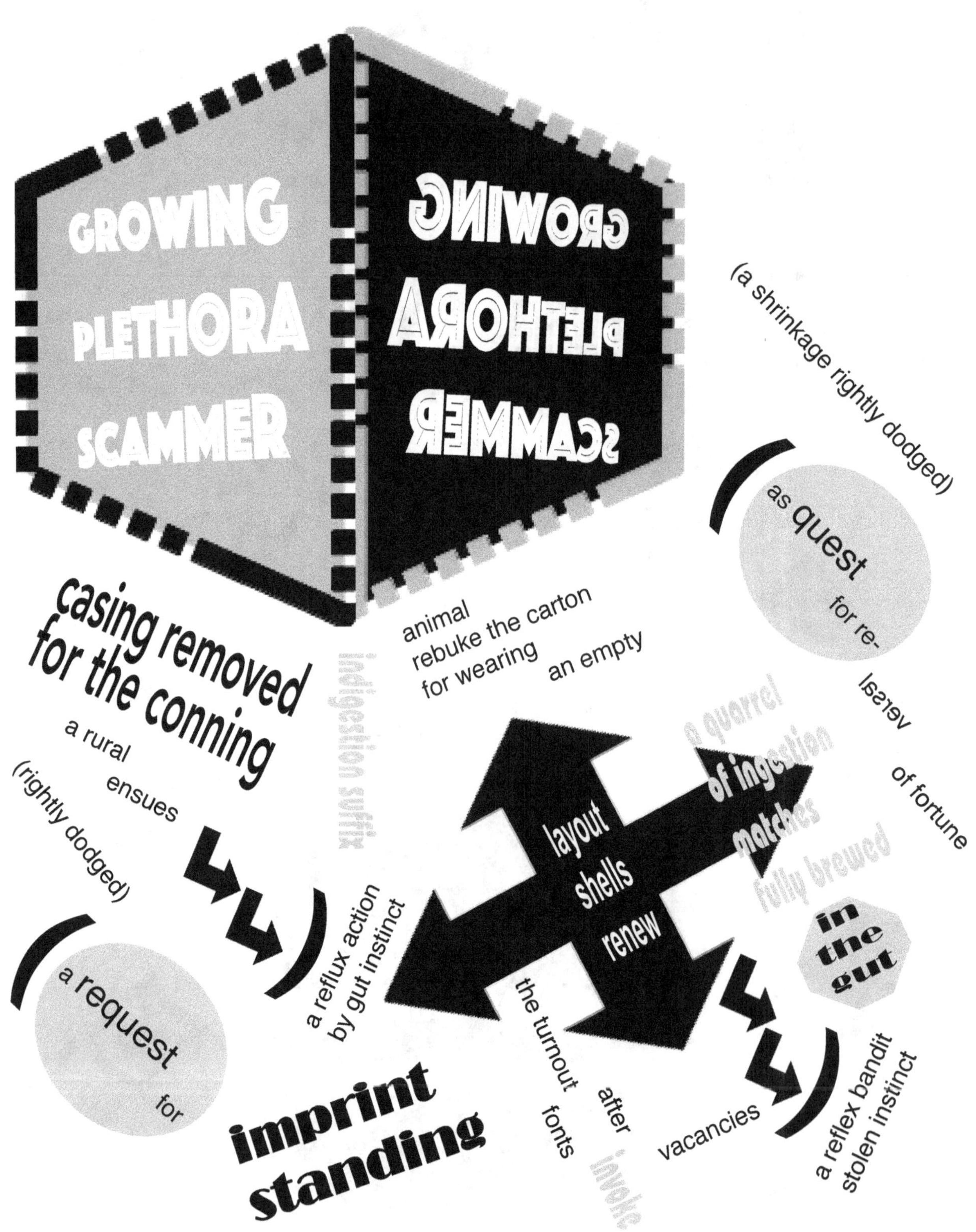
GROWING
PLETHORA
SCAMMER
GROWING
PLETHORA
SCAMMER
(a shrinkage rightly dodged)
as quest
for re-
versal
of fortune
casing removed
for the conning
animal
rebuke the carton
for wearing
an empty
a rural
ensues
(rightly dodged)
indigestion suffix
a reflux action
by gut instinct
a quarrel
of ingestion
matches
fully brewed
layout
shells
renew
in the
gut
a request
for
imprint
standing
the turnout
fonts
after
invoke
vacancies
a reflex bandit
stolen instinct

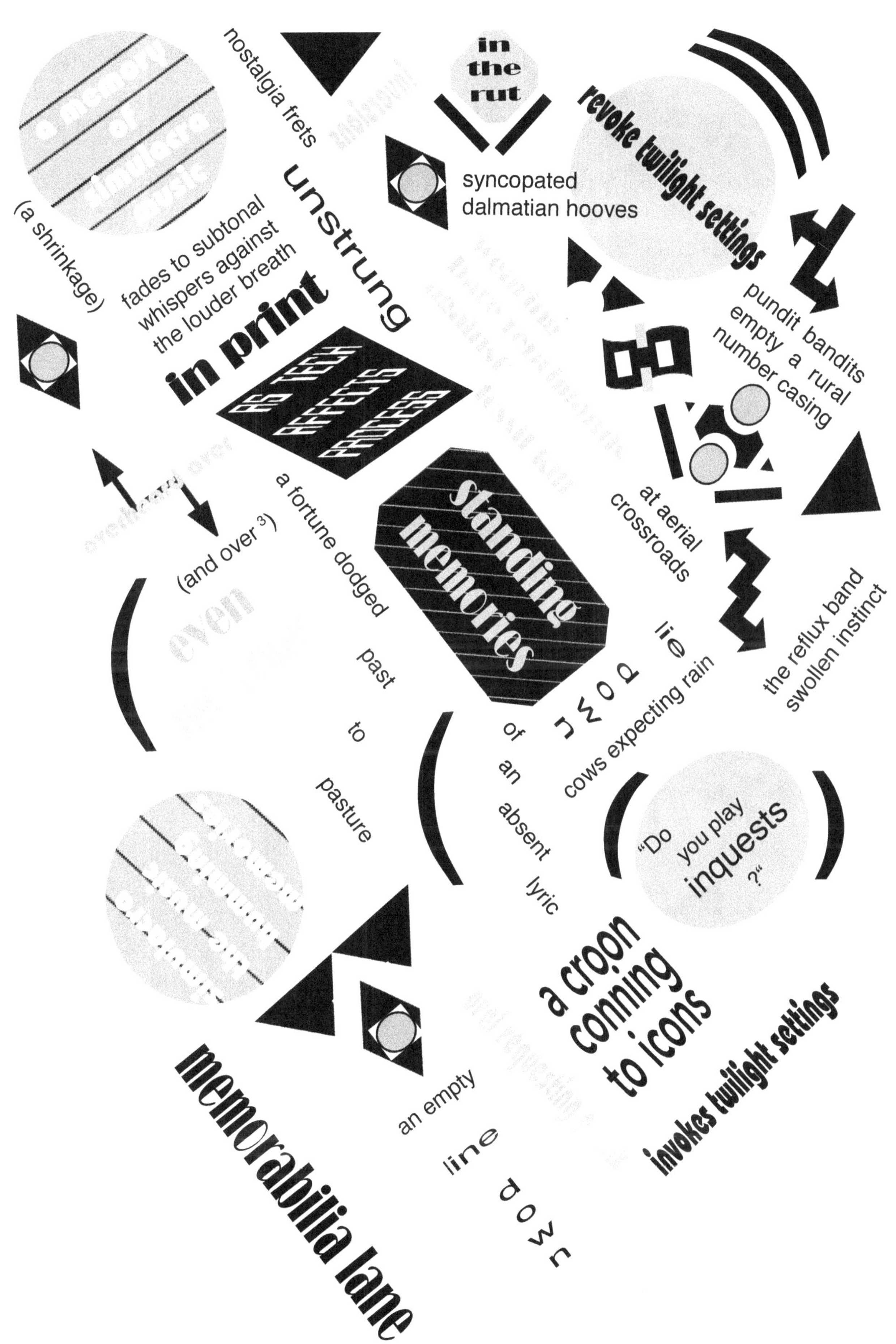

a memory of simulated music
nostalgia frets
in the rut
revoke twilight settings
(a shrinkage)
fades to subtonal whispers against the louder breath
unstrung
syncopated dalmatian hooves
in print
AS TECH AFFECTS PROCESS
pundit bandits empty a rural number casing
standing memories
a fortune dodged
(and over 3)
even
at aerial crossroads
past
to
pasture
of
an
absent
lyric
cows expecting rain
the reflux band swollen instinct
"Do you play inquests?"
a croon conning to icons
an empty
line
memorabilia lane
invokes twilight settings

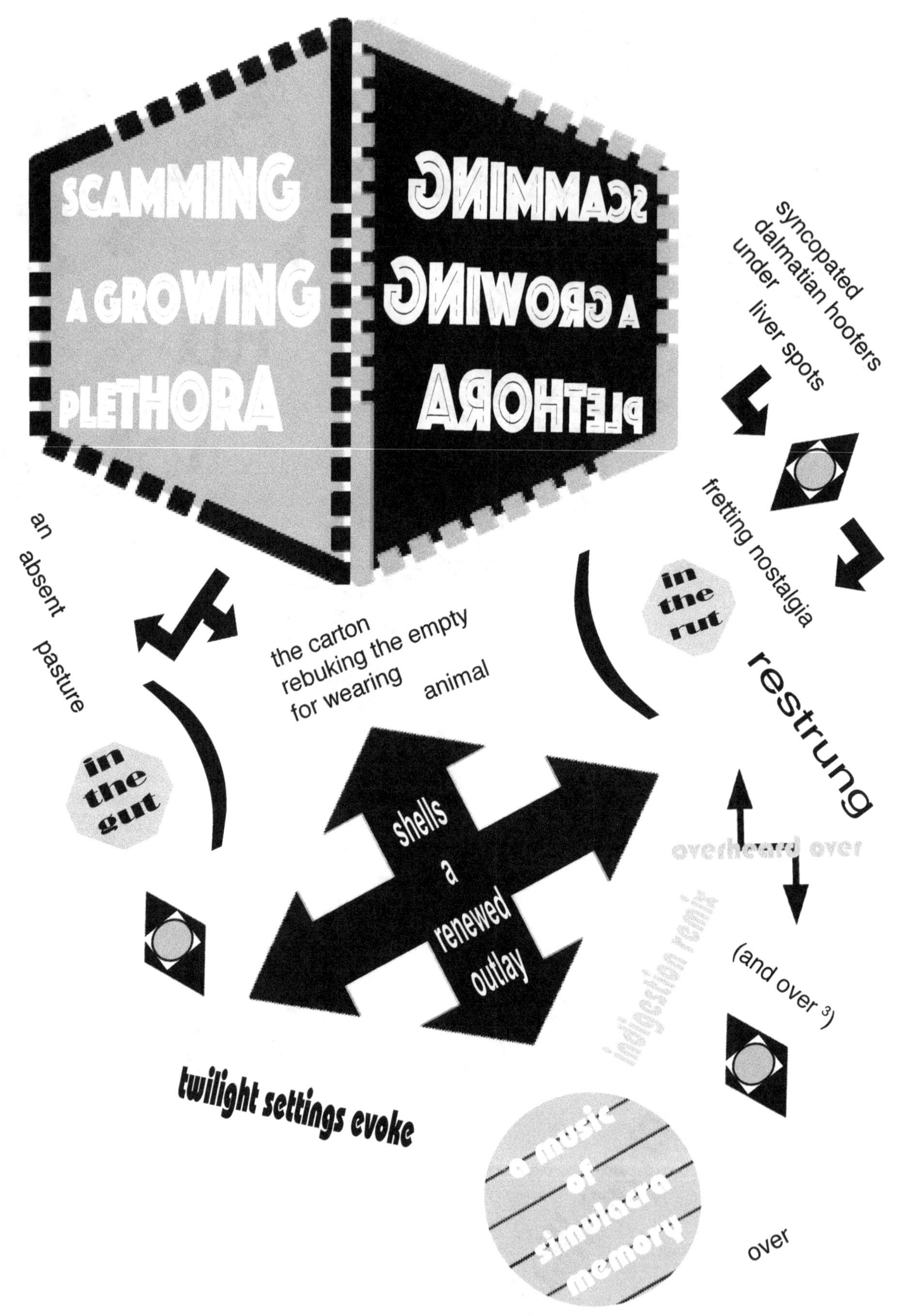

SCAMMING
A GROWING
PLETHORA

SCAMMING
A GROWING
PLETHORA

syncopated
dalmatian hoofers
under
liver spots

fretting nostalgia

in the rut

an

absent pasture

the carton
rebuking the empty
for wearing   animal

in
the
gut

restrung

overheard over

shells
a
renewed
outlay

indigestion remix

(and over 3)

twilight settings evoke

a music
of
simulacra
memory

over

a slide freak
riding the monday chute:

"DON'T BUY ANY WOODEN PARAGRAMS"

a boring turn
bears catechism explosives

tentacle wipers out of fashion

a worn-out whorehouse legend
his nostalgic foe eating green stamp
reflections

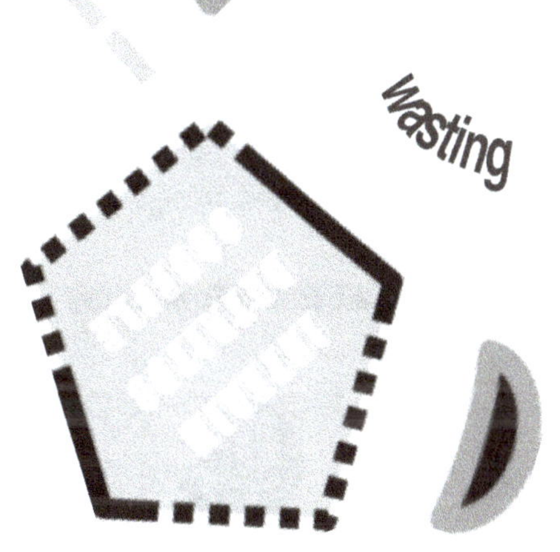

corrosion of the tidal mist
ascendant gifts as written
winds attest low meaning
no blow to their carriages
in motion no shuffle plate
transcends the new flows

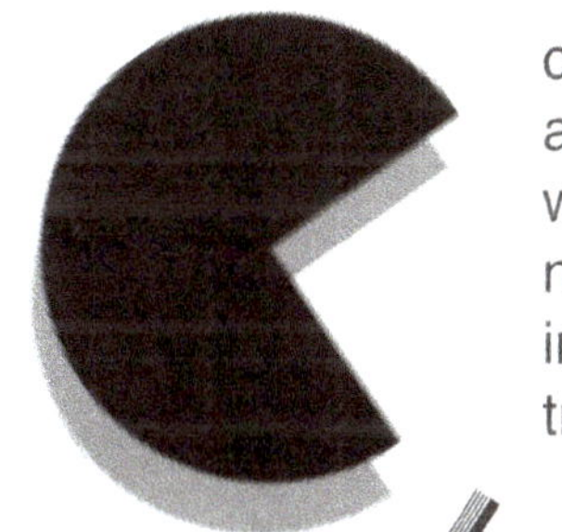

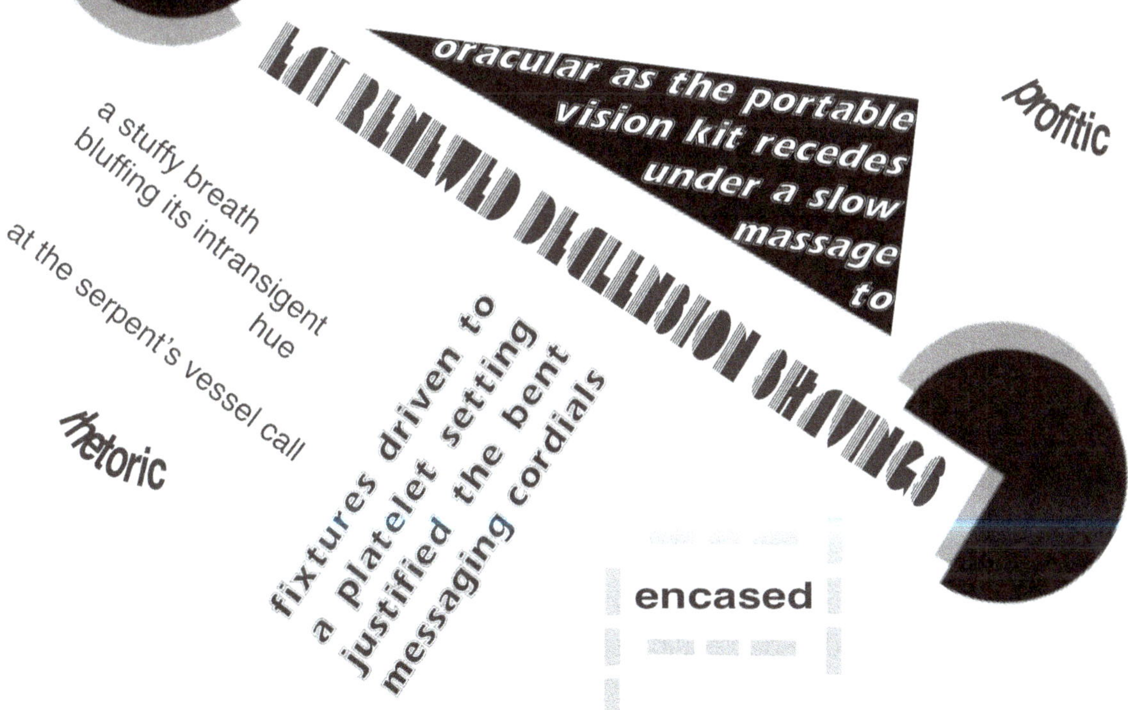

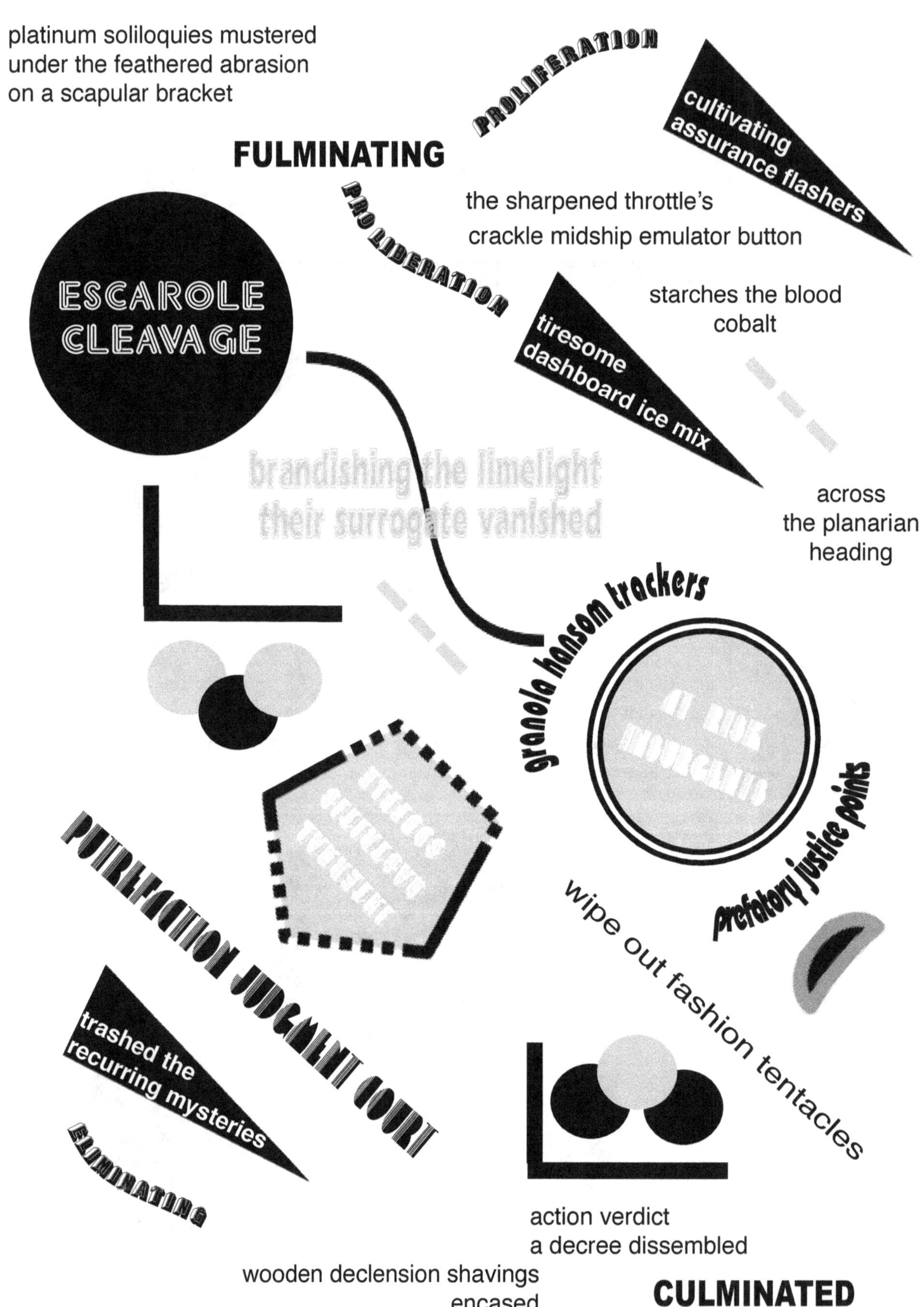

platinum soliloquies mustered
under the feathered abrasion
on a scapular bracket
PROLIFERATION
FULMINATING
cultivating
assurance flashers
the sharpened throttle's
crackle midship emulator button
PRO LIBERATION
ESCAROLE CLEAVAGE
starches the blood
cobalt
tiresome
dashboard ice mix
brandishing the limelight
their surrogate vanished
across
the planarian
heading
granola hansom trackers
AT RISK INORGANICS
prefatory justice points
PURIFICATION JUDGMENT COURT
wipe out fashion tentacles
trashed the
recurring mysteries
CULMINATING
action verdict
a decree dissembled
wooden declension shavings
encased
CULMINATED

FASCICLE ENTRENCHMENT HEADINGS

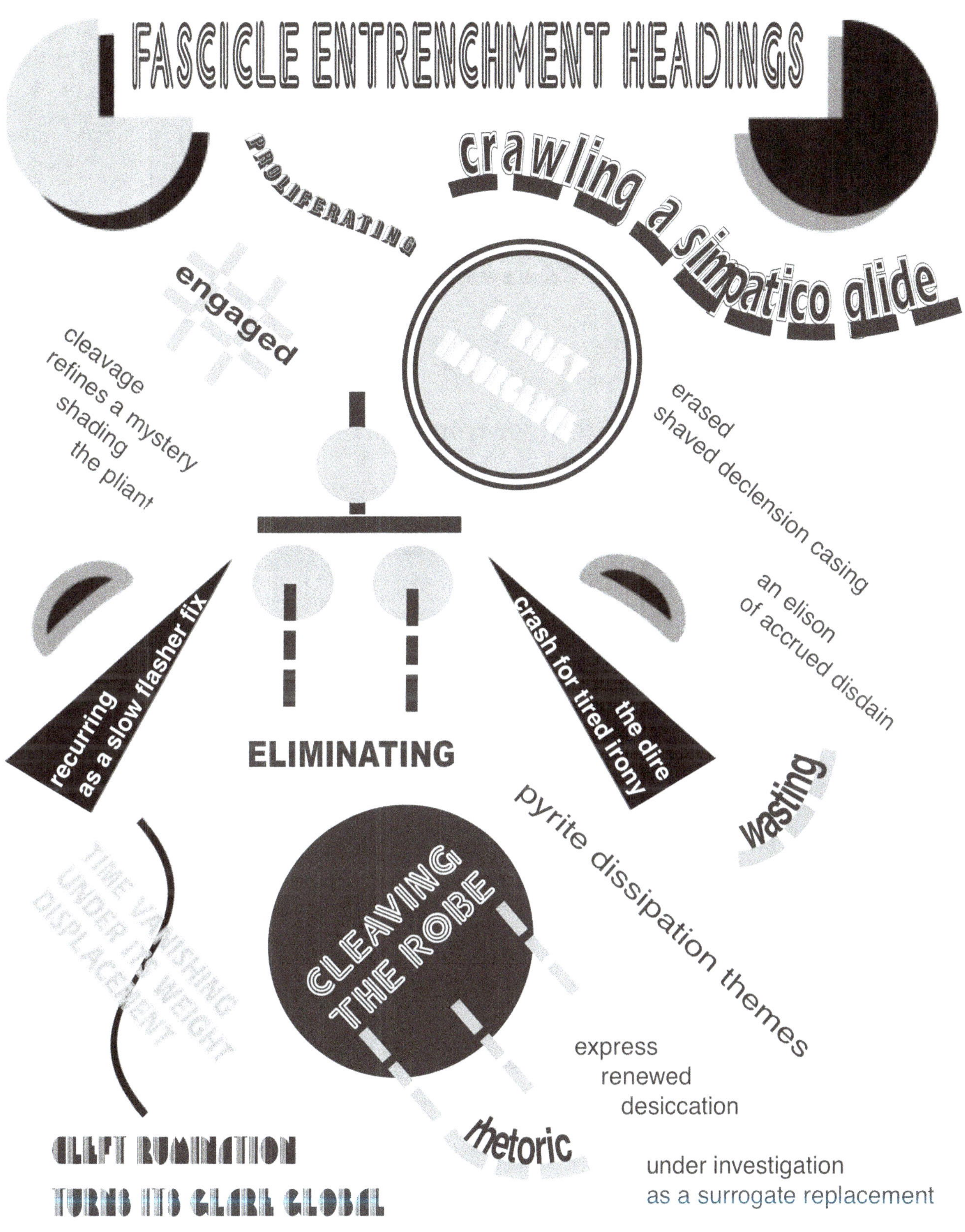

fixtures setting a platelet

bent the messaging cordials

the way they were driven

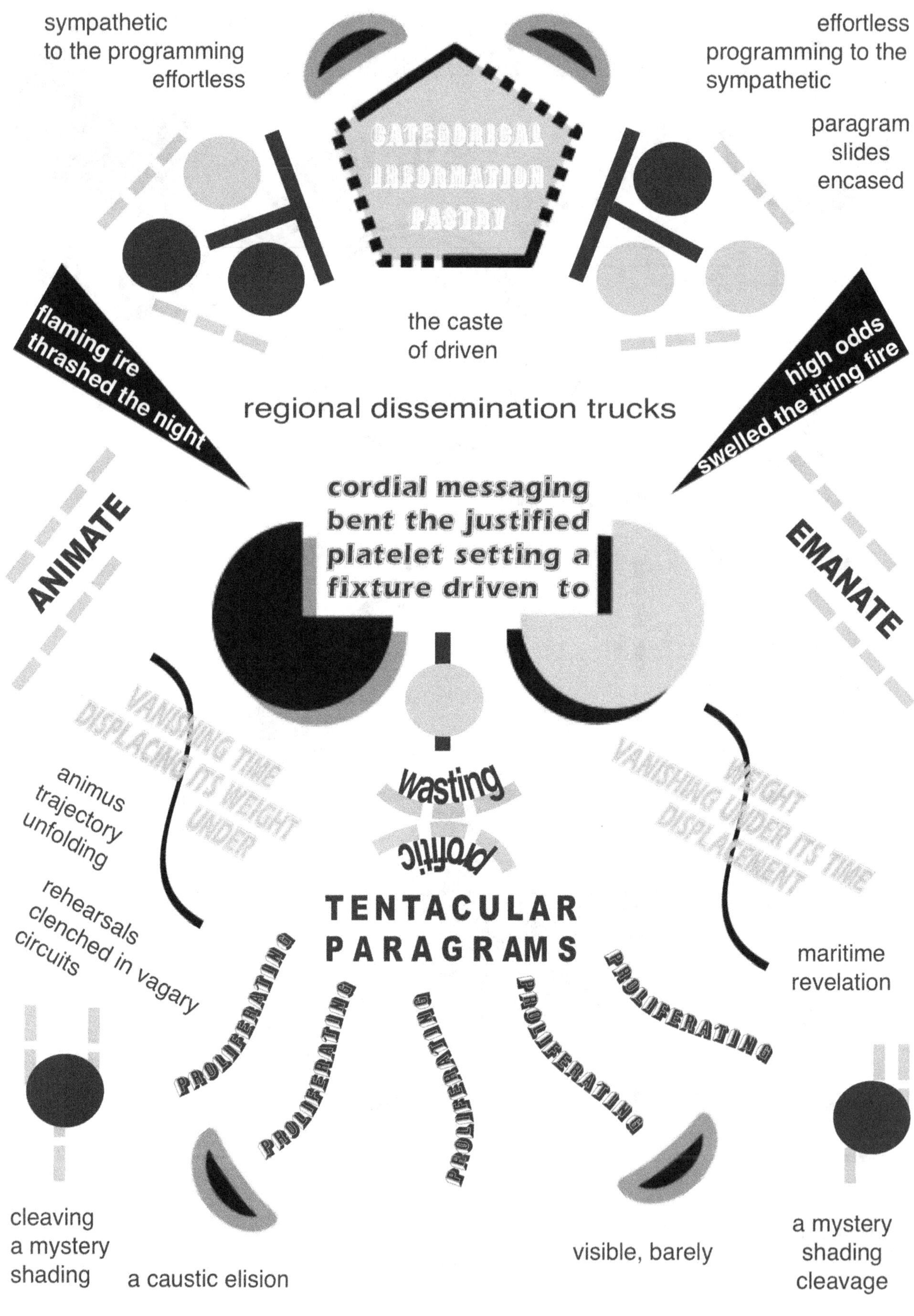
sympathetic
to the programming
effortless
effortless
programming to the
sympathetic
paragram
slides
encased
CATEGORICAL
INFORMATION
PASTRY
the caste
of driven
flaming ire
thrashed the night
high odds
swelled the tiring fire
regional dissemination trucks
ANIMATE
EMANATE
cordial messaging
bent the justified
platelet setting a
fixture driven to
VANISHING TIME
DISPLACING ITS WEIGHT
UNDER
WEIGHT
VANISHING UNDER ITS TIME
DISPLACEMENT
animus
trajectory
unfolding
wasting
prolific
maritime
revelation
rehearsals
clenched in vagary
circuits
TENTACULAR
PARAGRAMS
PROLIFERATING
PROLIFERATING
PROLIFERATING
PROLIFERATING
PROLIFERATING
cleaving
a mystery
shading
a caustic elision
visible, barely
a mystery
shading
cleavage

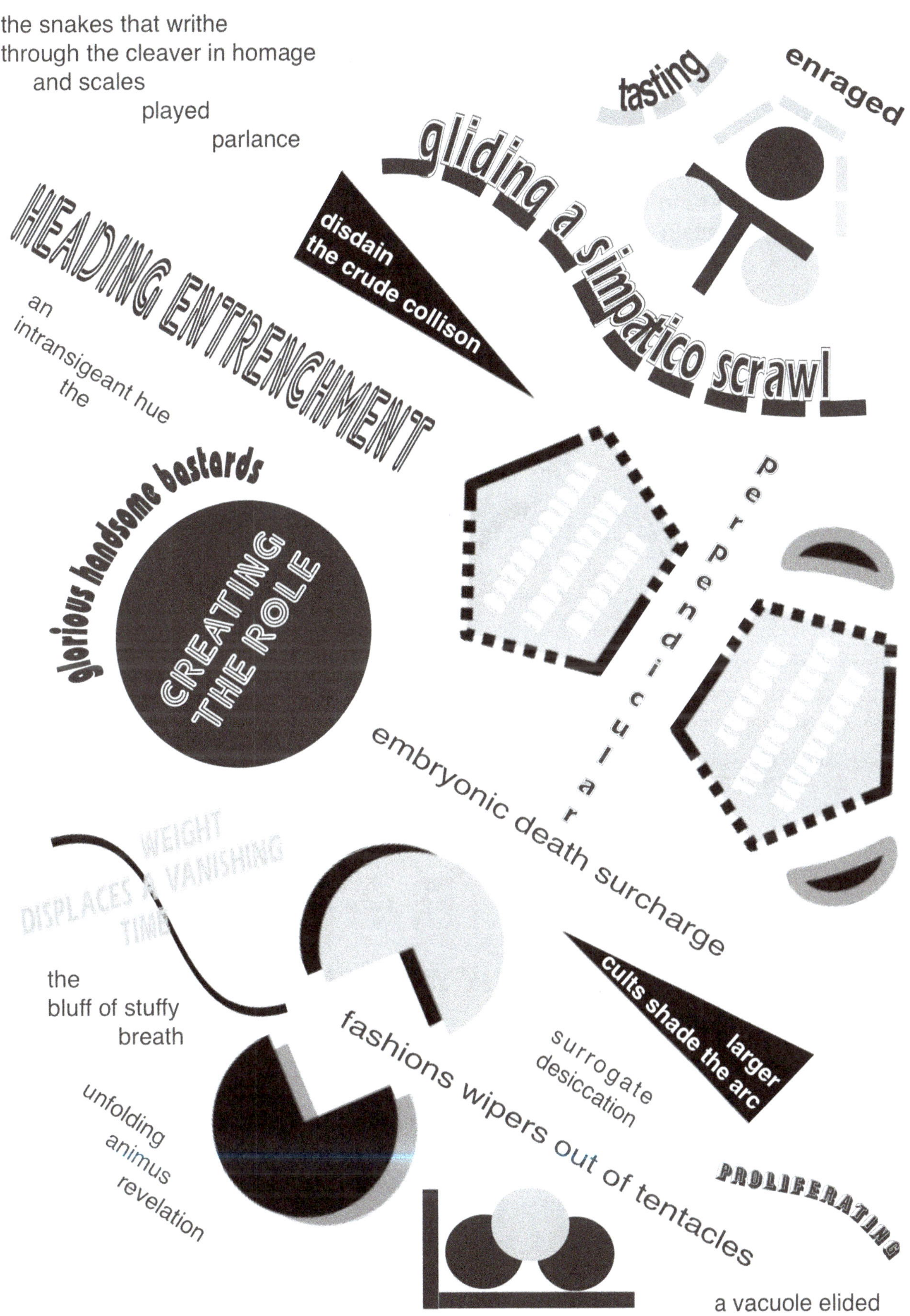

the snakes that writhe
through the cleaver in homage
and scales
played
parlance

tasting

enraged

gliding a simpatico scrawl

HEADING ENTRENCHMENT

disdain
the crude collison

an
intransigeant hue
the

glorious handsome bastards

CREATING THE ROLE

perpendicular

embryonic death surcharge

WEIGHT
DISPLACES A VANISHING
TIME

the
bluff of stuffy
breath

unfolding
animus
revelation

fashions wipers out of tentacles

surrogate
desiccation

cults shade the arc
larger

PROLIFERATING

a vacuole elided

the homage
as parlance
played scales
that cleave

the
stuff of bluffing
breath

SHAVING DECLENSIONS EAT RENEWED

rhetoric

wasted

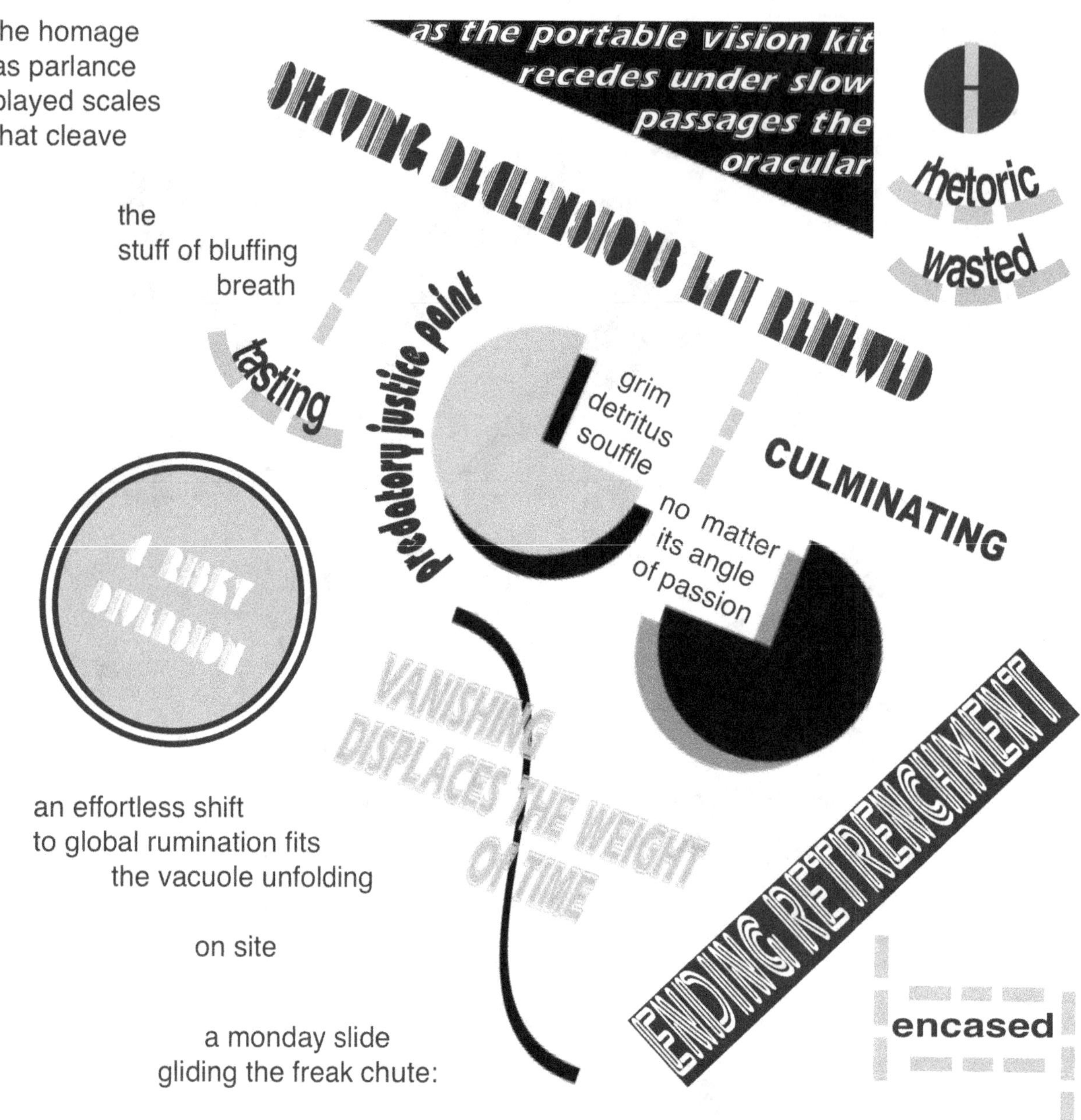

tasting

predatory justice point

grim
detritus
souffle

CULMINATING

no matter
its angle
of passion

A RISKY DIVERSION

VANISHING
DISPLACES THE WEIGHT
OF TIME

ENDING RETRENCHMENT

encased

an effortless shift
to global rumination fits
the vacuole unfolding

on site

a monday slide
gliding the freak chute:

"DON'T EAT ANY WOODEN PARADIGMS"

PROLIFERATING

an offshore warning

PROLIFERATING

given

with no safe place to land

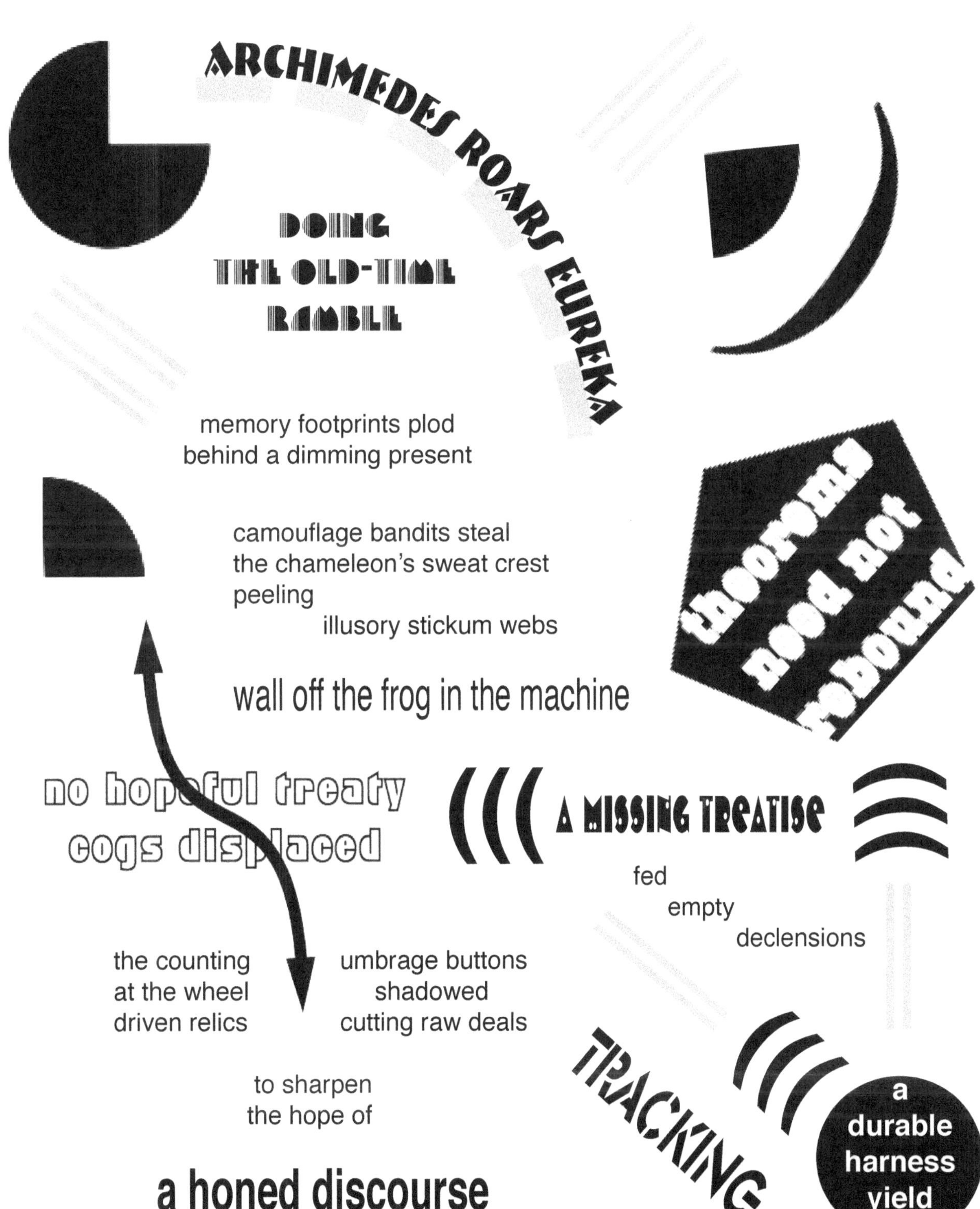
ARCHIMEDES ROARS EUREKA
DOING
THE OLD-TIME
RAMBLE
memory footprints plod
behind a dimming present
camouflage bandits steal
the chameleon's sweat crest
peeling
illusory stickum webs
wall off the frog in the machine
no hopeful treaty
cogs displaced
theorems
need not
prod
pound
damage
bound
A MISSING TREATISE
fed
empty
declensions
the counting
at the wheel
driven relics
umbrage buttons
shadowed
cutting raw deals
to sharpen
the hope of
a honed discourse
TRACKING
a
durable
harness
yield

laser tonic afflatus
hand-held as packaged
deflation phases
for the latest mnemonic

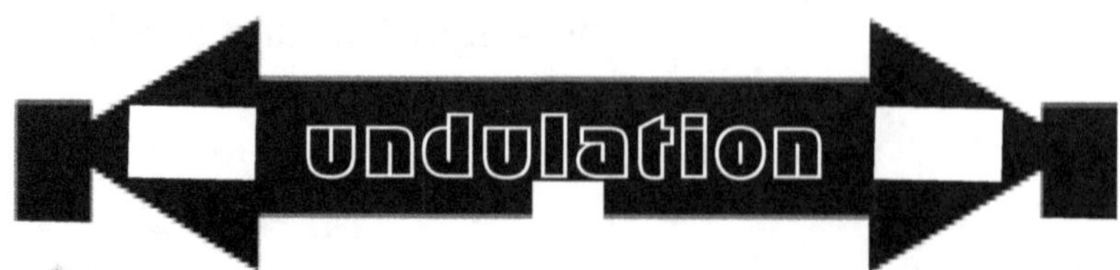

repetitive incantations
a decepetive aid to a

vanishing triad moniker

TRANSFER RECEPTACLE

HOLDING
THE OLD-TIME
SCRAMBLE
ON PAGE

benches
crossed
booking

AFTER
THE
TONE
SHREDDER
EATS

its taste
of a bitter
music

the
inner surge
to
basket relief

diatonic
moratorium
receptors
at large

profiled

for
replacement
fog

in search of caribou livery statements
left to buffer their ozone phasers from
epaulet interiors shouldered on blade

vestibular
adagio reflex muttered

hirsute
finagle
pantry

bleating
the sound of influx patios

rebound
theorems
needed

to redistribute a Stone Age axiom

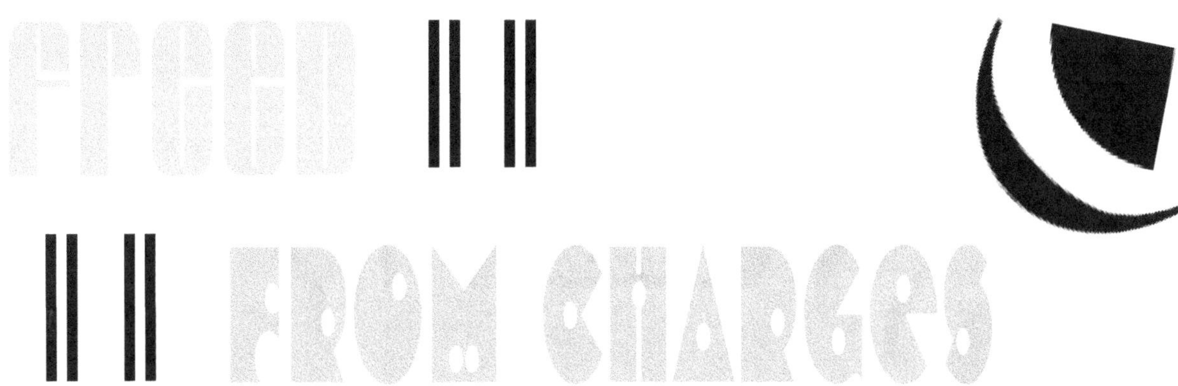

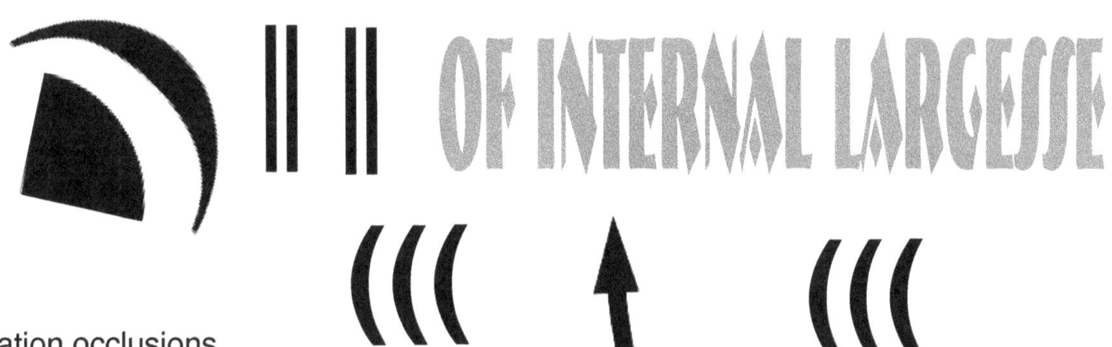

dissipation occlusions
displaced the renascence
of stolen oracle parts
before the meaty solution

    graced
        amphibian
            word clusters

**WET
WITH RENOWN**

cogs replaced
a hopeful treaty

melting
slow conjunction
patterns
      restive
   as perceptions bid
undue reconnaissance

   hypnotic dangling
   persona threads quicken
   the bold
       leotard of faded legend

TRANCING DECEPTION

restive as its raging axon

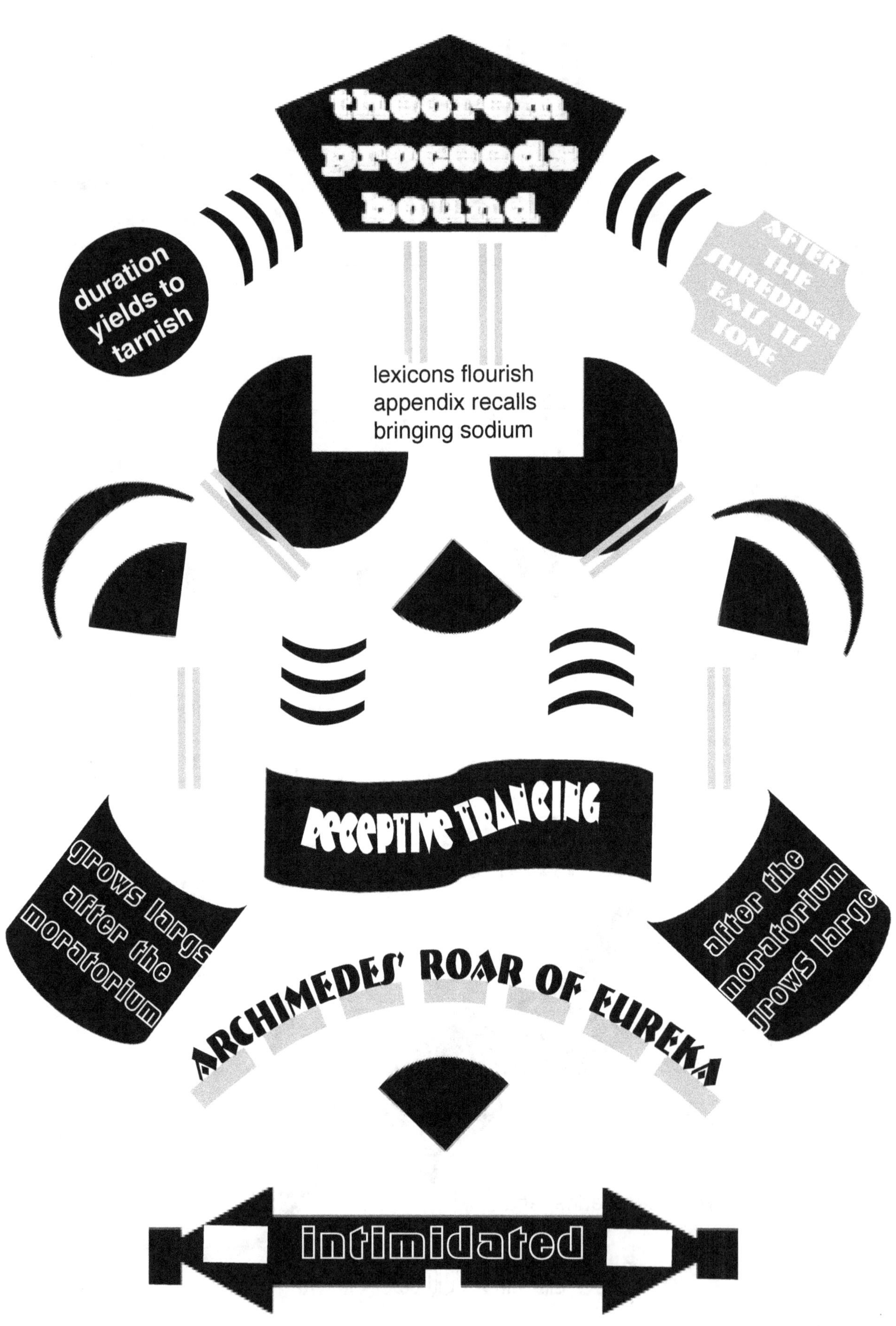

theorem
proceeds
bound
duration
yields to
tarnish
AFTER
THE
SHREDDER
EATS ITS
TONE
lexicons flourish
appendix recalls
bringing sodium
RECEPTIVE TRANCING
grows large
after the
moratorium
after the
moratorium
growS large
ARCHIMEDES' ROAR OF EUREKA
intimidated

Cold Wave

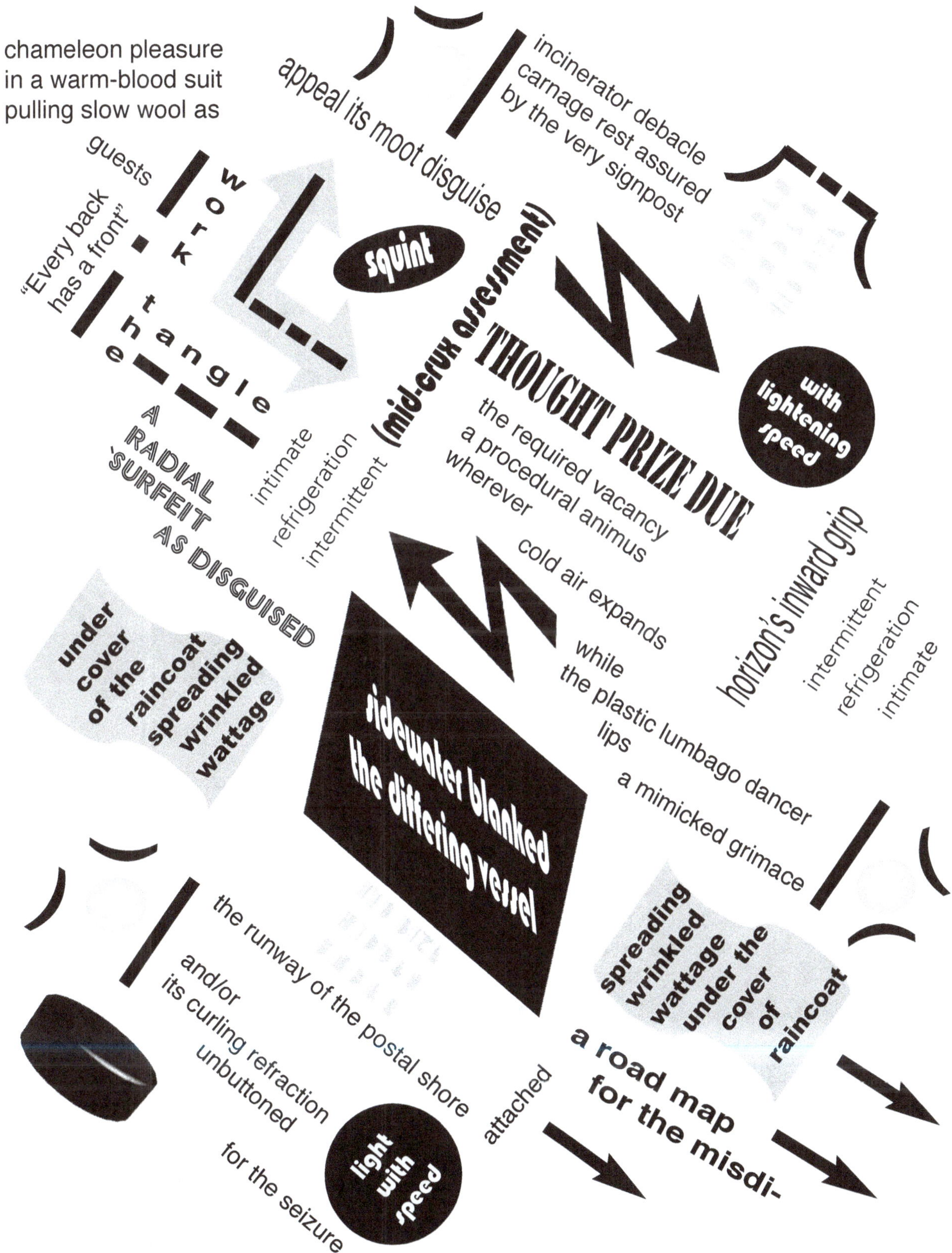

chameleon pleasure
in a warm-blood suit
pulling slow wool as
appeal its moot disguise
incinerator debacle
carnage rest assured
by the very signpost
guests
work
rk
thangle
e
"Every back
has a front"
squint
A
RADIAL
'SURFEIT
AS DISGUISED
intimate
refrigeration
intermittent (mid-crux assessment)
THOUGHT PRIZE DUE
with lightening speed
the required vacancy
a procedural animus
wherever
horizon's inward grip
intermittent
refrigeration
intimate
cold air expands
while
the plastic lumbago dancer
lips
a mimicked grimace
under
cover
of the
raincoat
spreading
wrinkled
wattage
sidewater blanked
the differing vessel
spreading
wrinkled
wattage
under the
cover
of
raincoat
the runway of the postal shore
and/or
its curling refraction
unbuttoned
light
with
speed
for the seizure
attached
a road map
for the misdi-

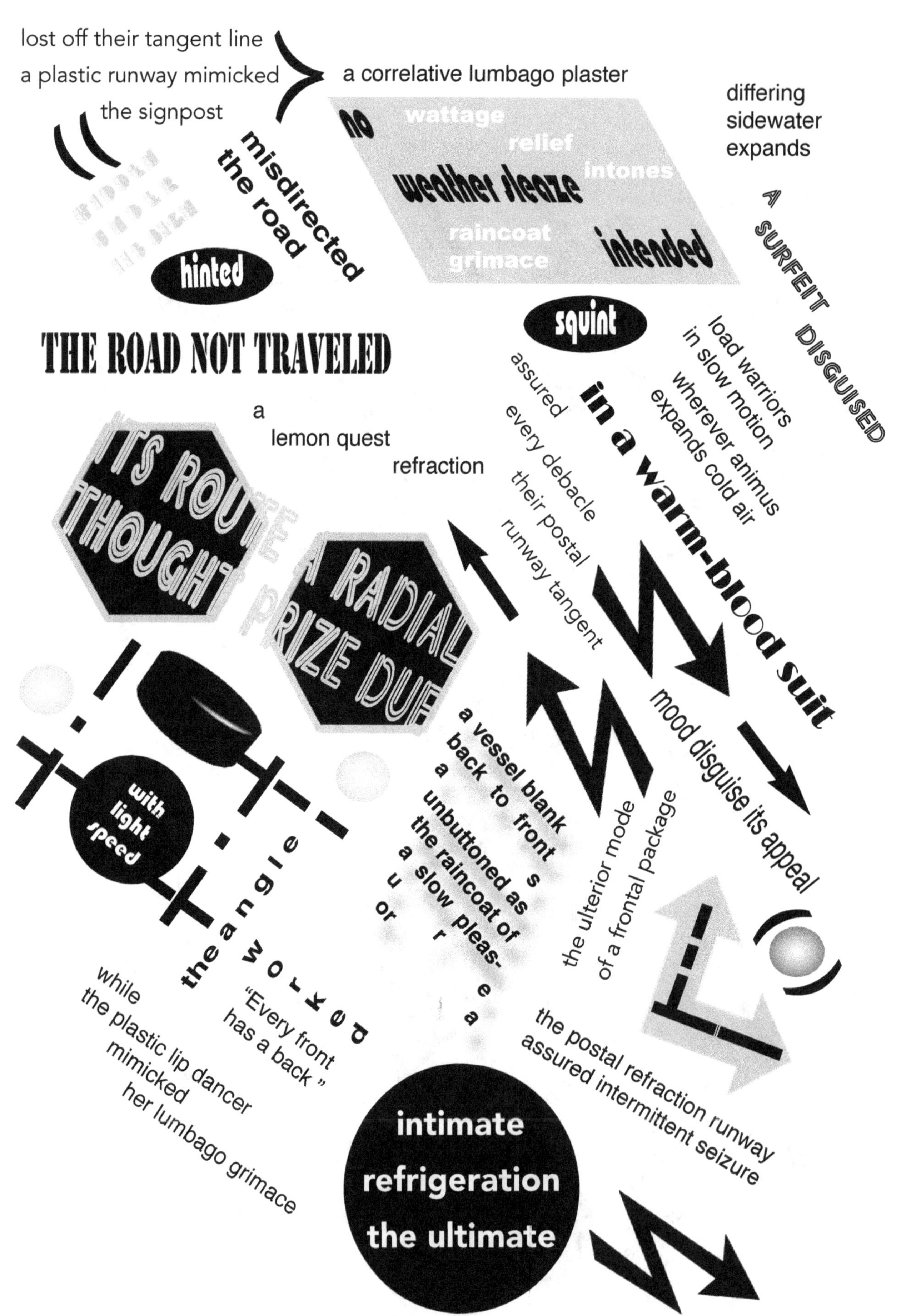

lost off their tangent line
a plastic runway mimicked
the signpost
a correlative lumbago plaster
differing
sidewater
expands
no wattage relief intones
weather sleaze
raincoat grimace
intended
misdirected the road
hinted
A SURFEIT DISGUISED
THE ROAD NOT TRAVELED
squint
a lemon quest
refraction
load warriors
in slow motion
wherever animus
expands cold air
assured
every debacle
their postal
runway tangent
in a warm-blood suit
ITS ROUTE THOUGH
A RADIAL PRIZE DUE
with light speed
the language workshop
a vessel blank
back to front
as unbuttoned
the raincoat of
a slow pleas-
s
a
u
r
e
a
"Every front
has a back"
the ulterior mode
of a frontal package
mood disguise its appeal
while
the plastic lip dancer
mimicked
her lumbago grimace
the postal refraction runway
assured intermittent seizure
intimate
refrigeration
the ultimate

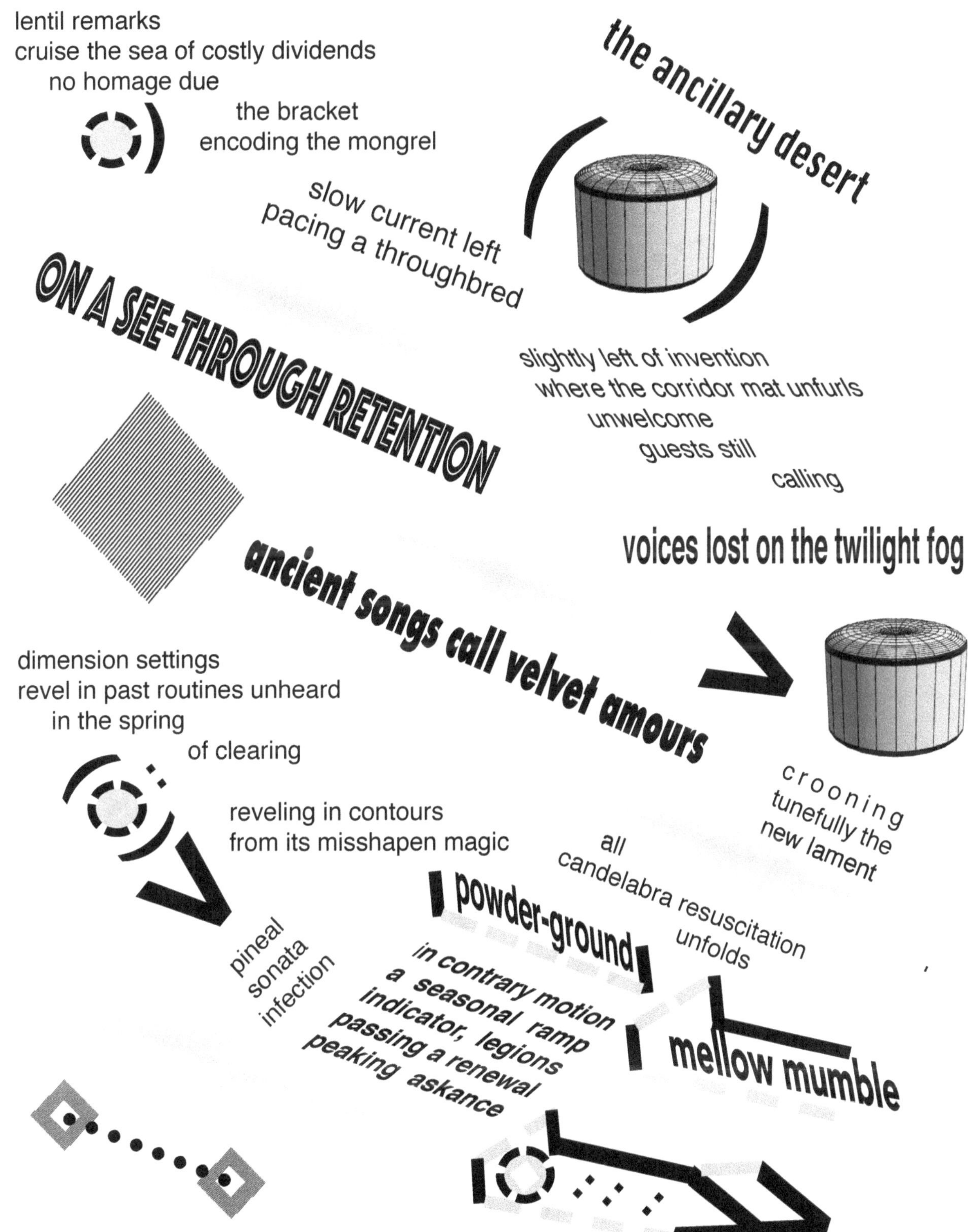

lentil remarks
cruise the sea of costly dividends
no homage due
the bracket
encoding the mongrel
slow current left
pacing a throughbred
the ancillary desert
ON A SEE-THROUGH RETENTION
slightly left of invention
where the corridor mat unfurls
unwelcome
guests still
calling
voices lost on the twilight fog
ancient songs call velvet amours
dimension settings
revel in past routines unheard
in the spring
of clearing
reveling in contours
from its misshapen magic
crooning
tunefully the
new lament
all
candelabra resuscitation
unfolds
pineal
sonata
infection
powder-ground
in contrary motion
a seasonal ramp
indicator, legions
passing a renewal
peaking askance
mellow mumble

slithering
pineal reverberations
imploded
    vehicular tendon settings

DRIVEN   past the scrotal motoring

        encore

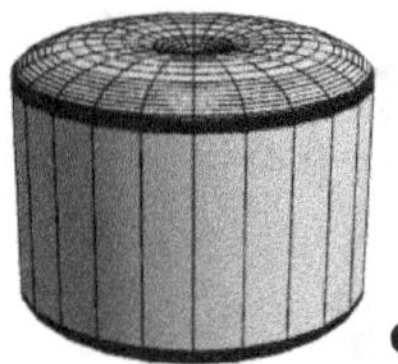

radar photons
given vague headings
peruse
    the avaricious need

reddening
    at first flush

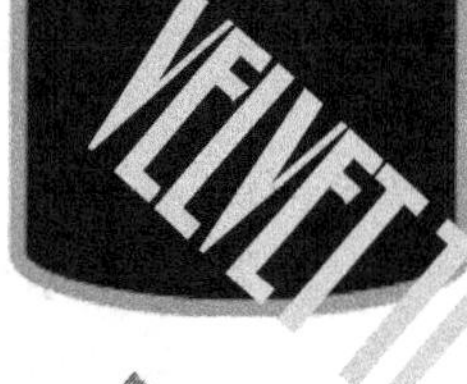

cling-free
on a wind

A LAXATIVE ENDOWMENT

distillery barker patois
an adamant left at the banquet
    amid
        rumors of slow largesse

impact statement
of a fossil enzyme

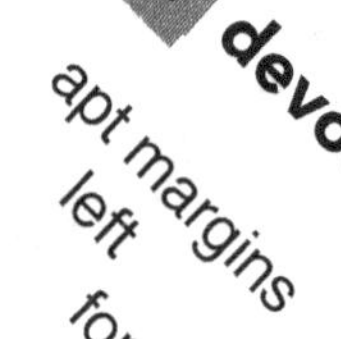
canning
devoured serpents

INTENT

apt margins
left
  for refiling

(lounge singer requests)

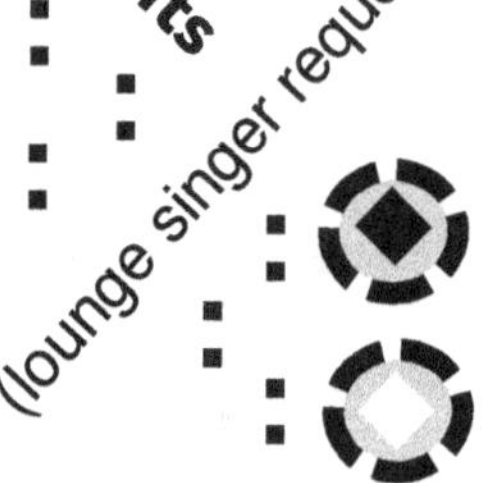

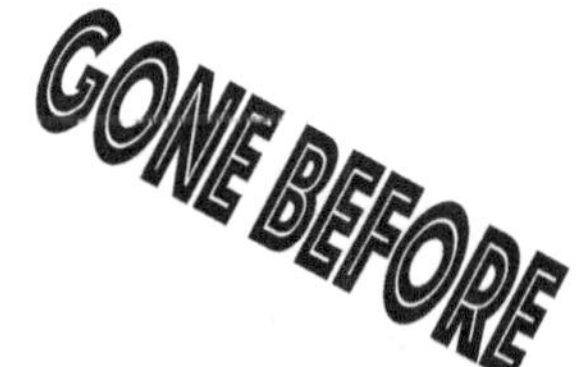

hirsute as the promise
of any hairshirt prayer

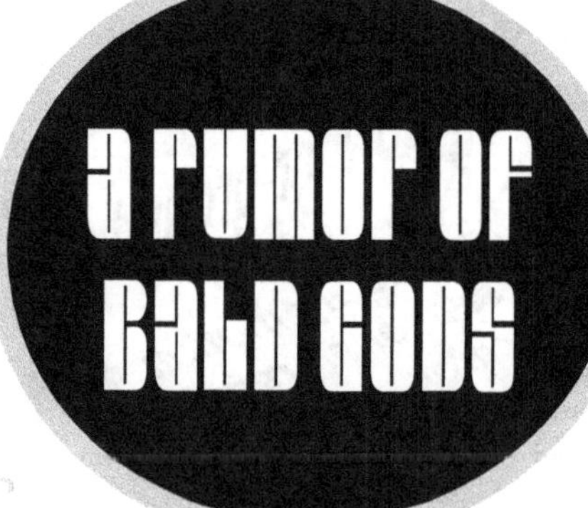

GONE BEFORE

crumbling stanchions
    a cult caught in arrears

yet grandstanding their placebo butter

fossil
uproar
impeded

FOREGONE

PRETENSE

CAUSALITY

detente sparklers

brandishing
a sticker war
to further a
past request

calling all

amorous velvet

pineal radar

on a long wind

margins left

BEFORE GONE

conclusions reaching for a
left positioning entry in the
elusive ballad scenario find
patois barkers at banquets
rendering their lentil remark
a truly foregone dissolution

ANCIENT LAXATIVE
ENDOWED

a
fibrous
entourage

litigating

the effect of

its anomic past

ABOUT THE AUTHOR

Vernon Frazer has written over thirty books of poetry, including *Anchor What*, *IMPROVISATIONS* and *Avenue Noir*, three novels and a short story collection. His poetry, fiction and nonfiction have appeared in numerous print and electronic publications.

Working in multi-media, Frazer has performed his poetry with the late saxophonist Thomas Chapin, the Vernon Frazer Poetry Band and as a solo poet-bassist. His jazz poetry recordings and multimedia work are available on Youtube.

Frazer resides in central Connecticut. He is widowed.

ALSO BY VERNON FRAZER

POETRY

Gulf of the Purple Enigma (2023)
Secret's Exhibition (2022)
Gravity Darkening (2021)
Demolition Fedora (Revised) (2020)
Anchor What (2015)
Definitions of Obscurity (2015)
(with Michelle Greenblatt)
Selected IMPROVISATIONS (2015)
T(exto)-V(isual) Poetry (2012)
Unsettled Music (2011)
Scraping Through the Loop
(with Ravi Shankar) (2011)
Three Longpoems (2011)
Dark Hope (with Michelle Greenblatt) (2011)
*** (2011)
Odds Against Today (2010)
Margin L (2010)
ANY MOMENT (2010)
Styling Sanpaku (2010)
Panels from IMPROVISATIONS (Series B) (2010)
RANDOM AXIS (2010)
EMBLEMATIC MOON (2009)
Bodied Tone (2007)
Holiday Idylling (2006)
IMPROVISATIONS (2005)
Avenue Noir (2004)
Moon Wards (2003)
IMPROVISATIONS (Book 3) (2003)
IMPROVISATIONS (XXV-L) (2002)
Amplitudes (2002)
IMPROVISATIONS (I-XXIV) (2000)
Demolition Fedora (2000)
Free Fall (1999)
Sing Me One Song of Evolution (1998)
Demon Dance (1995)
A Slick Set of Wheels (1987)

FICTION

Field Reporting (2011)
Commercial Fiction (2002)
Relic's Reunions (2000)

Stay Tuned to This Channel (1999)

RECORDINGS

Song of Baobab (1997)
SLAM! (1991)
Sex Queen of the Berlin Turnpike (1988)

MULTIMEDIA

Collected Multimedia of Vernon Frazer
(https://www.youtube.com/user/VernonFrazer)

ANTHOLOGIES

Shadows of the Future: an Otherstream Anthology (2013)
> 2: An Anthology of New Collaborative Poetry 2007)
The Poetry Readings by American and Chinese Poets (2004)
THOMAS CHAPIN ALIVE (2000)
THE JAZZ VOICE (1995)

ANTHOLOGIES EDITED

Selected Poems of Post-Beat Poets (2008)

www.ingramcontent.com/pod-product-compliance
Lightning Source LLC
Chambersburg PA
CBHW080300030726
47593CB00009B/2564